AFRICAN AMERICAN WOMEN IN THE NEWS

The hypersexual Jezebel. The emasculating Sapphire. The respectable Black lady. The bad Black bitches for whom crime and illegal drug use constitute a lifestyle. And now the Powerful Black Bitch, a recognition of African American women's growing influence as well as a warning about the dangers of allowing them real power.

These stereotypes, some older than others, are evident in news coverage of Black women. However, the goal of *African American Women in the News* is not simply to ask whether their representation reflects stereotypes commonly depicted in popular culture. Nor is it just to determine whether the findings of previous news studies apply to Black women. Rather, the broader intent of this book is to explore the portrayal of African American women from an intersectional perspective in a variety of news formats, platforms, and contexts. Who, in fact, are these women? How might they be characterized within different media formats and platforms? How does the intersectionality of gender, race, and class affect representation? And what can their portrayal in a variety of news contexts tell us about the status of African American women in society today?

Marian Meyers is Associate Professor in the Department of Communication and an affiliate of the Institute for Women's, Gender and Sexuality Studies at Georgia State University.

AFRICAN AMERICAN WOMEN IN THE NEWS

Gender, Race, and Class in Journalism

Marian Meyers

Routledge
Taylor & Francis Group

NEW YORK AND LONDON

First published 2013
by Routledge
711 Third Avenue, New York, NY 10017

Simultaneously published in the UK
by Routledge
2 Park Square, Milton Park, Abingdon, Oxon OX14 4RN

Routledge is an imprint of the Taylor & Francis Group, an informa business

Library of Congress Cataloging in Publication Data
Meyers, Marian, 1954–
African American women in the news : gender, race, and class in
journalism / by Marian Meyers.
       pages cm
    1. Blacks in television broadcasting – United States. 2. Women in
    television broadcasting – United States. 3. African American women
    journalists. 4. Blacks on television. 5. Journalism – United States –
    History. 6. Stereotypes (Social psychology) in mass media. I. Title.
    PN1992.8.A34M49 2013
    384.55´4´08996073–dc23   2012047213

ISBN: 978-0-415-87572-1 (hbk)
ISBN: 978-0-415-87573-8 (pbk)
ISBN: 978-0-203-85994-0 (ebk)

Typeset in Bembo
by HWA Text and Data Management, London

Printed and bound in the United States of America by Publishers Graphics,
LLC on sustainably sourced paper.

For Emma and Talia

CONTENTS

ACKNOWLEDGMENTS

This book has been a long time coming. And, as is usually the case with books that take a protracted route to conclusion, many people have graciously lent a helping hand along the way. Graduate research assistants Trayce Leak, Shajobia Keys, Darcey West, John Sewell, Melissa Miller, Kyle Sears and Katherine Tippins have contributed in multiple ways over the years, and for that I am extremely grateful. No matter how tedious the task – and transcribing TV newscasts ranks right up there – they were unflaggingly cheerful and dependable. This book would not have been possible without them.

I also want to thank the Organization for Research on Women and Communication, which provided a research grant to aid completion of this book. ORWAC's support is both affirming and very much appreciated. I am grateful, as well, to David Cheshier and the Department of Communication, as well as Mary Ann Romski in the College of Arts and Sciences at Georgia State University, for a summer research grant that allowed me to focus on finishing this book as opposed to teaching in the summer of 2012.

I would be remiss if I did not acknowledge dear friends who were not only supportive of my work, but also graciously tolerated my unavailability on more than a few occasions while I was working on this book. Their love, understanding and friendship sustained me through the inevitable frustrations attendant in the research and writing of this book. And so I thank Barbara Simpson, Jenny Warburg and Sharon Miller – and promise that the long-delayed road trips and visits await.

My children, Talia and Emma, have been a consistent source of inspiration, information, joy and love – as well as the occasional mug of hot tea and much-needed diversion – throughout the writing of this book. I am eternally grateful for all that they bring to my life and my work. In addition, I owe an incalculable debt to Lauren Rich for providing love, friendship, motivation and a keen editor's eye for typos as well as ill-defined arguments. Her readings of multiple drafts have resulted in a vastly improved manuscript, and her unwavering belief in the importance of *African American Women in the News* and in me have made all the difference.

Finally, I am indebted to the scholars who have gone before me, both the Black feminist scholars who have provided me with the theoretical tools that made this book possible and the news scholars whose work in race and representation provided the motivation for this book.

1

THE MISSING BLACK WOMAN IN THE NEWS

An Introduction

We have learned a lot about the representation of African Americans in the news over the past 25 years. Research has taught us that African Americans are rarely used as news sources, and when they appear in news coverage, they are primarily portrayed as a problem and a threat – as impoverished, as criminals, as self-serving politicians and, in general, as deviants straining the social fabric that binds us as a nation.[1] This depiction hasn't changed significantly over time. About 20 years ago, Fair (1994) proclaimed that: "Studies of media coverage of race suggest that non-whites and non-white culture have long been neglected in U.S. media except for activities that are criminal, violent or confrontational" (p. 35). More recently, Campbell, LeDuff and Brown (2012) revisited earlier studies of race, myth and the news to conclude that "news coverage continues to perpetuate the same myths about race that it has for at least 15 years" (p. 17) – specifically, myths that link African Americans to crime, reinforce their marginality and proclaim that barriers to assimilation no longer exist. Other news scholars also agree that the news reflects "modern racism,"[2] which denies the continuing existence of systemic racial bias and discrimination against African Americans, while attributing their lack of economic and social equality to deficiencies in personal responsibility and initiative.

So it appears we know quite a bit about the portrayal of African Americans in the news. *Or do we?*

It seems that we do know quite a bit about the representation of African American *men* in the news, but very little about African American women. Previous studies of African Americans in the news have by-and-large ignored Black[3] women. While some have clearly stated their focus is on African American men, others have elided gender, ostensibly including both men and women in their discussion of African Americans in the news. But are African American women, like African American men, similarly represented as impoverished and a threat to society? Are they, as studies indicate, over-represented as criminals and under-represented as victims? And are they blamed, as modern racism proclaims, for their lack of success and therefore denied assistance because any failing is seen as their own doing?

This book attempts to answer these questions – and others – through six discrete studies examining the representations of African American women in the news over the course of the past 15 years. It employs qualitative, textual analyses – principally discourse analysis, narrative analysis and the constant comparative method – to explore various aspects of their portrayal in local broadcast and national cable network news, in Black and mainstream[4] newspapers, and in YouTube video clips. The over-arching research questions are: (1) how are African American women portrayed in the news; and (2) how does this coverage reflect intersectionality – that is, the complex and varied ways that gender, race, class and other markers of social identity are inextricably linked within a hierarchy of dominance. In short, this book provides an in-depth look at the representation of African American women in the news from an intersectional perspective that integrates gender, race and class.

African American Women in the News is an attempt to remedy the gap in our knowledge of race and the news, as well as contribute to our understanding of the ways that race, class and gender shape representation. Examining the representation of African American women in the news from an intersectional perspective can tell us much about the current status of African American women in society, as well as whether the conclusions of previous research are applicable to African American women. As the chapters in this book make clear, intersectionality is central to representation – and conclusions based on studies that ignore the complexities of intersecting aspects of identity are, inevitably, limited and limiting.

This book takes as its starting point the notion that representation matters, that the cumulative effect of mediated popular imagery on the public imagination is to instill certain understandings and beliefs that have specific and anticipated outcomes. This position is supported by numerous studies. Dixon's (2008b) research into the effects of network news on racial attitudes found that exposure is associated with racism and the belief that African Americans are poor and intimidating. Gilliam and Iyengar (2000) similarly concluded that when Whites are exposed to crime news in which there is a Black perpetrator, they are more likely to hold more punitive attitudes toward crime, as well as exhibit higher levels of racism. Oliver's (2003) review of research concerning the effects of media portrayals of African Americans and crime indicates that viewer bias "not only reflects existing stereotypes of black men as 'dangerous and criminal,' but also likely serves to reinforce stereotyping in ways that can implicate essentially *any* black man as potentially threatening or violent" (p. 11). Dixon's (2008b) assessment of the research likewise found that the association of people of color with criminality on local news programs "can activate crime stereotypes regarding African Americans that can be used (by viewers) in subsequent judgments" (p. 321). And while audiences can interpret the news in various ways, "for the most part the media's audience lacks the time, resources, and information to independently construct alternative definitions and frameworks" (Potter and Kappeler, 1998, p. 18).

Although the above research did not address the representation – or audience perceptions – of African American *women* in the news, this book takes as a given that, like race, gender makes a difference, as do class and other signifiers of social identity. And because the news shapes public attitudes and discourse as well as public policy (Kraft and Furlong, 2010; Vavrus, 2002), news coverage involving African American women also has material consequences – socially, economically and politically. For example, the stereotype of the hypersexual, promiscuous Black Jezebel affects whether African American women who are raped are treated as legitimate victims or blamed for their victimization, which influences their prospects for justice. Whether the news media perpetuate stereotypes and negative images has implications not only for how the majority population thinks about and acts toward African American women, but also for how the African American community – women and men – sees them.

This book is indebted to Black feminist theory for its conceptualization of the multiple ways that intersectionality structures representation and popular imagery. It also draws on critical cultural studies[5] for its understanding of the role of mainstream media – in this case, the news – in maintaining and supporting the social, economic and political status quo, while at the same time existing as a site of struggle over competing ideologies and meaning.

Methodologically, *African American Women in the News* employs qualitative textual analysis because it is, as Campbell, LeDuff, Jenkins and Brown (2012) note in their own book about race and the news, "an approach best suited for answering *how* and *why* questions" (p. x) – which is the central concern of this book. The goal here is not to quantify the various aspects of coverage, as in ranking the frequency with which particular stereotypes may occur, nor to address aspects of reception or production beyond, in some instances, a discussion of sources cited within the news or the noting of how differences in organizations that create the news may affect content. Rather, the intent of this book is to increase our knowledge of the myriad ways that intersectionality shapes representation within the portrayal of African American women in varied news contexts, as well as to better understand how those contexts affect representation. Toward this end, Chapters 2 through 7 look across a range of media, from mainstream newspapers to the Black press, from YouTube to local television, as well as cable network news.

Different news formats have different points of focus, which may be shaped by newsroom imperatives, economics, technology, social values and the routines of reporters, as well as the interactivity of online media and social networks. For example, network television coverage focuses on national politics and policy, while local television news tends to revolve around crime. Similarly, video clips on YouTube, an increasingly popular and important source for news as well as entertainment, provide images and other content that often extends beyond what is considered acceptable in most mainstream media outlets. By analyzing the news in varied media platforms, this book includes diverse media perspectives and foci. In addition, by conceptualizing race as inseparable from and simultaneously constituted by multiple aspects of social identity, *African American Women in the News* advances our understanding of racial representation in the news as both gendered and classed.

Cultural Studies, Race and the News

Guerrero (1993) points out that "race is one of the most emotionally and politically charged subjects in the American social psyche and media imagination," and that its social and political meanings "are not fixed but are matters of ongoing construction and contestation; whether in volatile debate or subtle transactions, the negotiation of racial images, boundaries, and hierarchies has been part of our national life from its beginning" (p. 41). Not only is the social meaning of race a matter of negotiation, but the news itself is contested ground, viewed by critical news scholars as a site of ideological struggle and competing worldviews and beliefs.

The field of British cultural studies early on recognized the uniqueness of the news's role in legitimating the dominant power structure through its claim to represent an objective reality (Hall, 1977, 1982; Hall, Connell and Curti, 1977; Hall et al., 1978; Hartley, 1982). News scholars working within this critical paradigm assert that the news acts as an agent for the social, economic and political elite, and as such the news acts to support the values, ideas and points of view that keep this elite in power by creating ideological consensus. Although the dominant ideology is frequently referred to in the singular, it actually consists of multiple interlocking ideologies – including, but not limited to, racism, sexism, heteronormativity and capitalism – that work together to sustain and uphold the status quo. However, the dominant ideology is neither monolithic nor secure, but must be continually fought for against the encroachments of alternative or oppositional ideologies (Hall, 1977, 1982; Hall, Connell and Curti, 1977; Hartley, 1982).

Social, political and cultural hegemony depend on a combination of force and consent, with hegemony most effective in winning the consent of the subordinated when its ideological underpinnings appear natural, normal and common-sensical (Althusser, 1971; Gramsci, 1971, 1983). The news therefore must appear neutral, disguising its ideological roots to effectively build and maintain support for the prevailing social order. This "neutrality" is won through a variety of mechanisms – the choice of words and use of language; the delimiting of arguments so that truly oppositional positions are never presented as legitimate considerations; and the framing of stories so that they appear not to be ideological at all, but instead seem natural, grounded in everyday reality. Although any number of interpretations are possible given the polysemic nature of texts – that is, their inability to close off alternative interpretations – some discourses are privileged and most likely to shape meaning because they carry the weight of cultural assumptions and expectations (Eco, 1990). The "preferred reading" of the news, produced through language and symbolization, reflects and becomes the basis of popular consensus (Hall, 1980).[6] As Hall (1977) states: "The media serve, in societies like ours, ceaselessly to perform the critical ideological work of 'classifying out the world' within the discourses of the dominant ideology" (p. 346). In this way, the news – and popular culture more broadly – is a battleground for the discursive struggle over meaning and ideology.

Black Feminist Thought, Stereotypes and Representation

Black feminist scholars have extended the concept of a dominant ideology by incorporating the idea of multiple, intersecting ideologies into their analyses of representation. Patricia Hill Collins (2005) notes that the "global mass media circulates images of Black femininity and Black masculinity and, in doing so, ideologies of race, gender, sexuality, and class" (p. 122). Those ideologies have been characterized by bell hooks (1992) as "white supremacist capitalist patriarchy" because the term signifies interlocking systems of domination. Collins, hooks and Angela Davis have been at the forefront of conceptualizing intersectionality, arguing that gender, race, nationality and class, as well as other socially constructed markers of identity, cannot be decontextualized or divorced from each other. Davis (1998) emphasizes that: "The objective oppression of black women in America has a class, and also a national origin" and that "the structures of female oppression are inextricably tethered to capitalism" (p. 185). For Higginbotham (1992) the "racialization of gender and class" means that "gender identity is inextricably linked to and even determined by racial identity" (p. 254).

This understanding of intersectionality, along with Black feminist thought more generally, is derived from the experiences of African American women as society's marginal "Others" (Collins, 1991). From this perspective, African American women define the boundaries of society, with their experiences considered central to social analysis. The social location of African American women as the "ultimate outsiders" (Alexander, 1995, p. 15), as "perhaps the most consistently marginalized segment of our society" in terms of economic and political power (p. 6), provides Black feminists with a unique vantage point for theorizing gender, race and class "as simultaneous forces" (Brewer, 1993, p. 16). The self-defined standpoint of Black women, Collins (1989) adds, provides the foundation of Black feminist thought and is characterized by two interlocking components:

> First, Black women's political and economic status provides them with a distinctive set of experiences that offers a different view of material reality than that available to other groups... Second, these experiences stimulate a distinctive Black feminist consciousness concerning that material reality.
>
> (pp. 747–748)

This vantage point has provided the theoretical foundation for Black feminist theorists to link the intersection of race, class and gender oppressions to stereotypes of African American women, which of necessity adapt over time to accommodate social and cultural change.[7] The ideology that produces images of Black femininity, Collins (2005) explains, is never static but "internally inconsistent" and therefore "constantly subject to struggle" as it works to maintain its dominance within a changing society (p. 148):

> In essence, the mass media has generated class-specific images of black women that help justify and shape the new racism of desegregated, color-blind America... This media constructed Blackness took class-specific forms that mirrored changes in actual social class formations among African Americans.
>
> (p. 147)

In theorizing the relationship between intersectionality and the popular representation and imagery of Black women, Collins provides a useful framework for understanding how stereotypes have maintained and supported the oppression of Black women over time. She initially pointed to four socially constructed and interrelated "controlling images of Black womanhood" that reflect "the dominant group's interest in maintaining Black women's subordination" (1991, p. 71): the mammy, who accepts her subordination; the matriarch, who symbolizes the strong mother who emasculates her husband and lovers; the welfare mother, who is responsible for causing her own poverty and that of her community; and "the Jezebel, whore, or sexually aggressive woman," who lies at the heart of attempts to "control Black women's sexuality" (p. 77). Defining African American women as "stereotypical mammies, matriarchs, welfare recipients, and hot mammas" works to normalize and naturalize racism, sexism and poverty (Collins, 1991, p. 67). The stereotypes of the Jezebel, the mammy and the welfare queen, Collins (2005) adds, helped uphold slavery, Jim Crow segregation in the U.S. South and racial ghettoization (p. 28).

Collins (2005) later updated these images to reflect societal changes and also to emphasize the ways in which they are classed, with poor and working-class Black women stigmatized with the word "bitch" to indicate that they "lack middle-class passivity and submissiveness," and therefore their "undesirable, inappropriate behavior justifies the discrimination they might experience in housing, schools, and public accommodations" (Collins, 2005, p. 138). Images of poor and/or working-class Black women converge around either the "Bad Black Mother," such as the "crack" mom who abandons her children, or the "bitch," who is "aggressive, loud, rude, and pushy" and serves to defeminize and demonize Black women (p. 123). The stereotype of the bitch is frequently tied to Black women's sexuality, so that she may be depicted as an updated Jezebel: "Whether she 'fucks men' for pleasure, drugs, revenge, or money, the sexualized bitch constitutes a modern version of the Jezebel, repackaged for contemporary mass media" (pp. 127–128). Other versions of the sexualized bitch are the "ho," who trades sex for money, drugs, jobs or other items, and the materialistic "female hustler," who uses her body to get whatever she wants (p. 128).

Much like Collins's poor or working-class bitch, the Sapphire image represents the myth of the "angry black woman" and has many different shadings and representations, including "the bad black woman, the black 'bitch,' and the emasculating matriarch" (Harris-Perry, 2011, p. 88). This stereotype, Harris-Perry (2011) explains, refuses to recognize that Black women's anger may be a legitimate response to inequality; instead, that anger is "seen as a pathological, irrational desire to control black men, families, and communities," and is also used against African American women if they "dare to question their circumstances, point out inequities, or ask for help" (p. 95). She adds that the stereotypes of the Jezebel, mammy and Sapphire adhere both to the notion that women are the legitimate guardians of society's morality and that African American women are, by virtue of their skin color, uniquely incapable of this task. These stereotypes "have been powerfully and regularly reproduced in political discourse and popular culture since the Civil War" (p. 97), and they continue to be used to blame African American women for "the 'degenerative conditions' of the race":

> Black women were described as insufficient housekeepers, inattentive mothers and poor educators of their children. Because women were supposed to maintain society's moral order, any claim about rampant disorder was a burden laid specifically at women's feet. If blackness was a shameful cancer, black women were the main carriers because they produced black children.
>
> (p. 114)

Unlike their working-class or poor sisters, middle-class African American women can be seen as modern mammies or Black ladies, with the latter achieving middle-class status by rejecting the promiscuous sexuality attributed to working-class Black women and by engaging in the workforce: "The arrival of middle-class 'Black' respectability, as evidenced by the strictures of the Black lady and the modern mammy, helped shape a discourse about racial integration and African American women's place in it" (Collins, 2005, p. 147).

For Collins (2005), the Black lady is exemplified by the character of Claire Huxtable of the popular *Cosby* television show, which aired from 1984 to 1992: a wife and mother, as well as a lawyer, she was "beautiful, smart and sensuous" (p. 139).[8] The asexual modern mammy, on the other hand, updates the loyal female servant to the White boss and "requires a delicate balance between being appropriately subordinate to White and/or male authority yet maintaining a level of ambition and aggressiveness needed for achievement in middle-class occupations" (p. 140). For Collins, Oprah Winfrey represents the "penultimate successful modern mammy whom African American and, more amazingly, White women should emulate" (p. 142), a woman whose ideology of individual social change counsels personal responsibility. A third, and newer, middle-class image for Black women is the "educated Black bitch." Unlike the mammy or the Black lady whose claim to middle-class status is her respectability, educated Black bitches have "money, power, and good jobs," and they are in search of men not for a committed relationship, but for sex (p. 145). The stereotyping of middle-class African American women as Black ladies, modern mammies and educated Black bitches justifies discrimination against them in the workplace and is "used to explain why so many African American women fail to find committed male partners – they allegedly work too hard, do not know how to support Black men, and/or have character traits that make them unappealing to middle-class Black men" (p. 146)

One way that Black women have rejected the myths and stereotypes used to define them is by constructing alternative images of themselves, of which the "strong, black woman is the most pervasive and widely accepted," says Harris-Perry (2011): "Whereas the negative iconography of black women as lewd, angry, or unnaturally devoted to their domestic employers is reproduced by the state and in mainstream popular culture, the image of black women as unassailable, tough, and independent is nurtured within black communities" (p. 184). The downside of this self-construction, Harris-Perry adds, is that Black women may not be allowed – and may be shamed for – human failings. This alternate image of the strong Black woman is largely missing from mainstream popular culture, including the news.

Class and Gender in the News

In addition to violence and crime, the equating of African Americans with poverty is a recurrent theme in the news (Heider, 2004). Gilens (2004) points out that 1965 was a turning point in the racialization of poverty within news media. Stories about poverty were both increasingly illustrated with images of African Americans and increasingly negative, as opposed to the more positive depiction of deserving Whites living in rural poverty that had been the norm in media portrayals previously.

The racialization and classing of people of color provide the foundation for the concept of modern racism, which news scholars[9] assert is inherent in the media's coverage of African Americans. A basic premise of modern racism, sometimes referred to as symbolic or enlightened racism,[10] is that racial discrimination and bias no longer impede the progress of people of color, and that if they have not achieved financial and social success, they have only themselves and their bad choices to blame. Embedded in these claims is the notion of post-identity with its insistence that we have arrived at a time and place where we are "post" or "after" oppressions linked to race or gender, and therefore past the politics of identity (Joseph, 2011).[11]

Dixon (2008b), drawing on the work of Entman (1990) and McConahay (1986), notes that modern racism is characterized by three components: "(a) anti-African American affect or a general emotional hostility toward African Americans, (b) resistance to the political demands of African Americans, and (c) the belief that racism is dead and that racial discrimination no longer inhibits African American achievement" (p. 322). Modern racism is used not only to justify social and economic inequality, but also to deny remedial actions or assistance because any inequities are seen as self-inflicted. In this way, a lack of success is linked to lack of personal initiative rather than systemic inequality and discrimination.

Because the above studies have not explored the representation and roles of African American women in the news, their findings cannot be generalized to Black women. However, a handful of studies have examined news coverage of individual African American women, such as civil rights leader Fanny Lou Hamer (Bramlett-Solomon, 1991), former U.S. Senator Carol Moseley-Braun (Berry and Manning-Miller, 1996) and Anita Hill (Fiske, 1994; Morrison, 1992; Steiner, 1999; Hill and Jordan, 1995). Women who were not racially identified also have been examined in a few news studies but, here again, no conclusions can be drawn about the portrayal of African American women in the news more generally. For example, a study by Fourth Estate (2012) found that in the 2012 election news coverage, men overwhelmingly outnumbered women as quoted news sources, even about issues that primarily affect women, such as birth control and abortion. This finding echoes those from almost 20 years earlier, when the Women, Men and Media Project (1994a, 1994b) concluded that female news sources are less often quoted and female reporters less likely to receive bylines than men. These research projects, however, did not note racial distinctions in their findings. In addition, Rakow and Kranich (1991), in examining women as semiotic "signs" in TV news, found that "only white women are allowed to signify as 'women'" (p. 19) because the meaning of "woman" is bound to an assumption of Whiteness. Rakow and Kranich note that the signification of women of color differs from that of White women, but their study did not explore the specificity of this difference.

A few case studies have looked at news coverage involving African American women within a limited context or event from a perspective that incorporates gender, race and class (see, for example, Liebler, 2004; Cole and Jenkins, 2012). In an example of a case study that successfully incorporated gender, race and class into its analysis, Liebler (2004) compared news coverage of two female college students – one African American, the other White – in separate communities who went missing, She found inequitable media coverage across class lines was attributable to the middle-class, media-savvy parents of the White student, who had the resources to keep the story of their missing daughter in the news.

In addition, paternalistic racism, as opposed to modern or enlightened racism, was reflected in news studies that drew on an intersectional perspective in their analysis. Paternalistic racism assumes that African Americans need the assistance of Whites, particularly the White middle class, to help them achieve equality or other goals. This seemingly "benign" form of racism was found in the *Washington Post*'s coverage of the Truman administration's attempt to integrate the military in 1948, when the *Post* reported events in ways that promoted integration (Meyers, 1996). Paternalistic racism was subsequently noted in the analysis of a newspaper series about mothers addicted to "crack" cocaine. The mothers, all of whom appeared to be African American, were portrayed as in need of assistance from a White, professional, middle class to save them and their children from their addiction and destructive behaviors (Meyers, 2004b). A version of this study appears in Chapter 7 and provided a foundation for the research in other chapters in this book that found paternalistic racism in news coverage.

About this Book

The six discrete studies in *African American Women in the News* examine the representations of Black women over the course of 15 years through qualitative, textual analyses of the news. The research in Chapters 2 through 7 examines national and local Atlanta news, including local broadcast and cable network television news, mainstream and Black newspapers, and YouTube. Because of differences in the methodological approaches of the six studies, the specifics of their methodology are contained within the chapters; the overarching theoretical approaches of critical cultural studies and Black feminist theory are contained within this introductory chapter since it remains the underlying orientation throughout the book. The types of qualitative, textual analysis employed include discourse analysis, narrative analysis and the constant comparative approach. As with other types of qualitative research, the findings of textual analysis are not generalizable. However, the goal of this book is not generalizability, but to better understand the social and cultural meanings behind the images and portrayals of African American women in the news.

Intersectionality is addressed throughout the book. For example, Chapter 6 looks at news coverage of violence against African American women during "Freaknik," a weekend spring break for African American college students. Among that chapter's conclusions are that many of the victims were portrayed in the news as hypersexual Jezebels who provoked their assault. This enduring stereotype of the promiscuous, highly sexualized Black woman is classed as well as raced, with seemingly poor and working-class women who were the victims of violence blamed for causing the attacks while presumably middle-class college students were portrayed as innocent victims.

Atlanta was chosen for the study of local news coverage because it is both a majority Black city and a regional, national and international media hub with global reach and influence. The headquarters for CNN and TBS, as well as Cox Enterprises Inc., which owns Cox Communications and Cox Media Group, are located there. According to Nielsen Media (2012), Atlanta's designated market area for television was ranked 8th in the U.S. in 2011, and 9th in the U.S. in spring 2012. Local Atlanta news also is more likely to include stories that feature African American women than would be the case in cities with a proportionately smaller Black population. According to the U.S. Census Bureau, 32 percent of the Atlanta metro area's population is Black, placing Atlanta second among U.S. cities in terms of Black population. In addition, the State of Georgia has a 30 percent Black population – the fourth largest in the nation (DeShay, 2010). Atlanta's and Georgia's relatively large African American populations mean that local television news can be expected to include more African American women than national television news programs, which tend to limit coverage of African American women to events or activities involving a small number of high-profile women – for example, Oprah Winfrey or Michelle Obama – or to the reporting of tragedies involving well-known celebrities, such as the death of singer Whitney Houston.

Depending on the reader's preferences, the chapters can be read sequentially or in a different order. However, the chapters are grouped in ways that hopefully will facilitate connections as well as highlight contrasts. For example, Chapters 2 and 3 both explore the general representation of African American women in television news, with Chapter 2 examining local news while Chapter 3 looks at national cable network news. Both of these chapters attempt to ascertain whether the findings of previous news studies are applicable to the portrayal of African

American women, as well as to determine more generally how Black women are represented. The remaining chapters provide a more in-depth look at specific women or issues in the news. Chapters 4 and 5 each examine the representation of a prominent African American woman within different contexts and formats: Chapter 4 looks at Michelle Obama's portrayal on YouTube, and Chapter 5 analyzes coverage in Black and White newspapers of domestic violence involving nationally renowned televangelist Juanita Bynum. The next two chapters return to Atlanta in examining TV coverage involving violence against African American women in Chapter 6, and a newspaper series about mothers addicted to crack cocaine in Chapter 7. Finally, Chapter 8 concludes with a summary of the previous chapters' findings that synthesizes and extends their individual contributions, providing a fuller picture of how African American women have been portrayed in the news in studies conducted over the course of 15 years, as well as the factors that shaped representation.

This introductory chapter has attempted to make the case for a close examination of the representation of African American women in the news, and to provide the theoretical grounding for the chapters to come. In Chapter 2, the roles of African American women in local Atlanta TV newscasts were examined through the constant comparative method. This study found that they are most frequently represented as victims, and that the frequent inclusion of middle-class, professional African American women as spokespersons or experts tended to dispel negative stereotypes of African American women.

Chapter 3's discourse analysis of CNN and FOX News similarly found that, while African American women are rarely in the news, they are far more likely to be the victims of crime than the perpetrators. Among the most salient of several themes that emerged in cable network news programming were poverty, violence, victimization, crime and dysfunction.

Chapter 4 recognizes the blurring of the line between traditional news outlets and alternative sources of news, such as YouTube, and uses the constant comparative approach to ascertain the roles and stereotypes in the representation of Michelle Obama. Those roles ranged from the First Mom in clips uploaded by the White House or Obama campaign (and sometimes reused by national news networks), to that of the Powerful Black Bitch as indicated in video posted by conservative or right-wing individuals and organizations.

In Chapter 5, a comparison of the assault on popular televangelist Juanita Bynum by her husband in Black and White newspapers found that the Black press drew on socially conservative voices within the Black church to portray both Bynum and her husband as equally responsible for the violence. The White press, on the other hand, more clearly represented her husband as at fault and, in a few instances, included a feminist perspective on domestic violence.

Chapter 6, which is adapted from a previously published article in the journal *Critical Studies in Media Communication* (Meyers, 2004a), provides a discursive analysis of local Atlanta television coverage that involved violence against African American women during Freaknik. This chapter argues that class – as defined by educational status – was a primary determinant of whether the victims were represented as innocent or guilty.

Chapter 7, adapted from an article that appeared in the *Journal of Communication Inquiry* (Meyers, 2004b), provides a narrative analysis of a series about "crack babies" and their mothers that appeared in the *Atlanta Journal-Constitution*. The chapter argues that the news reflected paternalistic racism in presenting the story of a Black female underclass in need of saving by an altruistic, White, professional middle class.

None of the research in this book would have been possible without the theorizing of Black feminist scholars who laid the groundwork for our understanding of gender, race, class and other signifiers of social identity as indivisible and interconnected. Taken together, the studies in *African American Women in the News* indicate that, in short, the findings of previous research cannot be applied wholesale to the representation of African American women. The images of African American women in the news are far more complex, diverse and multifaceted than previous studies suggest. *African American Women in the News* challenges as well as augments the extant academic literature, arguing that African American women are not over-represented as criminals and deviants, but are instead more likely to be portrayed as victims. In addition, they speak loudly in local Atlanta news, where their appearance is a reflection of the city's large Black middle class. Furthermore, while modern racism may characterize some news stories about African American women, Black women also may be depicted through the lens of paternalistic racism. And while many of the popular images of Black women – such as the poor and/or working-class Jezebel, bitch and Sapphire, and the middle-class Black lady and modern mammy – are present in the news, the study of Michelle Obama's portrayal in YouTube clips heralds the arrival of a new image, that of the Powerful Black Bitch.

2

AFRICAN AMERICAN WOMEN IN LOCAL TV NEWS

An old adage about local TV news is that "if it bleeds, it leads." In practical terms, what this means is that if the reporter or cameraperson has obtained video involving death and violence – whether in the form of crime, disasters or accidents – in which a good deal of blood can be seen, that video has intrinsic news value and stands a good chance of opening the evening's newscast. Indeed, crime, accidents and disasters are among the most common – and easily acquired – stories in local TV news, with crime the most consistently reliable source of footage.

Institutional bias toward reporting "bad" news, Gandy (1998) explains, "all but guarantees that stories about racial minorities will emphasize the negative outcomes, the failures, and the misbehavior of members of minority ethnic and racial groups" (p. 159). In crime news, in particular, the tendency to focus on African American males "has produced a widely held belief that Black males are dangerous" (Gandy, 1998, p. 23). This depiction, Stabile (2006) points out, has been consistent since the earliest days of commercial news reporting in the U.S. Her analysis of crime news concludes that it has overwhelmingly constructed African American men as criminals but denied them the status of victims.

Crime news, like all news, is a construction, "built from the work of reporters in the field and influenced by the perspective of editors, who are anticipating the reactions of consumers" (McCormick, 2010, p. 9). Heider and Fuse (2004) similarly emphasize that the content of local broadcast news is shaped by journalists who understand the economic imperatives of the news organization and whose target market is the well-to-do, rather than those without significant financial resources. While all news "actively creates opinions and impressions about the world," crime news, in particular, trades upon and recreates "certain subtexts – law and order, discipline, danger, fear, authority," McCormick states (2010, p. 9). The underlying themes in crime news, he adds, "implicitly define the boundaries of society and have an effect on how people think and live their lives" (p. 9).

A number of news scholars have concluded that the underlying themes in local TV news work to reinforce negative stereotypes and White fear of African Americans by primarily portraying them as "the source of crime and chaos" (Dixon, 2004, p. 137). The bad news about African Americans in local news is echoed in multiple studies that examined the representation of African Americans in cities across the United States. For example, in Pittsburgh, 80 percent of the references to Blacks were negative, compared with less than two-thirds for Whites in local television news (Klein and Naccarato, 2003). In the Los Angeles area, Blacks were over-represented as perpetrators of crime compared with arrest records, while Whites were under-represented as perpetrators and over-represented as victims (Dixon and Linz, 2000). This overemphasis on African Americans as crime suspects also was found in New Orleans and Indianapolis news coverage (LeDuff, 2009).

Moreover, African American politicians in local news receive more negative coverage and appear more self-serving than White politicians (Entman, 1990, 1992; Entman and Rojecki, 2000; Gilliam and Iyengar, 2000; Jeffries, 2002). And, in a resounding indictment of local reporting, a study involving 12 television markets in different geographic regions found that African Americans were rarely used as news sources, particularly when a story contained only one news source, so that local news "continues to report from a mostly White perspective" that has not improved significantly over the past 50 years (Poindexter, Smith and Heider, 2003, p. 534).

None of the above, however, tells us much about the ways that African American *women* are portrayed in local news. Do they similarly lack a voice as news sources? And if crime stories are a staple of local news, do they most often appear as criminals, as the studies would suggest?

The goal of this chapter is to answer these questions by exploring the portrayal of African American women in local Atlanta news through the constant comparative method. As noted in Chapter 1, Atlanta was chosen for the study of local news because the large population of African Americans in the metropolitan area virtually guaranteed their inclusion in coverage, which would not be as likely in cities with a smaller Black population. Local news also is more likely than national news to provide diverse representations of African American women, particularly in a majority-Black city with a large Black middle class.

Methodology

In examining the representation of African American women in local Atlanta TV news, four station affiliates of the major national networks were included in this study. They are WSB (ABC), WXIA (NBC), WGCL (CBS) and WAGA

(FOX). These stations' weekday, half-hour 11 p.m. news shows were recorded and then transcribed. The 11 p.m. timeslot was chosen in an attempt to find relatively comparable news shows which aired at the same time and for the same duration, which was not possible with earlier programming. These shows were taped for two weeks in February 2009, Monday through Friday, from Feb. 16 through Feb. 27, for a total of 20 hours of local news programming.

Any story in which an African American woman or girl appeared, either in the background or as an individual featured in a story, was transcribed and analyzed. The women and girls were identified as African American based on their skin color and other signifiers of racial identify where appropriate. Class markers such as grammar and language usage, mannerisms and behavior, as well as appearance – which include clothing and hair style – were noted. Sports stories were not examined in this study, although African American female athletes would have been included if they appeared during the regular news programming as opposed to the sports news segment.

The constant comparative method (Glaser and Strauss, 1967) was utilized to look for patterns and themes concerning the representation and roles of African American women. In this method, texts are compared with each other so that tentative categories emerge, and as more texts are compared with other texts and existing categories for their fit, new categories are defined while previous categories may be eliminated or combined until final categories are established. This deductive approach allows the categories to be determined by the texts rather than being predetermined, as is generally the case in quantitative content analysis. Some stories contained multiple African American women in different roles. In this event, the stories were coded in multiple categories. This was the case, for instance, in a story about an elderly African American woman who was murdered. Because the story also contained footage of her friend, it was counted within the category of "victims" to represent the role of the elderly woman, but also "crime commentators" to account for her friend. On the other hand, if two women in a single story are both victims, that story will only count once in the "victim" category. Thus, although the number of stories within the final categories is noted, that tabulation does not reflect the total number of stories analyzed in this study, nor the total number of women in the news stories. Instead, it reflects the number of stories with specific representations of African American women; if more than one category of representation is present in a particular story, the representations are included in more than one category. The goal of this study was not to determine with statistical accuracy the prevalence of specific roles and representations, but to ascertain the types and variations of the roles represented within local TV news. In addition, because the focus of this study is Atlanta news, the findings are not generalizable to other cities. However, Atlanta's local news does reflect news conventions commonly adhered to in TV newsrooms in large, urban centers across the United States. In this regard, the news may not be that different than that in other urban media markets with similar racial and class demographics.

Findings

In applying the constant comparative method to the news, several categories emerged. The largest category, with 30 stories, involved African American women who appeared in the background, either as illustration for a story or simply because they just happened to be there when the cameras were rolling. However, the next largest category, with 22 stories, featured African American women who were victims, primarily of crime or bad weather. Other categories were: criminals, with 9 stories, three of which involved the same woman who was not actually charged with any crime but was linked to illegal activity through her relationship with her boss; crime commentators, who were somehow connected to a victim or criminal, with 13 stories, three of which involved the same friend of a murder victim; spokespersons, with 11 stories; public officials, with 8 stories, seven of which involved (now former) Atlanta Mayor Shirley Franklin; workers, with 4 stories; consumers, with 4 stories; celebrities, with 4 stories; experts, with 3 stories; residents, with 3 stories; and the unemployed, with 2 stories.

Victims

Crime

Twelve of the 22 stories involving victims were about victims of crime, with half of those stories about murder victim Kathryn Johnston, a 92-year-old African American woman who was shot by three White Atlanta police officers during a botched drug raid based on a bogus warrant. The six stories primarily revolved around the trial and conviction of the officers, who planted drugs in Johnston's home after shooting her. Photos of the elderly Kathryn Johnston were shown in these stories on all four stations.

Other murder victims included an 11-year-old girl, shown smiling in a photo, whose father was convicted of "brutally beating" her to death, and an unidentified woman whose photo was also shown. The audience was asked to call "crime stoppers" with any tips about this murder.

The other crime victims were not identified. They included: a woman – interviewed with only the back of her head and her hands shown – who stated she had been raped by two Atlanta police officers after being stopped for suspected drunken driving; a fire and burglary victim whose apartment was robbed by security guards after fire damaged her home; and – in the only non-local news story about a victim – a Kansas City woman whose "tight hair weave probably saved her life" when her former boyfriend shot at her through the back window of her car. The weave stopped the bullet. Although there was no identification or photo of the shooting victim,[1] video showed the damaged car window and the immediate area, which included several African American women standing next to a rundown storefront in what appears to be a poor neighborhood.

The remaining crime victim – the only one who was identified while still alive – was a church employee who "keeps track of the finances at St. Paul's A.M.E. Church." She was interviewed about a scam in which bogus checks were written from the church's bank account. Poised and well-spoken, she describes the phone call she made to the scammers: "I said, 'I just want you to know we're on to you already. We know that you are defrauding St. Paul A.M.E. Church here in Atlanta, and we've turned it over to the proper authorities. So your game is over as far as we are concerned.'"

Weather

Nine of the stories involving victims included women whose property had been destroyed or damaged by severe storms or tornadoes. Almost all the women interviewed appeared intelligent and well-dressed. Renee Jackson was picking up her children from daycare when her car was damaged by "baseball-sized hail." She describes the scene: "All of a sudden, we looked outside and all we could see was white falling, and it was just something out of a movie scene." In another story, Katie Barnes was said to have come "home from work to find her home destroyed" by a tornado. She states: "I was just panicked. I just broke down in tears. I mean, my home is gone. It's shredded." An unidentified woman in that same story, commenting on the destruction of her church, describes how "that church has been my rock and my family." In a different story, Virginia Johnson – who was described as a "mother of eight" in one station's newscast and having "eight people in the house" in another's – survived a tree crashing into her bedroom during a storm. According to the WSB reporter, she "is lucky to be alive." She is quoted in that story as having told everyone to get into the hallway as the storm approached.

Tiffany Hunter appeared in three stories with her 6-year-old daughter, Jordan. The two climbed into the bathtub for safety after Hunter identified what sounded like a train as an approaching tornado. The twister downed trees in Hunter's yard and tore power lines from her house. Hunter is well-spoken and attractive, and her daughter, standing next to her, is adorable – which no doubt prompted the reporter to ask her what she did when the tornado was approaching. "I just ran into the bathtub, and it just came," the girl said.

Other tornado victims included women whose church had been destroyed. They were shown in pews in a nearby church, where they were said to be "comforting each other, promising to be faithful." In a separate tornado story,

Charlotte Moss, identified as a grandmother, was said to be "one of the many lucky residents of Hancock County who escaped without serious injury." The reporter goes on to explain that: "A tree slammed through the ceiling of the room she and three grandchildren were sleeping in, narrowly missing their beds." Moss is then shown stating: "I just kept calling on the Lord. I kept saying, 'Lord, just help me.'" The fact that Moss and her grandchildren share the same bedroom indicates they are likely poor, and the children probably are being raised by Moss.

Accident

In only one story was an African American woman said to be the victim of an accident. An unidentified woman was shown trapped in her car while rescuers were attempting to get her out. She was injured as a result of what was described as a "freak accident" in which a metal gate crashed through the windshield.

Criminals

Nine stories involved African American women who were criminals or connected to a crime, but few fit the stereotypes associated with Black women and criminality. Contrary to popular conceptions and the Jezebel or Black bitch stereotypes, none were prostitutes, and only a few were involved with drugs or guns. In addition, three of the nine stories in this category involved a woman who was not actually accused of any crime, although she might be perceived as complicit. In these stories, Keisha Williams is identified as a top aide to DeKalb County Police Chief Tyrell Bolton, who is accused of breaking the law by allowing Williams to use an unmarked police car and giving her a badge that she was unauthorized to wear. In one story, she is shown in the photo as an attractive, light-skinned African American, possibly in her 30s. The two other stories ran video of Williams coming out of or going into a car that presumably is at the center of the investigation into the police chief's misuse of county property. The relationship between Williams and the police chief is not defined, other than the reference to her as a "top aide," but the implication is that it may be sexual. Within the context of the chief's actions, it seems a plausible explanation. The possibility of an illicit affair places Williams within the stereotypic role of the Jezebel or bitch (Collins, 2005) who is the cause of the chief's downfall.

Murder was the most serious crime in this category, and women were implicated in two murder stories. However, in one instance, the death appears to be accidental, and in the other, it is actually the woman's husband who committed murder. The latter story involved the stepmother of the 11-year-old girl whose father was convicted of murder for "brutally beating" the child. The stepmother, shown in what looks like a jail photo, was scheduled to go to trial for murder. A photo of the child, smiling, ran with the story. In the other crime report, Shirley Ogelby, shown in what appears to be a police photo, was said to be behind the wheel of a car that hit and killed a 7-year-old boy in front of a school building.

Only two brief stories included women stereotypically involved with drugs and/or guns. In one story, gunfire in a neighborhood resulted in eight people being taken into custody; one Black female and one Black male were shown handcuffed and being taken to a police cruiser. The other story was about drug arrests for crack and powder cocaine. This included four head-shots of the suspects, two of whom were women.

Other stories about African American women charged with crimes included a woman arrested and charged "with providing alcohol" to teenage boys, one of whom died in a car crash presumably caused by drunken driving. The other story was about a teenager hoping to become a soldier who was not allowed to deploy until a felony charge was dismissed. The young woman is said to have paid back the $10,000 she stole while working as a grocery store cashier, but the charge was not dismissed due to bureaucratic delays. "I am a good person," she says. "I just know I made a terrible, terrible mistake."

Crime Commentators

More African American women were interviewed in relation to a crime than were criminals. The 13 stories in this category included women who were related to, neighbors of or friends of the victim or criminal – or even just happened to be in the area when they were approached by a reporter. In the only story in which a neighbor of an alleged criminal appeared on camera, Gloria Lawrence, the former neighbor of a man "accused of killing a cancer researcher," stood outside her well-kept home in what looked like an upscale residential area and stated, "I'm in shock. I can't believe it. He's such a nice, young man."

All other crime commentators were African American women who were either related to or friends of the victim, or simply were in the area where the crime occurred. Kelly Hill, a friend of murder victim Kathryn Johnston – the 92-year-old African American woman killed in a botched police raid – was said to have called Johnston once a week and regularly took her grocery shopping. Hill, considerably younger than the elderly Johnston, said Johnston "reminded me of my grandmother, so we connected pretty quickly." Attractive and well-dressed, Hill appeared in three stories aired by three different stations. Commenting on the police officers convicted of killing of her friend, she said: "They seem remorseful – some of them took more responsibility than others. But I'm sure this has been a difficult process for their families… I really believe it's [the killing] more systemic than anything. I believe it could have been any Atlanta police officer on that day, but unfortunately it was them, and they didn't make the right decision. So they're going to be held accountable."

Relatives of murder victims included two mothers: the unidentified mother of a 7-year-old boy, shown in a photo with both parents, who was killed in a car accident in front of his school, as well as the mother of a woman who was killed. This mother was interviewed in the news report, and the audience was urged to call "crime stoppers" with tips. In another story, Denise Martin, a relative of a teenage boy who was beaten by police, defended the boy by stating: "I can't see him saying or doing anything to warrant this type of abuse. So what happened this night [with the police] – was it just like any other? We don't know." The implication is that Atlanta police routinely may be beating innocent, young Black men.

Four of the stories in this category involved residents of a neighborhood where a crime occurred, and a fifth story contained interviews with two women on a street in Midtown, an upper-middle-class Atlanta neighborhood where a woman was murdered in her condo. However, it is not clear in this story whether the two women live in that neighborhood or not.

Among the stories that featured residents of neighborhoods where a crime had occurred was one about a community meeting in the working-class Ormewood Park area to protest a judge's sentence that sent a criminal to drug court rather than jail. In this story, an unidentified African American woman appears on camera expressing concern about crime in the area. Other stories included interviews with a resident of an apartment complex where a home invasion has occurred, and with a mother worried about a pedophile in her working-class neighborhood. The mother states: "I make sure that my son knows that, you know, you don't get into a car with a stranger, and if someone says they're sent by me, that you make sure you talk to me first." In addition, two women in another story who live in a neighborhood where a church has been vandalized are interviewed. The first to comment on the vandalism is Sandra Smith: "I feel that somebody's got a serious problem, and they need help if they're going to go and destroy a church or any other building anywhere, no matter where you live." In one of the rare instances in which an African American woman appears on camera using non-standard English grammar, the second woman then states: "It shocked me. I don't know. I don't know why they wanna do that. A person who do that, that's wrong. They'll get punished by God."

In addition, a student is interviewed outside her high school about a man who attempted to grab other students at the school and pull them into his car. She states: "For me, it's really scary because they could have gotten kidnapped – or anything could have happened to them, and no one knows [who grabbed the students] 'cause there wasn't a camera at the parking lot."

Spokespersons

African American women appeared on camera in 11 stories as spokespersons, most often for a local county police department or other public agency. All were professionally attired, well-spoken and seemingly middle class. They included Lt. Rebecca Brown of the Clayton County Police Department, who commented on two stations about a prostitution sting operation; Mekka Parish of the DeKalb County Police Department, who was interviewed twice about a contractor scam involving an elderly resident, as well as the lockdown at a high school where a boy brought a weapon; and Cpl. Illana Spellman of the Gwinnett County Police Department, who was interviewed on two stations for a story about a home invasion.

Andrea Coleman, a spokesperson for the Metropolitan Area Rapid Transit Authority (MARTA), was interviewed in two stories: when a MARTA bus smashed into a Chevy, and when an elderly couple was killed after a speeding truck clipped a MARTA bus and landed on the couple's car. Other African American women who were spokespersons represented: Mercer–Atlanta University, in discussing a lab explosion in which two students were injured; Kroger Supermarket, where customers can now load e-coupons to their cell phones; and an exhibit about a civil rights activist in Atlanta.

Workers

Four African American women appeared in stories in which they were either interviewed about their former jobs or were heard on camera speaking in the context of their jobs. Two former employees had worked at the Peanut Corporation of America in Blakely, Georgia, which was the source of tainted peanuts that resulted in a national salmonella outbreak. They were interviewed in separate stories. In the first story, the employee defended the company, claiming that she didn't remember any tests that found salmonella, "but if they found salmonella, the product was put on hold." In a story aired on the same station two days later, a former plant sanitation supervisor acknowledged that she had no training and sometimes no staff, and was never told about positive salmonella tests. She said that every week, she told management they needed to shut down the plant for a thorough cleaning, but that cleaning never happened.

Two other stories showed women at work. A policewoman in an undercover prostitution sting operation is shown leaning into the driver's side window of a car and asking the driver if he's "Looking for a date?" Later in the story, she is heard asking, "How much you wanna give me?" and still later, she tells someone, "I'm looking for a date. I ain't looking for a ride." Finally, in a story about auditions for the TV reality show *American Idol*, a woman appears on stage singing one line of a song, and then walks off stage.

Experts

African American women were interviewed as experts in three stories. Acting Public Health Director Dr. S. Elizabeth Ford was interviewed about flu season in Georgia and urged viewers to "wash your hands." In a story about women with eating disorders, psychologist Judi-Lee Webb described the symptoms: "They over-exercise or they restrict food or they binge and purge. And, in reality, they're not in control at that point; they are very out of control." And Atlanta Public Schools superintendent Beverly Hall, named National Superintendent of the Year,[2] defended her replacement of most of the district's principals to improve the system.

Unemployed

Despite the relatively large number of stories linked to unemployment that focused on job fairs and expos, only two stories contained interviews with African American women who were unemployed. In both cases, the women did not appear to be from the ranks of the long-term unemployed, but, rather, they seemed to personify the struggles of the middle class laid off from well-paying jobs during the recession. Jobs fair attendee Debbie Doshire, attractively attired in a royal blue suit, was "offering free interview coaching while she looks for a job, too." Her goal, she said, was to: "Shake their hand, leave a great resume – and hopefully I'll get a phone call."

In a feature about "one woman who lost her job and now she's trying everything to save her home," an unidentified woman, shown in shadows, acknowledges: "It's embarrassing, it's humiliating. I have never been through it before in my life." The inside of her home seems spacious and tastefully furnished. The reporter notes that because she has been without a job for four months, her water and electricity have been cut off. She is shown reading from a bible by flashlight.

Public Officials

Seven of the eight stories involving public officials involved Atlanta Mayor Shirley Franklin, and most of those stories were about the city's finances. In these stories, she met with President Obama concerning stimulus money for Atlanta; sought federal funding to generate jobs; brushed off a reporter who asked to speak to her about a city loan scandal, replying "No. No, not right now" as she was approached by the reporter in a hallway and just kept walking; spoke about the effect of city furloughs on the fire department; presented a new budget proposal; and called for the governor to accept federal stimulus funds after he said he would refuse to do so. The only other public official in this category was Acting Police Chief Karen Anderson of DeKalb County, shown in a photo, who was reported to have been told by the county CEO to fire Keisha Williams, the top aide to Police Chief Tyrell Bolton.

Celebrities

A standard news value guiding reporters' choices for what constitutes news is the prominence of those involved. As the president's wife and daughters, Michelle, Sasha and Malia Obama appeared in four stories, three of which were about the girls getting the dog promised to them by their parents. These stories, from different stations, ran the same footage of the first lady and the girls walking onto a stage with their father on election night. In the fourth story, Michelle Obama is shown with the president in a story about troop withdrawal from Iraq.

Consumers

The four stories in this category represented area residents as consumers of corporate or city services. In one, two airline passengers were interviewed at the airport about bag fees: Johncie Butler complained about having to pay for a checked bag: "If I pay a certain fee for the fare, I should at least be allowed at least one bag – at least one bag to be able to check in." And Mary Rogers stated: "I understand why the airlines are doing it. I understand it, but I don't like it."

Another story, about rising gas prices, included two women, one of whom was unidentified and stood next to her car at a gas pump. She states: "I'm not understanding. I mean, the price per barrel is the lowest it's ever been, but yet the gas [price] is steadily going up." Lashonda Washington, shown filling the gas tank of her car, comments: "I travel through two counties every, you know, Monday through Friday, to go to work. So I'm paying for it – literally."

Two other stories included Atlanta residents complaining about hikes in their water bills. At a legislative hearing, an unidentified woman is described as being angry by the reporter: "This woman among the angry Atlanta water customers here to tell state lawmakers their problems and demand answers." However, the woman speaking does not indicate anger in her demeanor or comments. She states as part of her testimony: "No leaks indicated from my plumber, but the city supervisor, inspector came out and said, 'Oh, it's your toilet.'" Norma Smith also was described as an angry water customer who had been "slapped with $1600 bills and shut off notices." Again, there is nothing about her demeanor or words that evoke anger: "I still call [the water department], and I think that I might call the water company's hotline. But I still don't get an answer. I'm still, I still have to pay my bill." In a separate story about the water problem, Helen Ellis, shown outside her home, is said to have received a monthly bill for nearly $3,000 when her usual water bill is about $30 per month. She hired a plumber who didn't find any leaks, and she describes the bureaucratic run-around she has received. As in the other story, she does not sound angry, as she was characterized by the reporter, but is measured in her comments: "When you talk to the call center, you get one answer. When you talk to the actual people at the water department at city hall, it's a completely different answer... I don't know about the rest of Atlanta, but I cannot afford a $3,000 – much less a $2,000 – water bill. So right now, I'm just in limbo. And I'd really rather not try to take out an equity home loan just to pay my water bill."

Residents

Three stories included women who were residents of Atlanta and were interviewed about city services. Fatima Muhammed described the closing of a fire station as affecting the safety of her neighborhood; an unidentified woman, who could have been a teacher or a parent, objected to school budget cuts at a school board public hearing; and, in a story about the city seeking funding for streetcars, Angelique Jackson comments: "If you look at how much they would have to kind of break up the road just to add the streetcar in it, it might be just more beneficial to just widen the streets – you know, just like you would on a highway, just to have more lanes."

Background

As might be expected, most of the African American women who appear in local TV news are in the background. The 30 stories in this category involve women who do not have a speaking role and are not identified by name, and they appear in a wide variety of contexts. They showed up either in large crowds, in small groups, or as individuals who just happened to be near someone being interviewed or within the camera's view. Their presence was often used to illustrate a story, but their appearance also could be irrelevant and incidental.

Crowds

African American women frequently appeared in predominantly Black crowds to illustrate the unemployment problem in metro Atlanta. In these stories, they often were shown in long lines inside or outside buildings at job fairs and job "expos," while they waited, often holding papers or portfolios, to be seen by a potential employer or job counselor. They also appeared in the waiting room of an unemployment office.

Other crowd scenes showed African American women: at a "huge, semiannual consignment sale," where they stood in the cashier's line with their arms loaded with clothing; in lines at the airport in a story about airline industry fees; at a town hall meeting of community residents protesting police brutality; and at a school board public hearing about budget cuts. In addition, they could be found in an audience of soldiers or as pedestrians on city streets.

Younger African American females frequently were shown in classrooms or school auditoriums. They appeared in a middle school auditorium, in a mixed-race audience listening to an astronaut guest speaker; in a predominantly Black high school audience where rapper T.I. talked to them as part of his community service for weapons charges; and at their desks during a lecture by a guest teacher.

African American female students also were shown in smaller groups of two to four: making signs and approaching cars to help raise money for their historically Black school, Morris Brown College, which was facing a financial crisis; singing in a school auditorium; milling around outside their high school after a student brought a weapon to school; playing musical instruments in a high school band; and as high school cheerleaders.

Adult African American women who were not students also appeared in groups of two to four. They included three women standing outside a building, perhaps a motel, in a story about a prostitution sting operation. It was unclear whether these women were undercover female police officers involved in the sting operation, bystanders or prostitutes. Other stories in which two to four women were shown included: NAACP members, shown in a photo with male members of the group, in a story about the organization protesting a racist *New York Post* editorial cartoon; women looking at a civil rights exhibit; women walking a picket line comprised mostly of men; unemployment office workers behind desks helping clients; and women sitting in court when rapper T.I. is ordered to pay more in child support to the mother of two of his children.

Individuals

African American women also appeared individually to illustrate stories. These women included: a ticketing agent helping a passenger in a story about the airline industry; a lab technician for a story about sperm banks; a patient getting tested for flu; and a cashier at a Target store in a story about the economy. And, in an example of a woman whose presence seemed wholly unrelated to the story, the woman was simply standing next to a minister whose house has been "set on fire."

Discussion

What is clear from this study is that the overwhelming representation of African American women in local Atlanta news does not fit the stereotypes traditionally ascribed to Black women. Nor do they fit the stereotypes found within previous news studies that did not attend to gender distinctions, for the women in this study were far more likely to be victims than criminals. In addition, they overwhelmingly appeared to be intelligent, well-dressed and attractive. In appearance and behavior, they reflect middle-class tastes, behaviors and mannerisms. Even when they were unemployed, they seemed educated and displayed the trappings of a middle-class lifestyle, whether in their home furnishings or in their demeanor and appearance. As opposed to the stereotype of the angry Black woman, even when the reporter chose to describe as angry those women at a public hearing to protest exorbitant water bills, their comments were well-reasoned and their demeanor moderate in expressing the frustration and annoyance anyone might experience had they encountered bureaucratic stonewalling after receiving $3,000 monthly water bills.

In one of the few instances in which an African American woman used less than "proper" grammar – which usually signifies a working-class or poor economic status – the woman was commenting on the vandalism of a neighborhood church. Another example of a woman likely considered to be poor by viewers was the grandmother said to be "lucky" to be unharmed after "a tree slammed through the ceiling of the room she and three grandchildren were sleeping in, narrowly missing their beds." In this case, poverty is signified by their shared bedroom. Stories about jobs fairs and the unemployed also connote poverty, although they could also imply a struggling economy in which even middle-class workers may find themselves jobless.

African American women appeared to be working class when they were shown in the context of working-class jobs, as in the story about salmonella contamination at the peanut factory, or where they were shown in the background, unidentified and without speaking roles, as a cashier at Target or an airline ticketing agent. However, the class status of some workers who appeared in the background was less clear in a number of instances, such as workers at unemployment offices or job fairs.

Nonetheless, examples of African American women who could be considered poor were notable for their rarity. African American women in local Atlanta news coverage overwhelmingly appeared middle class, well-educated and attractive. The number of stories in which African American women are spokespersons underscores their professional status, as do the stories, fewer in number, in which they are interviewed as experts. The fact that the city's mayor was an African American woman also emphasizes the professional stature of African American women in Atlanta. Whether they are in the news commenting as residents, consumers or the friends or neighbors of victims or criminals, they by-and-large appear middle class.

They do not, however, appear to reflect the middle-class controlling images of the modern mammy, the Black lady or the educated Black bitch (Collins, 2005). The absence of indicators for these images is likely a reflection of the fact that local TV news is, by definition, an abbreviated construction of events. The characterization of someone as a criminal is fairly clear-cut – the stated connection to drugs, guns or crime in general, or the display of handcuffs or a mug shot, immediately signal that this person has likely broken the law and is therefore deviant and likely dangerous. However, within the extreme time constraints of local news, there is little room for character development and fewer ways to convey to audiences the stereotypes of middle-class African American women; it is difficult, if not impossible, to tell within the brief narratives of local news, for example, whether African American women who are spokespersons or experts are "educated Black bitches" who "work too hard, do not know how to support Black men, and/or have character traits that make them unappealing to middle-class Black men" (Collins, 2005, p. 146). Within the context of a police department spokesperson commenting on a prostitution sting, or a physician advising people to wash their hands to avoid the flu, there is nothing to tie them to the stereotypes with which African American women are routinely assailed. Indeed, the African American women portrayed in local Atlanta TV news provide a remedial contradiction to these harmful stereotypes. The demographics of Atlanta, with a large African American population that includes a substantial middle class, no doubt plays a significant role in their portrayal. Also likely affecting representation is the heightened sensitivity of Atlanta reporters, many of whom are African American and have worked to educate their White colleagues about the dangers of racial stereotyping over the years. For example, in a previous study involving interviews with Atlanta area journalists, reporters and editors emphasized that the demographics of the city necessitated sensitivity toward race in their news coverage (Meyers, 1997). As one reporter stated: "We try to be careful about that because we are in a city that has a minority population that is the majority" (Meyers, 1997, p. 95).

However, African American women do, at times, fit the working-class stereotypes of the Jezebel or the bitch, such as in the reports of the prostitution sting operation, as well as the two crime stories involving drugs and guns. But those stories are the anomalies. The studies that claim African Americans are over-represented as criminals and deviants in TV news are, quite simply, wrong when women are taken into account. African American men may, indeed, be over-represented by these stereotypes, but when it comes to the African American women in this study, those stereotypes do not hold up. Rather than criminals, they are over-represented as victims. This category was the largest in which *individual* women appeared (as opposed to them being in the background of stories). But even when they are criminals or associated with criminals, as in the case of the aide to the DeKalb County police chief, they are for the most part not portrayed as stereotypical prostitutes or crack addicts. Their crimes may more likely be providing alcohol to underage teenagers or accidentally killing someone while driving.

In addition, given the largely middle-class and often professional status of the women in this study, claims that the news reflects modern racism in its depiction of African Americans do not correspond as neatly to the representation of women as they seem to for men, who are more often portrayed as criminals. Jhally and Lewis (1992) found in their study of audience responses to the *Cosby* television show, which featured an upper-middle-class African American family in which the father was a doctor and the mother a lawyer, that White audiences tended to view the show as evidence that barriers to racial discrimination no longer existed. The "enlightened racism" that Jhally and Lewis found among White audiences similarly may be triggered by the presence of professional, successful African American women in the news. Thus, while local news can be considered one of the bright spots in mediated popular culture in terms of the depiction of African American women challenging the expected negative stereotypes so common in other genres and forms, the double-bind of this progress is that these portrayals may result in a White public assuming that Black women no longer face racial or gendered bias. This dilemma is cause for further research, as is the question of why African American women in local news coverage in Atlanta are predominantly portrayed in ways that connote middle-class lifestyles. It may be that, in a city that is predominantly Black, journalists are sensitized to the working-class and poverty stereotypes of African Americans and go out of their way to not perpetuate them. The findings of this study are not, as noted previously, generalizable to other media markets or cities. But they do provide evidence of some progress – and some problematics – in the representation of African American women in local TV news.

3

CNN AND FOX NEWS

African American Women in Cable Network News

While local news focuses on crime coverage, network news centers on issues of policy and politics (Dixon, 2008b, p. 332), often within the context of a problem in need of fixing. Along with informing (or misinforming) audiences about national and international events and concerns – such as health care, the economy, war, terrorism and Supreme Court deliberations – network news provides us with images that shape our understanding of our social environment, the world and the people in it. And what audiences see on network news – whether viewing it from mostly White Idaho or majority Black counties in the Mississippi Delta – are images that, according to news scholars, reinforce stereotypes of African Americans as dangerous and impoverished.

Studies of African Americans in network news have found that the news perpetuates stereotypes of African Americans as hostile, intimidating and poor (Dixon, 2006a, 2006b, 2008b; Gilens, 1996). Network studies have concluded that African Americans are associated with crime, drugs and violence (Entman, 1994), as well as sports (Entman and Rojecki, 2000). In addition, Black politicians in network reports often appear more concerned with special interests than their White counterparts (Entman, 1994). Summing up the scholarship on network news, Dixon (2008b) states that "African Americans typically occupy roles as poor people, loud politicians, and criminals" and are most often "associated with poverty, complaining, drugs, and crime" (p. 322).

In addition, a number of these studies[1] indicate that network news – as is the case with local news – reflects modern racism. While modern racism rejects traditional claims of White supremacy and its corollary, the inherent inferiority of people of color, it instead posits that racial discrimination and bias are in the past, that systemic barriers to equality have been lifted, and, as a result, if

African Americans have not achieved middle-class success, they have no one but themselves to blame. Byerly and Wilson (2009) note that enlightened racism, while "more subtle than overt racism... nonetheless generates animosity among the races and tends to reinforce white resistance to the political demands of blacks and other racial minorities" (p. 215). Because network news focuses more on policy and politics than on crime, it is more likely than local news to address social and policy issues that "encourage viewers to locate blame for societal problems such as income disparity and lack of education" (Dixon, 2008b, p. 332). This blame, in turn, is often the basis for modern racism.

The questions raised in this chapter are similar to, and build on, those raised in the previous chapter about local news, but from the perspective of cable network news: Are African American women in network news associated with poverty, complaining, drugs, violence and crime, as studies involving network news claim? Does the portrayal of African American women in cable network news differ from what appears on local TV news, as indicated in the previous chapter? Does network news reflect modern racism in its depiction of African American women? And are African American women even represented in national network news as politicians, given the scarcity of Black women in national politics?

Methodology

This study of cable network news applies discourse analysis to CNN and FOX News coverage involving African American women. Those networks were chosen because of their standing as leaders in cable network news.[2] In an attempt to find two relatively comparable news shows on CNN and FOX during the same time period, the morning weekday news programs were chosen for analysis. FOX's *America's Newsroom* and *CNN Newsroom* during this morning slot were billed by the networks as presenting news rather than opinion. FOX's evening programs feature opinion shows with Bill O'Reilly, Sean Hannity and Greta van Susteren. In addition, morning TV news shows are important in introducing news stories and establishing their significance for the rest of the day.

FOX News's and CNN's news shows were taped from 9 to 10 a.m. for four weeks, Monday through Friday, from Oct. 5 through Oct. 30, 2009. In all, 20 hours of news were taped for each station, amounting to 40 hours in total, during which any story or promotion for an upcoming story[3] in which an African American female appeared, either in the background or as an individual featured in a story, was transcribed and analyzed. African American women were identified in this study based on their skin color and other signifiers of racial identity where appropriate.

This study combined discourse analysis with the constant comparative method (Glaser and Strauss, 1967) to first determine the themes and patterns within news coverage, and then to provide a deeper analysis of how language is used within news to shape certain meanings and understandings. In applying the constant comparative method, this study looked for patterns and themes concerning the representation of African American women. Discourse analysis was then conducted to examine how ideologies are expressed in written, spoken and visual texts, as well as how language and representation produce meaning and construct identities and subjectivities (Hall, 1997). In news studies, discourse analysis looks at topics, schematic structures, semantic strategies and implicitness, which may be "even more important, from a critical point of view, than what is explicitly said or meant" (Van Dijk, 1991, p. 17). The combination of discourse analysis with the constant comparative approach allows for an in-depth examination of selected articles within specific categories. In addition, applying a perspective informed by Black feminist theorists ensured that gender and class, along with race, were central to this analysis. As is the case with other qualitative textual analyses of this type, including those of other chapters in this book, the findings here are not generalizable but are meant to provide insight into the portrayal of African American women within cable network news.

Findings

In 40 hours of news programming, African American women appeared in 40 news stories or promos – 18 for CNN and 22 for FOX. The total length of time for these stories was approximately 23 minutes on CNN and 60 minutes on FOX. These times are deceptive in that, for many of the stories – particularly the longer stories – African American women appeared only fleetingly.

African American women primarily appeared as background illustration for the news, but they also appeared as victims and, albeit rarely, as criminals. The primary themes were victimization, dysfunction, poverty, crime and violence. While poverty, crime and violence were similarly found to be primary themes in previous news studies, victimization and dysfunction tied to family, community or individuals were not. In addition, African American women were more likely to be represented as victims or the mothers of victims than as criminals. And in the rare instances in which they appeared as a lawbreaker, their crime was family-related or non-violent – and therefore did not constitute the threat to social order as indicated by previous studies. However, when African American women appear in large, mixed-gender crowds that are predominantly or exclusively Black, those gathered are likely to be represented as a violent or threatening presence, which suggests that the presence of Black males constitutes the danger. While modern racism was evident in some news stories, so, too, was paternalistic racism, which views African American women as in need of and deserving assistance from a White public.

Background Illustration

African American women rarely were featured in the two morning news shows on CNN and FOX; in the majority of news stories, the presence of African American women was limited to background videos or crowd scenes, where their presence served to illustrate the topic being covered. In these stories, the women appear as mute visuals beneath the voice of the anchor, reporter or newsmaker.

Their appearance in stock video footage was particularly prevalent in stories involving health care reform or H1N1 flu – so-called "swine flu." At the time of this study, the health care reform debate was occupying Congress and "swine flu" had reached epidemic proportions, with the president declaring a state of emergency. So, for instance, in two separate stories about health care reform on FOX – one a six-minute telephone interview with Republican Senator John Barrasso of Wyoming and the other a four-minute phone interview with Democratic House member Martin Frost of Texas, African American women appear fleetingly in video aired over the interview, as either patients being attended to by physicians or as nurses performing their duties. Similarly, in an Oct. 15 CNN story about a White nurse suing the state of New York because it mandated that health care workers receive an H1N1 flu shot, background video included: two Black women who appear among a group of about a dozen supporters on the steps of a courthouse; a Black nurse loading vaccine into a syringe; and a second scene of supporters at the courthouse in which one Black woman is visible. Another CNN story, on Oct. 20, about precautions that hospitals are taking in the wake of the swine flu outbreak, as well as an Oct. 26 CNN story about the nation's response to the virus, also contained background video, with voice-over, showing Black nurses rolling hospital beds into a room or down a hallway, as well as Black patients and family members in a hospital waiting room. An Oct. 28 FOX story about a shortage of H1N1 vaccine likewise included background video of a Black female patient receiving the vaccine from a Black female nurse.

African American women and girls also appeared in the background in stories that were about events that would directly affect them or in which they were present at the scene of the story being covered. For example, an Oct. 8 CNN story about a plant shutting down in Winston-Salem, NC, included brief background video of an African woman and man working inside the factory. The implication is that they will be among the 905 people who will lose their jobs. In a FOX story on Oct. 7 about "schools in Florida in a tight budget squeeze," numerous videotaped scenes of students in classrooms were shown, including ones with African American girls at their desks. And in an Oct. 7 story about new cell phone technology, a montage of young adults on cell phones included African American women.

And in one of the few instances in which a small group of African American women appeared together, four women were featured in a "flash mob dance" in downtown Miami as part of a promotion for the city's Seaquarium. Video showed the students dancing to Michael Jackson's song, "Thriller."

African American women also appeared within large, racially mixed gatherings, such as a campaign rally. Stories about President Obama often included crowd scenes in which African American women were present (CNN, Oct. 16). For example, in FOX stories about the Virginia (Oct. 28) and New Jersey (Oct. 30) governor's races, crowd shots of President Obama speaking at rallies showed African American women in the audiences.

Additionally, in the only story to explicitly address racism, CNN reported Oct. 27 that six male, African American college students were not allowed into a bar because, the students said, they were wearing baggy pants. Video showed a multi-racial audience with male and female students in a college lecture hall where students "are considering mounting a protest."

Violence and Poverty

Stories involving large, predominantly or wholly Black crowds in which African American women were present invariably highlighted poverty and violence. For example, a promo Oct. 8 on CNN began with a video of a large crowd of people, all of whom appeared to be Black, while the anchor stated: "Long lines and short tempers for thousands of people seeking federal housing assistance in Detroit. Applications for money for the homeless – or those about to be homeless – were being handed out." Scenes of African American women and men in long lines, filling out paperwork or handing out applications, included a shot focusing on two African American women sitting down while filling out paperwork as the reporter continued: "The deadline to submit the applications was originally yesterday. Well, stress over that deadline led to scuffles and some injuries. And, as you saw, massive lines. We'll have more on this story coming up in our next hour."

Stating that "applications for money for the homeless were being handed out" is code for "government handouts," which conservative groups tend to view as undeserved and a drain on hard-working taxpayers' dollars. From this perspective, recipients of this assistance are seen as unworthy of help, particularly given their seeming proclivity for violence. However, even when there is no violence, the threat of violence seems to hang over African Americans in large groups when Black males are included. For instance, a FOX promo Oct. 9 for a story about "hunting for jobs in Detroit" showed video of an all-Black crowd inside a large hall. The anchor notes that Detroit has "30 percent unemployment... the worst in the nation." Although no violence is shown, a Black male official can be heard yelling that: "We need everybody to calm down, get in line. Everybody will receive an app [application]." The appeal for calm indicates the potentially explosive nature of the crowd. In this story and the one above, it appears that when Black women are in large gatherings with Black males, the possibility of violence is ever-present.

Victims

When African American women were featured in the news as individuals rather than in the background or in crowds, they were often portrayed as victims or a relative of the victim – most often the mother. In a number of cases, these stories highlighted poverty and dysfunction. For example, an Oct. 7 CNN report focused on the "young victims" of "Chicago's deadly violence" by telling the story of 6-year-old Martrell Stevens, who was shot and partially paralyzed "while sleeping in the back seat of his mother's car" by a gunman whose "target was someone near the car." Martrell's mother, an African American woman named Lakeesha Rucker, tells the reporter, Gary Tuchman, that people – herself included – know who the shooter is, but she and others in her South Side neighborhood are afraid to talk. Tuchman later tells the audience that "what keeps this mom happy is her son's progress." Over video of the boy as he uses a walker to navigate among the chairs and desks of his school classroom, Tuchman notes that he "is a fast wheelchair rider" and is "in first grade at a public school that specializes in special needs children." Martrell is later shown moving across a stage with his walker to accept his diploma as he graduates from kindergarten, and Tuchman explains that the boy received "what his mom hopes is the first of many diplomas." The reporter states that "Martrell's mom dreams he will have a bright future" and knows her son "is going to be able to walk again." At the end of the story, video shows Rucker, holding her toddler daughter, with Martrell and another son. Tuchman concludes: "But she worries every day about the safety of all three of her children. She's a janitor and has another dream [here the video cuts to Rucker pushing her son in a wheelchair toward their home] – about the day she can afford to move her family into a safer neighborhood."

Rucker appears to be a single mother, and while she may not fit the stereotype of the welfare mother given her job as a janitor, she appears to be a poor, unmarried Black mother with several children who is trying her best to care for them in a hostile environment. Although devoted to her son, she is unable to protect her children – which is arguably the primary and most important responsibility of a parent. Rucker holds out hope for a better future for her son and family, but the story provides no indication that they will ever have the resources to escape the cycle of poverty and violence that permeates their lives and neighborhood. She knows who shot Martrell, drives by him daily, and yet does nothing about it, allowing her son's attacker to possibly endanger others. While this may be a logical choice given the probable consequences from gang members, as well as the long history of ineffectual and even destructive responses by the police and courts in dealing with crimes against African Americans, Rucker appears inadequate as a mother. She wants to protect her children, but she can't. She appears to need help that does not appear to be forthcoming from her African American community, which is presented as the source of her problems. Her only hope, then, lies outside her community, presumably from the larger, White viewing public.

In a different story that included an African American mother of a victim, a Tennessee newborn was reported "kidnapped from his Nashville home" but "found safe in Alabama" three days later. This CNN story indicated that the mother may have been involved in the kidnapping – which, it appears, is what the authorities initially thought. At the beginning of the story, an African American woman, presumably the mother, is shown holding a baby as the anchor states that: "An Alabama woman is in jail, facing a federal kidnapping charge." The mother later is shown again, this time without the baby but with cuts and bruises to her face. The juxtaposition of the visual image of the mother of the kidnapped child with the anchor's words makes it appear as though the mother was behind the kidnapping of her own child and is the one in jail. The anchor continues the story by noting that "the Associated Press reports there are allegations a family member was arranging to sell the boy," and the camera remains on the mother's bruised face. The next-day follow-up to that story began with the anchor announcing:

> Checking the top stories now. A Tennessee mom has been reunited with her newborn baby after he was kidnapped and later placed in state custody. Still, police say they have a lot of questions about the case. The baby was found in Alabama last week after being abducted during a knife attack on the mother. The Associated Press reported the state took custody of the baby and her siblings after someone claimed a family member had tried to sell the baby. Police now say they don't think the parent had anything to do with the kidnapping.

During this brief update on what was introduced as a "top story," the "parent" apparently is the mother since there appears to be no father or other parent involved. The same image of the mother holding her baby that aired in the previous day's story is shown again. In both stories, the mother appears to be the victim of a crime, although she also was suspected of the kidnapping and sale of her child. The first story adds another dimension: an Alabama woman, presumably a relative, has been arrested on kidnapping charges. Thus, this story presents both an African American woman – the mother – who is a crime victim (as well as the mother of a crime victim), and an African American woman – the relative – who is a criminal. Not only did the "family member" steal the baby in an attempt to sell it, but she attacked the mother with a knife. The mother also is said to have three other children, initially removed from her custody by the state "after someone said a family member tried to sell the baby."

The mother appears to be unmarried with multiple children and a dysfunctional, violent family. Given the historical association of this image with the stereotype of the "welfare mother," many viewers would assume that she is on welfare or, at least, poor. In addition, given the much-publicized link between the sale of children – even babies – for sex in exchange for "crack" cocaine, the implication of this reference to the selling of a newborn is that drugs may have been involved.

Another story, featuring an African American woman who had been raped as a child, was aired Oct. 19 on CNN. In this story, about the release of "20 convicted rapists and murderers" given life sentences but scheduled to be released from North Carolina prisons, an unidentified African American woman who was kidnapped and raped in 1978 by one of the convicts when she was 9 years old is interviewed. In video footage in which only her hands on a desk are visible, she states, apparently in response to a question: "What would I say to him? It's not what would I say to him – it's what would I do to him, because I feel like he shouldn't be living on this earth." Her rapist, Steven Wilson, appears to be African American in a photo and is said to have "racked up 18 infractions while in prison, including attacking another inmate with sexual intent." The reporter concludes the report by noting that the state "is now scrambling to find a way to keep them [the convicts] behind bars."

In this story, the reporter implies that the "convicted rapists and murderers" – signified by Wilson – remain dangerous and should not be released. The story does not address the psychological harm Wilson caused his victim, although the emotional and physical toll are hinted at when the victim states that Wilson "shouldn't be living on this earth."

And in a story with a pseudo-familial connection, CNN reported that the former fiancé of a cast member on the reality TV show *The Real Housewives of Atlanta* had been fatally injured in a fight outside "a strip club in Atlanta." "Housewife" Kandi Burris was engaged to the victim until August, the anchor noted. Although she was not related to the victim, this story has a pseudo-familial connection given their long-standing engagement on the show. The reference to the strip club provides a somewhat seamy aspect to the story, while also underscoring the violence within Atlanta's African American community.

Dysfunction, Poverty and Crime

Other than the CNN stories about the kidnapped Tennessee baby, the only other story that involved an African American woman as a criminal was a FOX News story about a woman who claimed to have won the lottery and offered to pay for the purchases of customers in an Ohio store. Significantly, both of these stories reflect the intertwined themes of crime, dysfunction and poverty.

The Ohio story was introduced in a promo early in the news hour with video of an African American woman getting out of a limousine with a checkbook in her hand. She is then shown talking to a woman and later is inside the store, talking on a cell phone. While this video is being shown, the anchor states: "Hey, a woman in a stretch Hummer sets off a feeding frenzy inside of a store. She offers to buy everyone inside a winter coat." The screen transitions to a still photo of the woman while the anchor continues: "But, boy, you should see the number of people that turned out." At this point, the story appears to be about the "feeding frenzy" caused by the announcement of free coats; the reference to "the number of people who turned out" indicates the store was mobbed by those seeking something for nothing. About half an hour later in the newscast, a second promo shows video of a crowd of people, predominantly Black, standing outside a Burlington Coat Factory store while White, male police officers appear to be talking to them. The anchor states: "From shopping frenzy to shopping fury, a woman says she won the lottery and wants to share her riches. But find out what happened when the truth came out." The screen then cuts to a White male who says he "grabbed a laundry hamper" so that he could put what he could grab into it, and then cuts to a young, African American female who says: "I don't even need the clothes. I said, 'I just need some, uh, assistance with my rent.' She said, 'Well, how much is it?' And she just promptly wrote out a check." About 10 minutes later, a White, female anchor presents the full story: "Alright, wait until you hear this story. There was chaos at a Burlington Coat Factory store in Ohio when Linda Brown rolled up in a stretch limousine. She walked in and announced that she had won the lottery and was paying for everyone's purchases."

The story continues with the woman, on camera, announcing: "I won the lottery for half a million dollars. Thank God! I don't want none of it, really. Five hundred dollars – tell your friends, tell your family." The screen cuts to video of a crowd, predominantly Black, standing outside the store while police officers appear to be explaining something to them, and the anchor states that: "The customers inside the store called their friends and relatives to come on down, and soon the store was flooded with people. Does this sound too good to be true? Well, if so, that's because it is. Brown took the limo, which turned out to be rented, to an ATM to take out the supposed cash, and she returned empty-handed. Word spread quickly of the hoax." The anchor later states that "a riot started in the store," with "angry customers" throwing clothes and running out of the store "without paying." Brown, meanwhile, "took off in the limo, while cops struggled to control the crowd."

As the news story unfolds, various video shots of the woman are shown, her face blurred, as well as taped interviews with store customers and police officers asking the crowds to leave. Toward the end, the anchor announces, "Linda Brown is now behind bars. She was turned over to police by her limo driver after he realized that she doesn't have the cash to pay the $900 she owes him for the limo."

In this story, which was heavily hyped during the hour with two promos, Brown's actions are presented by FOX as a "hoax," which implies intentionality. However, the fact that Brown went to an ATM to get money and then returned empty-handed indicates that mental illness rather than deception and fraud may have been the cause. Brown's actions imply that she may well have been delusional and believed she had the money she claimed to have won. In either event, her crime was clearly non-violent and non-threatening. However, the actions of the "angry" mob include rioting and looting,

This story, like the CNN kidnapping report, links dysfunction, poverty and crime: the young, African American woman needed help with her rent, and Brown, herself, had neither the $900 for the limo nor, presumably, the cash to make bail. However, in neither the kidnapping nor the "hoax" story does the African American woman accused of crime represent a threat to society at large – although the crowd of predominantly Black looters and rioters do. Rather, she serves as a sign of poverty, as well as dysfunction – mental or familial. While Linda Brown and the Tennessee mother do not appear to be violent, the mother's family and the store mob are both linked to crime and violence.

In a few stories, the relationship of the woman to crime is more tenuous and may not, in fact, even exist. These appear to be one-off stories of guilt by implication, but they suggest that African American women are not to be trusted and are, in fact, inclined to skirt the law. For example, in one such story, Megan Williams, who is African American, recanted her 2007 accusation of rape and torture in an Oct. 22 CNN story. Over video of Williams entering a courthouse with her family and legal counsel, the anchor states: "A woman who claimed she was raped and tortured in a racially motivated attack now says she lied." Williams had claimed that for several days she was held captive in a trailer by seven White people, all of whom confessed and pleaded guilty. Six were sent to prison. The anchor concluded by noting that: "Williams, now living in Ohio, says she recanted the story because she no longer wanted to live a lie. Prosecutors have dismissed Williams' new claims. Attorneys for the defendants would not discuss their plans."

Whether Williams was the victim of rape and torture is unclear, particularly given that the suspects all confessed and pleaded guilty. What is clear is that Williams is a liar – either at the time of the alleged rape and torture or more recently with the recantation of those charges. In addition, if she did lie initially, as she now claims, she is guilty of a crime. However, given the confessions of those convicted, it may be that Williams really was raped and tortured, and has some other, unnamed reason for recanting her story. Not only does her retraction lend credence to the idea that women lie about rape, but it also supports the notion that African Americans unjustly claim racism when it does not exist.

In another guilt-by-implication story, FOX aired two promos Oct. 6 about the soon-to-be-released results of an internal investigation "nearly a month after a nationwide scandal nearly brings down that left-wing political group ACORN [Association of Community Organizations for Reform Now]." The anchor reminded viewers that ACORN workers "were caught on camera advising a supposed prostitute how to fake out the feds and the IRS and set up a brothel." With this, the screen shows a still photo of two women, one a scantily dressed White woman with her back to the camera, and the other appearing to be a middle-aged African American woman, dressed more conservatively in a tank top, with her hands on her hips, talking to the White woman. The photo seemingly illustrates the interaction between the White "prostitute" and the Black ACORN worker who illegally advised the fake prostitute in what was, but is not described as such by FOX, a sting operation conducted by right-wing activists. The second promo, 20 minutes later, uses the same still photo to announce ACORN's release of an internal investigation, which will be aired "live, top of the hour."

The next day, FOX aired another story involving ACORN, this one critical of a decision by the Department of Homeland Security to provide $1 million in funding to the group from "money typically earmarked for fire departments all across the country." ACORN again is described as a "left-wing group," and two video-taped scenes are shown with voice-overs from two anchors discussing the story. Both videos are of ACORN rallies – in one, an African American man is leading a chant, and in the other, two Black women are visible among a crowd marching in a circle with signs stating "Stop Foreclosures: Foreclosure Free Zone: ACORN." One of the anchors continues the story by stating: "Apparently, DHS is having second thoughts… We understand the money has been frozen, so ACORN has not received the money. It's been awarded, but it has not been doled out. They cannot cash that check." Both anchors agree to "keep you posted" on this story. As in the previous day's promos, ACORN is demonized as a left-wing, corrupt organization, in this case taking money from firefighters who need it. And, as with the promos, the African American women shown appear to be involved in a radical organization engaged in unlawful and morally objectionable activities. The photo of the "prostitute" and ACORN worker is used to implicate the African American woman in the illicit scheme.

Foil for FOX

While the above story suggests that the African American woman in the ACORN video is somehow engaged in criminal activity, it also places her in the position of a foil for FOX's conservative political agenda. In this and a number of other instances on FOX, the presence of African American women allowed the network to claim "balance" in a story that appeared motivated by a consistent corporate strategy aimed at undercutting President Barack Obama and his policies. One example of this was a FOX report on Oct. 15 in which the anchor opened the story by stating: "A New Jersey school landed in the national spotlight after a video of students singing President Obama's praises hit the Internet. Some compared this to political indoctrination." The school superintendent "faced a board meeting packed with parents and defended his teacher's actions." After a statement by the White superintendent claiming that "this was an innocent song performed by a class of small children to recognize and congratulate the first African American president of the United States of America. There was no attempt to promote a political point of view through this song," the anchor noted that: "Not only did many of the parents give him a standing ovation, they spoke out in support of this song, also." The camera then cut to an African American mother of a student at the school who states: "I think it was innocent. My daughter has gone to this school. She's at middle school now. But when she was here, she sang songs about other politicians, other presidents, and it was never an issue. So I'm kind of offended that because this president is an African American president that all of a sudden it's inappropriate for any type of politics or any of those type of things to be brought in the school."

After this brief comment from this African American mother, the rest of the relatively long – four-minute – story was primarily devoted to a telephone interview with another mother, this one presumably White. Leslie Gibson is not shown on the screen; her voice is heard against video of schoolchildren, their faces blurred, singing on a stage in what appears to be a school assembly. She is asked whether the principal or superintendent "apologized last night to parents for making kids sing this song about how wonderful President Obama is, as are some of his policies." Of course, the anchor knows an apology was not offered, but it gives Gibson the opportunity to state her dissatisfaction with the school's administration and how she believes "an official apology" should be given by the superintendent or school principal. When the anchor then suggests the woman "must have felt like a lone voice last night" after the superintendent got a standing ovation, she replies: "No – there were actually about 25 people who sat when he got that standing ovation, and I was one of those people." The anchor's response: "Good for you. So, but listen, the bottom line here is no one suspended, no one reprimanded, the principal supports this, the superintendent supports the principal. Are you satisfied now with the outcome, or what do you want to see happen?"

While it was clear from what Gibson previously had said about wanting an apology and being disappointed at the outcome, the anchor gave her another opportunity to state her opposition to what's being presented by FOX as the indoctrination of young students. Gibson then calls for the principal's suspension and claims that "if John McCain had won this election, they would never have done this song." She also blasts the principal for having shown "her political views by sending home stickers while the election was going on" and submitting "a picture of herself and her husband at the inauguration for our yearbook, so when I look back at my children's yearbook, there's a picture of herself and her husband… she let everyone know her political views that way." And after the anchor attempts to sign off, the mother states: "I want to say one other thing" and is given more time to vent her displeasure with the school's administration: "I've grown up in this town, lived here my whole life, and all of my brothers and sisters send their kids through school here. Not only has she [the principal] said this is a diverse community, but she has taken away American traditions here. I understand this is a diverse community. However, she has taken away Halloween from our children and can give us no clear reason why. And that's another major issue that I asked the board to look into."

In this story, Gibson is given a national soapbox to vent what appears to be a long-standing antagonism toward the school's administrator. The unidentified African American mother, on the other hand, is allowed to only briefly support the superintendent in what appears to be an attempt by FOX to claim balance by presenting both sides of the issue. The African American woman's comments are undercut by the lengthy interview with Gibson. Indeed, the anchor even applauds Gibson by stating "Good for you" when she says she sat while others gave the superintendent a standing ovation. The African American mother appears to have been used as a foil to claim balance in a story in which the overwhelming message is that children singing a song about President Obama is an unacceptable case of political indoctrination that needs to be punished.

In another example of an African American woman used as a counterpoint to FOX's conservative ideology, Claudia Fegan, the former president of Physicians for a National Health Program, was pitted against Dr. Marc Siegel, FOX News's medical correspondent, in what was billed by the anchor as a "fair and balanced debate" about "a powerful new post," the health choices commissioner, created by the House health care reform bill which has come to be known as Obamacare. Notably, Fegan was the only African American woman who was included in this study because of her professional expertise. The "debate," moderated by the anchor asking questions, allowed Fegan to make a cogent argument for the bill, even undercutting the FOX medical advisor's position that what's needed is "a national playing field for insurance companies so that they can compete and be held more honest…getting more government oversight, more government bureaucracy is not going to fix that because there's already too many backdoor deals going on." Fegan's response, that "the market has not done anything to help the number of people who are underinsured and uninsured," states what is for many Americans obvious. She concludes with a plug for the House bill and states that it will be a "treat" for the insurance industry, the pharmaceutical industry and the American public, "which is looking for a simple plan" – and, she adds, "We already have one – Medicare for all, and I think that's a simple way to expand coverage. If Medicare is enough for people over 65, then why is it not enough for people over 25?" In this story, Fegan appears to have bested the FOX medical expert by undermining his argument that a market free of government interference can solve the nation's health care problems, and by having the last word.[4]

Michelle Obama also appeared in a FOX story that, as its promo stated, is about "who's at fault for Chicago not getting the Olympic games" and concludes that it might be the president. Video shows President and Michelle Obama walking side-by-side at an Olympic event in Copenhagen, where they had gone with the U.S. delegation to support Chicago's quest to be the 2016 summer Olympics venue. In a second promo about 20 minutes later, they appear in background video on a stage in Copenhagen and, later, sit side-by-side as part of the Olympic delegation. About five minutes later, the four-minute story begins and contains a debate about whether Obama erred in expending "political capital" going to Copenhagen and whether Democrats are "making fools of themselves by continuously blaming things on George Bush." Videotape of the president and Michelle Obama walking to the stage was then shown once again.

Within the context of a story that implies the president should not have traveled to Copenhagen, the first lady's presence there also appears ill advised, suggesting she is both complicit in the president's mistake as well as irrelevant to the stated mission of the trip. Although never explicitly stated, the questions raised about the trip hint at the possibility that it was merely a junket for the president and his wife at taxpayers' expense.

Celebrity Families

African American women and girls also were newsworthy by virtue of their familial ties with a famous husband or father. Michelle Obama and daughters Sasha and Malia appeared in a few news stories, including one Oct. 28 on CNN about the girls receiving immunization shots for H1N1 flu. This story used a professional portrait of the first family as a graphic – most likely because the president and first lady have kept their children off-limits to the press. The stories involving the children serve to normalize the Obama family, presenting the mother and daughters as part of a stable, two-parent household – a relative rarity in the news for African American families. In addition, a report about Michelle Obama and Jill Biden, the wife of the vice president, attending the opening game of the World Series showed the women on video, embracing in front of a podium at what appears to be a White House press function. This story, too, presents both Obama and Biden within the context of their relationship to their famous husbands. It also normalizes Michelle Obama; she and Jill Biden are engaging in an all-American spectator sport enjoyed by baseball fans across the country – albeit, in the case of attending the World Series in person, one that may not be accessible to most.

In contrast to the seeming normalcy of the Obama family, and hence Michelle Obama, family dysfunction underscored a CNN report about the three adult children of the Rev. Martin Luther King Jr. – two sons and one daughter – who were said to have reached an out-of-court settlement over their parents' estate. Over courtroom video scenes of the three King children, including Bernice King, the anchor explained that they had "agreed to split the money from the estate that they've been fighting over. Bernice King and Martin Luther King III had accused their brother Dexter King of taking money from the estate."

Discussion

Contrary to previous studies that concluded African Americans in the news are over-represented as criminals and deviants, with their primary portrayal a threat to the social order, this study found that African American women are more likely to be the victims of crimes or the mothers of crime victims. In the rare instances in which they appeared as lawbreakers, their crimes either targeted their own families or involved non-violent behavior, such as a "hoax." Unlike African American males, the few African American women who are portrayed as criminals did not appear to be threatening or a serious challenge to law and order; their crimes were not connected to drugs or guns.

Nevertheless, the primary themes within news coverage of African American women were poverty, violence, victimization, crime and dysfunction, the latter related to family, community or individual. Poverty, crime and violence were frequent, conjoined themes, occurring in stories that highlighted individuals as the *victims* of violence, rather than the *perpetrators*, and in stories involving large crowds of predominantly or exclusively African American men and women. These crowds created "scuffles" and caused injuries when seeking housing or jobs, and they engaged in a "feeding frenzy" of rioting and looting at a store.

Aspects of modern racism appeared in some coverage, particularly when crowds seeking government assistance were engaged in rioting or looting. The violence as described in these instances underscores the violent and undeserving nature of those present and their lack of responsibility and discipline, which supports the premise within modern racism that they are to blame for their impoverishment and the violence in their communities. However, the story about Martrell Stevens and his devoted mother, Lakeesha Rucker, who dreams of better things for her children, points to a paternalistic racism that portrays some African Americans as deserving of help that is not forthcoming from the African American community and thus may only be available from White concerned citizens.

Furthermore, stories in which African American women appeared fleetingly in background video to illustrate stories – whether about health care or new cellphone technology or education – worked to normalize African American women and girls. Their appearance as nurses, patients, pedestrians or schoolchildren spoke to a color-blindness that naturalized their presence in ordinary, everyday activities in which Whites also engaged. They appeared to be no different from any of the other nurses, students, pedestrians and others who were similarly shown in background video. More than the stories which featured African American women individually, their presence in background video affirmed their equality.

No African American women appeared in cable network news as a spokesperson or politician, and only Dr. Fegan was allowed to serve as an expert, which occurred within the context of a debate over health care that showcased FOX's political and ideological conservativism. It was not the intent of this chapter to compare the coverage between FOX and CNN. Nevertheless, the conservativism with which FOX News framed stories involving African American women could not be ignored. FOX used African American women as foils to promote a conservative agenda that seeks to undermine the president, both personally and politically.

In addition, FOX's choice and framing of stories often reinforced stereotypes about African American women and men. This is perhaps best illustrated by a comparison of two in-depth reports produced by FOX and CNN: that of 6-year-old shooting victim Martrell Stevens and his mother, Lakeesha Rucker, and that of the much-hyped FOX story involving Linda Brown, the woman who claimed she had won a lottery and would pay for the purchases of strangers at a Burlington Coat Factory in Ohio. In the CNN story, Rucker is portrayed as poor, but hard-working and determined to make a better life for herself and her children in the midst of a dangerous neighborhood, with a disabled child and not enough money. The reporter appears compassionate and clearly sympathizes with her struggle, and she is represented as the victim of circumstances over which she has no control.

Brown, on the other hand, is an object of derision and scorn, if not outright contempt, from the anchors, as are the people involved in what was called a "feeding frenzy" touched off by the false promise of free shopping. Comments such as "Alright, wait until you hear this story" and "Does this sound too good to be true? Well, if so, that's because it is" emphasize both the anchor's incredulity at what happened, as well as the gullibility of those who would believe they could be getting something for nothing. In addition, references to the number of people at the store and the description of looting and chaos as a "feeding frenzy" work to frame African Americans as violent freeloaders and criminals – frames that contribute to modern racism within the news.

Some themes, such as poverty and violence, involved both African American men and women. But there were differences. African American women, unlike men, were more likely to be portrayed as victims than criminals, and news coverage of Black women reflected paternalistic racism and dysfunction, in addition to modern racism. Furthermore, the use of African American women as a foil for FOX to promote a right-wing ideological agenda speaks to the on-going struggle of a conservative elite to maintain dominance and control. It is no coincidence that FOX, rather than CNN, ran the story about Linda Brown, or conducted an extensive phone interview with Gibson, who was used to advance the network's anti-Obama agenda in a story that framed a children's song as an attempt at political indoctrination. This is not to say one-sided ideological reporting is limited to media controlled by FOX owner Rupert Murdoch. But it is to say that in the ideological struggle over meaning that gets played out daily in cable network news, FOX represents a conservative extreme poorly disguised as what its slogan claims it to be –"fair and balanced" news. Within this context, it is likely that negative stereotypes of African American women, as well as men, will be far more common on FOX than elsewhere in mainstream network TV news.

4

'TUBING WITH MICHELLE OBAMA

During the 2008 presidential election campaign, Michelle Obama became, as *The New York Times* reported, "a favorite target of conservatives, who attack her with an exuberance that suggests there are no taboos anymore" (Gibbs and Newton-Small, 2008, p. 28). She was said to be unpatriotic for commenting during the Wisconsin primary that: "For the first time in my adult lifetime, I am really proud of my country." Her senior thesis as an undergraduate at Princeton gave rise to a "slanderous e-mail rumor campaign" in which she was falsely accused of stating that America was founded on "crime and hatred" and that Whites were "ineradicably racist" (Katel, 2008). A false rumor also was spread by conservative radio talk show host Rush Limbaugh and others that a tape existed in which Michelle Obama referred to White people as "whitey." The FOX News channel referred to her as "Obama's baby mama"[1] – a term "rooted in the specific history of shaming black women as sexually immoral" (Harris-Perry, 2011, p. 273) – and also suggested that she gave her husband a "terrorist fist jab" when they bumped knuckles at a campaign rally in St. Paul (Pickler, 2008, p. A2). In addition, the cover of the April 21, 2008 issue of the conservative *National Review* featured a photo of her, scowling, with the caption "Mrs. Grievance: Michelle Obama and her discontent."

Seeking to both satirize and sum up this wellspring of ill-will that sought to paint Michelle Obama as a stereotypically angry, unpatriotic, militant and disgruntled Black woman, *The New Yorker* magazine ran an illustration of her and Barack Obama on the cover of its July 21, 2008 edition: Michelle is sporting a large Afro and combat fatigues, a gun and ammunition belt slung over her shoulder; a portrait of Osama bin Laden hangs over the fireplace, in which an American flag is burning; and Michelle and Barack Obama – he clad in a turban and what would likely appear to Westerners as an Arab-style robe – are bumping fists.

Less than a year later, as the first African American first lady, Michelle Obama's favorability ratings had soared to 76 percent, up 28 points since the previous summer, according to a *Washington Post*-ABC poll conducted in late March 2009. "Who could have seen this coming after the *New Yorker* cover and all the other negative press she received," asked Debbie Walsh, director of the Center of American Women in Politics at Rutgers University (quoted in Samuels, 2009, p. 40). Indeed, four years after the *New Yorker* cover, as Barack Obama campaigned for re-election in the summer of 2012, polls confirmed that his wife continued to be more popular than he, with 66 percent of Americans viewing her favorably compared with 52 percent for the president in a May 10–13, 2012 poll (Jones, 2012).

How did this transformation come about? Spillers (2009) suggests that the negative reactions to Michelle Obama "so stirred up the Obama campaign's PR machine that the future first lady had to be re-choreographed into a more palatable routine; in short, she appears to have been 'handled,' 'softened' in tone and image" (p. 308). Much of this re-choreography occurred in traditional news media, with newspapers, TV and magazines showcasing stories about Michelle Obama. However, the Obama campaign also skillfully employed YouTube videos to "soften" and shape news coverage of her. The campaign "was renowned for its sophisticated use of the Internet and YouTube," outmatching Obama's rivals in gaining internet viewers' attention on YouTube and Facebook so that viewers spent 1 billion minutes watching Obama videos (Strangelove, 2010, p. 139). YouTube clips served as virtual "video press releases" that had a greater chance of getting covered by news organizations than traditional campaign material (Palser, 2006, p. 90).

Given both the pervasiveness of racist and sexist stereotyping of Michelle Obama during the 2008 election, and the subsequent reversal in her approval ratings four years later, as well as the increasing prominence of YouTube in shaping political discourse, just how the first lady was portrayed in YouTube videos during the 2012 presidential election is worth asking. Were the stereotypes that dogged her four years earlier a part of YouTube discourse in 2012? Are there new and different images of the first lady? And how have the White House and Obama campaign sought to portray her? This study seeks to answer these questions through an examination of YouTube clips for the roles and representation of Michelle Obama during the presidential primaries. Michelle Obama's portrayal in Web videos uploaded by the White House and Obama campaign[2] is of central interest to this research given the success of the administration in bolstering the first lady's popularity. These clips served as a way both to reach the public without the mediating filter of news organizations, and to shape the content of traditional news. However, this study also is concerned with how she is portrayed in YouTube videos posted by others, including non-professional video producers – the user-generators who, as Strangelove (2010) states, produce amateur video that plays a significant role in how "elections are being fought, won, and lost online" (p. 141).

Because YouTube is, Strangelove explains, "a fierce battleground over public opinion and over the legitimacy of various groups and beliefs" (p. 155), a study of the representation of Michelle Obama on YouTube is expected to reflect this struggle. In addition, as Shoop (2010) notes, the position of first lady is one which "many people around the United States and the globe look to for clues about the appropriate role of women in society" (p. 807). Thus, she adds, "How the news media cover these high-profiled women may certainly impact the perpetuation or breaking down of gender stereotypes to a domestic and international audience" (p. 807). How Michelle Obama is portrayed in YouTube video clips therefore also should tell us something about the roles and status of African American women in society, as well as the various attempts to define the nation's first African American first lady.

This examination of YouTube video clips provides evidence of the ideological struggle over what it means not simply to be the first lady of the United States, but what it means to be the first African American first lady. In clips posted by the White House or Obama campaign, she appeared as a Black lady (Collins, 2005) in the roles of First Mom, First Wife, First Hostess, advocate and celebrity. However, a new image – that of the Powerful Black Bitch – was used to demonize the first lady and may be used as justification for denying African American women access to real economic, political and social power. This study also argues that format type is central to representation. When Obama appeared in unscripted, late-night talk shows, which allowed for a spontaneity denied her in more controlled environments, she was most able to speak in her own, authentic voice.

Literature Review

Michelle Obama grew up in a working-class family on Chicago's South Side and holds an undergraduate degree from Princeton University and a law degree from Harvard Law School. She met Barack Obama while working at the Chicago law firm of Sidley and Austin, but left corporate law in the early 1990s to work in the public service sector, later moving into a position at the University of Chicago, where she eventually became vice president of the University Medical Center (Parsons, 2008, p. 67). She married Barack Obama in 1992; they have two daughters, Malia and Sasha. In an often-repeated anecdote that is said to illustrate their egalitarian relationship, Michelle Obama reportedly told him as he was about to deliver the keynote speech at the 2004 Democratic National Convention: "Just don't screw it up, buddy."

As a role model for African American women and girls, Obama has been considered by some, "especially as she entered the various celebratory galas on January 2009 inauguration night, to (be) the political and historic embodiment of the first African-American princess" (Lester, 2010, p. 298). Lester (2010) also credits the first lady and her daughters with opening the door to "what used to be an exclusive FOR WHITES ONLY American White House" (p. 306). Obama's accessibility to the African American community is evident in interviews with publications targeting African Americans, such as *Black Hair*, *Ebony*, *Today's Black Woman* and *Essence*, which historically have not been routine venues for interviews with the first lady (Samuels, 2009, p. 40).

Indeed, Michelle Obama has arguably appeared on more magazine covers over a wider range of genres than any other first lady,[3] with cover stories in publications ranging from the health-oriented *Prevention* and the senior citizen *AARP Magazine*[4] to – and this is not an exhaustive list – *Vogue*, *People*, *Glamour*, *Good Housekeeping*, *Ladies' Home Journal*, *Oprah Magazine*, *Women's Weekly*, *Us Weekly*, *Time*, *Newsweek*, *More* and *Radar*.[5] In these and other publications, she is generally lauded for her common-sense approach to parenting, her intelligence and her "gift for easy elegance" (Sherr and Murphy, 2012) in her sense of fashion. She is, according to the *New York Times*, "arguably the most style-conscious first lady since Jacqueline Kennedy," and she is the inspiration for a book titled *Commander in chic: Every woman's guide to managing her style like a first lady* (Oliver, 2011). Her appeal – and reader interest in her – extends beyond the United States: she has appeared on the magazine covers of *Gala* in France, *Pani* in Poland and *Schweiser Illustrierte* in Germany. Even before Barack Obama's election to the presidency, the United Kingdom's *Times* gushed that everything about Michelle Obama:

> speaks to the modern, post-feminist[6] woman: she is manifestly clever, independently minded, attractive in a normal, accessible way... Her demeanour is a reassuring mixture of sassy and self-deprecating; her easy, confident dress sense neither too sexy nor too self conscious. Most of all, however, she appears to be the personification of sanity, a woman who, while clearly supportive of her husband's quest for world domination, is nevertheless not afraid to point out when he is in danger of drinking his own Kool Aid.
>
> (Vine, 2008, p. 8)

And, this article continued, Michelle Obama is the only wife of a presidential candidate in memory who "instead of playing herself down, played up the general uselessness of her husband in matters domestic – and in doing so not only held her ground intellectually but also reached out to all those women who, while devoted to their spouses, also find them slightly useless in matters of sock-tidying" (p. 8). In other words, Michelle Obama is a woman to whom other married women can relate.

As first lady, Michelle Obama has undertaken two signature projects: the "Let's Move" campaign to combat childhood obesity, and the "Joining Forces" initiative she is spearheading with Jill Biden, the wife of vice president Joe Biden, to support military families. In addition, she is the White House's self-proclaimed "Mom-in-Chief" who makes sure she is home when her children return from school. Her expertise as parent and role model for other parents has been highlighted in popular magazines and, in August 2012, she teamed with the women's online community website iVillage "to offer families helpful tips as their children are preparing to head back to school" (USA Today, 2012, p. B1). Jodi Kantor (2012), who covers the first family for *The New York Times*, has noted that the first lady is the primary disciplinarian, enforcing tough rules[7] for her children that have led some White House staff to "joke that they wish they could send their own children to Mrs. Obama's boot camp for training" (Sept. 7, p. A18).

Popular media accolades notwithstanding, Harris-Perry (2011) states that Michelle Obama is "the most visible contemporary example of an African American woman working to stand straight" in a room made crooked by the racism and sexism of American popular culture (p. 271). Because Obama's family history – from slavery to Reconstruction to the Great Migration of African Americans from the U.S. South to the urban centers of the North – reflects the quintessential Black American story, Michelle Obama seems to fit neatly into the racial framework of the United States and therefore "was readily subjected to the distorting images of the crooked room" (p. 273). This included "attempts to frame her within the common trope of hypersexuality," as exemplified by FOX News referring to her as "Barack's baby mama," as well as conservative commentators framing her as a stereotypical "angry Black woman" (pp. 274–275).

According to Harris-Perry (2011), Michelle Obama has been subjected to the myths about Black women in three areas: her body, her role as a mother and her marriage:

Each area maps onto one of the three primary myths about black women. Issues of hypersexuality lurk in the media obsession with Michelle's body; the specter of the angry black woman shadows discussions about her marriage; and national yearnings to depict black women as Mammy are embedded in public discourse about her black womanhood. In each case, she made a number of choices to deflect, resist, redirect, or accommodate these anxieties about her black womanhood. Because her efforts were so public, they provide insight into the efforts of one African American woman to stand straight in a crooked room. They also suggest the limitations of individual strategies to challenge deeply embedded myths.

(p. 277)

Harris-Perry (2011) adds that the "public dissection of Michelle Obama into body parts – first her butt and then her arms – is reminiscent of the treatment of Saartjie Baartman, the so-called Hottentot Venus" (p. 279).[8] Adding to the discussion of Obama's body, McAlister (2009) claims the media's fixation on it foregrounds class while sidestepping racial identity. This is evidenced, she explains, in the media's concern with Obama's atypical physicality, particularly her "buff biceps," as displayed in the first lady's penchant for sleeveless dresses, and the "long, lean" athleticism of her frame: "The bodily standards by which Obama is being measured are clearly gendered, but they are also classed, animated by anxiety over the sight of muscular arms (fit for menial labor, but unfit for display in polite company) on the figure of the First Lady" (p. 312). In addition, a comparison of newspaper coverage of Obama and Cindy McCain, the wife of the Republican presidential candidate during the 2008 campaign, found that Obama was coded as being more than masculine in appearance and behavior than McCain, as well as less traditional (Swan, 2010).

Other scholars also have looked at the media's portrayal of Obama, variously concluding, in one way or another, that her representation reflects the contours of what Harris-Perry (2011) refers to as the crooked room of racism and sexism. For example, Lugo-Lugo and Bloodsworth-Lugo (2011) situate the first lady within a post-9/11 framework of threat and the need to contain danger. Noting that the stereotypes of the mammy and the Jezebel "have been reconfigured to adapt to and reflect changing understandings of race" in the U.S. (p. 205), they argue that Obama has been rendered "unsafe" and a threat to Americanness in two ways: (1) she deviates from the safe stereotype of the mammy, who traditionally places the children of the White family she works for above her own Black children, through her "preoccupation with her daughters rather than with the campaign or the country," thereby rejecting the more acceptable (to Whites) image of the self-sacrificing Black woman (p. 210); and (2) she embodies the "threatening/unsafe stereotype of the Jezebel" in discussions of her alluring physical appearance, including the famously sculpted biceps, that earned her a spot on *Maxim* magazine's annual list of the 100 "hottest women in the world" (pp. 213–214).

Besides attending to the mediated representation of Obama, a number of scholars have focused instead on the first lady's efforts to reclaim her image from stereotypical depictions by shaping the popular narrative of herself, her family and race. Although Spillers (2009) laments the impact of "handlers" in muting the first lady to make her more palatable to the public, Joseph (2011) applauds Obama's skillful use of the tools of post-identity to undermine its claims of a meritocracy and a society that is "post"-racist. In reframing and redefining the meaning of "American" and "patriotism," as well as discussing race, class and gender in codes that articulate a counternarrative, Joseph argues, the first lady appears post-feminist while actually resisting a post-feminist and post-racist subject position so as to refute racism and sexism (Joseph, 2011). Kahl (2009) similarly points to Obama's use of herself and her family as signs of racial progress to combat stereotypes, melding the "colorblind wish of all mothers for their families" (p. 319) with the public and private aspects of her life to combat racial stereotypes. Obama's strategies for reclaiming her identity from the media's images of her included frequently identifying her children as her first priority, thereby reinforcing a nonthreatening focus on motherhood and the family; advocating for military families in a show of patriotism that benefits both herself and her husband; advocating work–life balance for working mothers to place her on the side of working women and families; and directly engaging the topic of race, using "her family's presence in the White House as a springboard for statements supporting racial inclusiveness" (pp. 317–318).

First Ladies

Shoop (2010) points out that the role of the first lady is complex and undefined, which leaves the White House room to delimit her actions and activities so as to present a public image in line with gendered social expectations, as well as the goals and agenda of the administration. To further its agenda, the White House "routinely restricts the performance repertoire, foreign policy voice, and political agenda of first ladies, thereby subjugating them to the conduct conventions of the so-called 'mythic first ladyship'" (Erickson and Thomson, 2012, p. 240). This mythic ideal – linked to feminine normativity and traditional notions of American womanhood such as motherhood and child-rearing – "summons expectations of faithfulness to female performance standards even though performing feminine normativity may pigeonhole first ladies as gendered political actors," forcing them to "balance the portrayal of their authentic voice against the role's objectifying myths and traditions" (p. 241).

While the earliest first ladies were restricted to the role of hostess, that mold initially was broken by Eleanor Roosevelt, who held all-women press conferences, wrote a popular newspaper column and addressed issues of public policy; Jacqueline Kennedy later employed various media strategies while campaigning for her husband, although she did not express any political opinions (Beasley, 2005; Shoop, 2010). Although Kennedy achieved icon status for her chic style, Hillary Clinton, who famously headed a failed attempt at health care reform when her husband was president, is likely the most criticized first lady in history (Beasley, 2005; Rivers, 2007). Perhaps having learned from the abuse Clinton experienced, Laura Bush "remained largely noncontroversial, representing family values and tackling such issues as education and reading" (Shoop, 2010, p. 809).

A number of studies have examined the roles and representations of first ladies – or potential first ladies – in the news media. Beasley (2005) notes that while "the first lady is the single most visible symbol of American womanhood (p. xix), she is generally ignored and her activities trivialized by the media, which "seem mired in outworn ideas about women's status" (p. 244). The result, she adds, is that the first lady is disregarded by the press "except as a celebrity political wife whose status is derived totally from her husband and consequently not worth thoughtful coverage" (p. 239).

Gardetto's (1997) analysis of the coverage of Hillary Clinton in *The New York Times* during the 1992 presidential campaign found three narrative themes: (1) "her strength–his weakness," which represented Hillary Clinton's intelligence and public speaking skills as a threat to her husband's power; (2) "comparing women/wifestyles," which compared Hillary Clinton with other politicians' wives; and (3) "new kind of marital partnership," which questioned whether a conflict of interest existed due to their dual careers (p. 226). In addition, Winfield (1997) found that the media framed first ladies in one of five ways: as their husband's escort; in a protocol role for leading various events; in a *noblesse oblige* role that involves charitable works; in a policy-making role involving formulation, development and influence; and in a power role tied to political influence (p. 241). Erickson and Thomson (2012) similarly developed a taxonomy of six first lady diplomacy role functions involving their performance abroad in international relations: escort, aesthete, surrogate, cultural emissary, goodwill ambassador and social advocate.

Shoop's (2010) framing analysis of news coverage of candidate wives Cindy McCain and Michelle Obama during the 2008 presidential election found that a significant number of articles addressed controversy involving the potential first ladies, with McCain's wealth and Obama's outspokenness central to the controversies surrounding them. Whether Michelle Obama continues to be the focus of controversy four years later on YouTube, and the nature of that controversy, is one of the questions to be explored in this chapter.

YouTube

YouTube was launched as a commercial Web site in June 2005 and purchased by Google in 2006 for $1.65 billion. Strangelove (2010) emphasizes that "YouTube's words and actions should always be interpreted in light of its primary position as an advertising platform and its need to keep its main client – corporations – reasonably happy" (p. 108). It earns $16.6 billion annually in online search advertising (Strangelove, 2010, p. 6) and claims that 20 hours of video are uploaded to its servers every minute, amounting to 365,512 videos per day, with 79 percent estimated to be user-generated content – that is, content uploaded by audiences in their dual roles as producers and consumers of videos (p. 19). YouTube allows viewers to comment on the videos they watch, as well as to post a video of their own in reply. Although anyone with a connection to the internet can view a YouTube video, uploading or posting video clips is limited to members who are registered with YouTube and have created a channel, which is essentially a YouTube page that acts as a repository for a member's uploaded videos. Regular channels are free, although partner channels, which provide special privileges, are available for a fee.

Steve Grove (2008), YouTube's former news director, has noted that all 16 of the one-time presidential candidates in 2008 had YouTube channels, with seven announcing their candidacies on YouTube (p. 28). In addition, almost five million people watched Barack Obama's 37-minute speech on race via YouTube, "shattering the notion that only short, lowbrow clips bubble to the top of the internet's political ecosystem" (Grove, 2008, p. 29). "If news organizations want to see how a particular piece of content will resonate with audiences," Grove (2008) added, "they have an automatic focus group waiting on YouTube" (p. 29). Strangelove (2010) similarly points out that a correlation exists "between blog discussion of a YouTube video and mainstream media coverage of that video" (p. 142). "Just as newspapers and television newscasts set the agenda for public debate," he states, "YouTube videos also establish themes and issues that become fodder for online debate" (p. 142). This, in turn, can find its way into traditional news outlets, as well as public discourse. As Grove (2010) points out, "Top videos – discovered and promoted by YouTube's grassroots community – are rebroadcast on TV and other platforms, especially when news organizations don't have their own footage of an event" (p. 50).

During the 2008 presidential election, YouTube was used by corporate lobbyists and public relations firms posing as amateur videographers, as well as by real amateurs "who recorded clips at political rallies and uploaded forgotten videos from past campaigns" (Strangelove, 2010, p. 138). Some of the more famous videos from the first YouTube presidential election were made by professional production companies, attracting "millions of online viewers and tons of press coverage" (Strangelove, 2010, p. 139).

While Web videos were relatively new to campaigns in 2008, they have become one of the primary ways that campaigns communicate with voters, allowing politicians to get their messages out quickly and, as Peters (2012) states, to:

> connect with people they know are engaged and not fast-forwarding through messages on their DVR players or flipping channels during commercials. And, perhaps more important, it offers them a way to disseminate their news into online communities where friends and family members share, discuss and debate. Campaigns believe that helps elevate their messages beyond propaganda.

Barack Obama kicked off his 2012 re-election campaign by "turning first not to a 30-second commercial but a 17-minute online documentary" he and staff hoped would be shared online through e-mail and social media (Peters, 2012). The documentary, "The Road We've Traveled," appeared on a new YouTube platform that enabled the Obama campaign to "turn the passive experience of watching a video into an organizing and fund-raising tool" with the technology necessary for viewers to post content to their Facebook pages and elsewhere from Obama's dedicated YouTube page (Peters, 2012).[9]

However, clips posted by amateur videographers also attempt to influence how events are portrayed and interpreted with non-professional online video that "produces and reproduces political discourses" (Strangelove, 2010, p. 142). The political dialogue on YouTube, Strangelove (2010) adds, is often obscene and hate-filled, with hatred "a dominant characteristic of the 'Tube'" (p. 148).

Methodology

This study applied the constant comparative method to Michelle Obama's representation in YouTube video clips in terms of her roles and asked whether those roles reflect the myths and stereotypes about African American women. All YouTube clips posted between March 15 and April 15, 2012, that were captured using "Michelle Obama" as the search term were saved to a file on April 15, 2012, and those that contained a visual imagery or a spoken reference to Michelle Obama within the video itself, either mentioning her by name or as the first lady, were included in this study. Clips of the same footage that simply had been reposted, some numerous times, were removed, as were all clips that did not contain evidence of any connection to the first lady even though they contained a reference to her in the title or written description. However, clips with the same or similar footage that were framed differently through their title or description were included in this study. Strangelove (2010) notes that a common method of YouTube political discourse involves individuals "simply uploading television content and adding a title or description that frames its meaning" in a way that alters the original meanings of the materials uploaded (p. 147). A variation of this approach involves combinations of "television content, annotations, still images and a recording of the amateur videographer or other YouTubers" providing commentary (Strangelove, 2010, p. 147).

The removal of duplicate video resulted in a list of 80 video clips, a number of which included at least some of the same footage. The 80 video clips then were transcribed, and an additional 19 clips were removed from this study because, despite titles or descriptions that referenced Michelle Obama in some way, 12 clips did not actually mention or provide a visual image of her, and seven were in a foreign language. In the end, 61 videos were included in this study, ranging from just over a minute to just over an hour in length.

The representation of Michelle Obama in YouTube clips was examined using the constant comparative method (Glaser and Strauss, 1967) in which themes and patterns emerged from the videos. As tentative categories emerged, and as more video clips were compared with other clips and existing categories for their fit, new categories were defined while previous categories were eliminated or consolidated. Many of the clips reflected multiple roles for the first lady and so may be represented in multiple categories. For example, in welcoming guests with the president to a White House function, the first lady appears as both wife and hostess. The final categories derived from this inductive process were then examined for their correspondence with existing stereotypes of African American women as described by Collins (2005) and others. Examples from the videos were used to illustrate the roles and categories.

It should be pointed out that, although YouTube ranks video clips by number of views, those numbers can be significantly inflated or understated:

> Often, there are many copies of the same video under different names. Sometimes a highly viewed video is deleted and then reposted, which causes the view count to start over at zero. Since view counts include repeat viewings, they only approximate the actual audience size. In cases of highly popular videos, the total size of the online audience can be larger than YouTube's view count by a factor of ten to twenty.
>
> (Strangelove, 2010, p. 21)

For this reason, and because the focus of this study is on the representation of Michelle Obama and not the popularity of certain videos, the YouTube clips were not analyzed in terms of view count. In addition, as a result of editorial concerns about the potential interruption to the flow of this chapter from the placement of video citations throughout, the YouTube citations will only appear in a separate section at the end of this chapter.

The Black Lady

Through YouTube clips, the White House and Obama campaign successfully cast Michelle Obama within traditionally feminine and domestic roles tied to the myth of the first ladyship. From this restricted position, the first lady graciously welcomed guests to the White House, offered advice to parents and provided encouragement to children. Obama's activities and responsibilities, even in relationship to celebrities, remained connected to children and family. She is the embodiment of Collins's (2005) Black lady – respectable, smart and attractive, while also committed to her children and marriage (p. 139). Indeed, Obama even serves as a metaphor for middle-class propriety in a YouTube clip that features a semi-pornographic rap song named after her. In this song, rapper Semi Duce sings that his girlfriend may be a "nice little freak" when "she climbs in the sheets," but she is "Michelle Obama when we ride with the streets" –

that is, she has the respectability and proper behavior of Michelle Obama when out in public. Here, Semi Duce combines the contrasting stereotypes of the hypersexual Jezebel and the hyper-respectable Black lady into the single body of his girlfriend – a feat that is difficult if not impossible for most women to accomplish but is apparently a common fantasy for some men. [10]

The roles that defined Michelle Obama as a Black lady in the YouTube video clips are that of the First Mom, the First Wife, the First Hostess, advocate for women and families, and celebrity. Her designation here as the "first" mom, wife and hostess denote the significance of her status as first lady, for she is not just any mother, wife or hostess. The fact of her marriage to the president of the United States elevates these roles beyond the ordinary. However, the designation of "first" also is meant to connote her exceptionalism in that she appears to excel in all these roles – she appears to be the perfect mother and role model for other parents in her interactions with children, balancing encouragement and support with a no-nonsense approach; she is the perfect wife in a modern, egalitarian marriage, always supportive of her husband, but never in a way that undermines her own authority within the home or her independence; and she is the ever-gracious hostess. Yet, despite her status as first lady and the exceptionalism of her skills as mother, wife and hostess, the representation of Michelle Obama in these YouTube clips attempts to deny this atypicality by emphasizing the normative behaviors of a more conventional wife and mother.

The First Mom

Although the White House and Barack Obama campaign represented the first lady variously as a mother, wife and hostess, as well as an advocate for children, women and military families, her primary role was as the First Mom, a champion of not just her own children, but an advocate for all children. A cornerstone of that advocacy is Obama's two signature projects, the "Let's Move" campaign to combat childhood obesity by encouraging children to exercise and engage in physical play, as well eat more vegetables and less junk food, and the "Joining Forces" initiative to support military families. In clips posted by the White House and Obama campaign, it is clear that while Barack Obama may be the president of the United States, within the domestic sphere, it is Michelle Obama who calls the shots.

As the First Mom, Michelle Obama often appears surrounded by children – her own and others. Her interactions with them, as well as her comments to adults about children and parenting, establish her as a no-nonsense yet nurturing authority on parenting. For example, in videos involving the "Let's Move" initiative, the first lady often offers advice to parents about raising children and being their role model. In one such clip, she emphasizes that children need to be physically active "to burn off that steam" and well-nourished if they are to succeed in school. And, she states, she will continue to be visible as a role model for children, "hopefully running and playing and jumping a little double-Dutch and making a fool out of myself with kids so that we can show them that we, as our kids' first, best role models, aren't afraid to move ourselves. They kind of do what we do." After Obama's comments, the program moderator affirms the first lady's role as a mother above all else: "This first lady, as you can tell, is committed to this from her heart and as a mom first."

Michelle Obama also was featured prominently as she engaged with children in the White House Easter Egg Roll. In different videos, the first lady is shown: with her family, welcoming participants to the annual Egg Roll; reading to young children; helping a youngster roll her egg on the lawn with a long-handled wooden spoon; hugging children; or sitting next to her husband while he reads to children.

The various activities during the Egg Roll also provided the first lady with the opportunity to demonstrate her parenting expertise by providing advice to other parents. In a cooking demonstration with children and a "celebrity chef" during the day's events, the first lady suggests the vegetables be cut into small pieces so that children will not know they are eating vegetables: "Sometimes you have to fool them," she says. Then, after explaining that buying fresh vegetables in season or frozen vegetables out-of-season is less expensive than fresh vegetables out-of-season, she adds: "I tell my children, vegetables aren't really a choice… There are certain things we are just not supposed to dump into our bodies… You've got to eat vegetables every single day." Obama, explaining that parents are their children's best role models, also adds: "We're not setting our kids up for success" unless they're eating vegetables.

In her interactions with children, Michelle Obama unfailingly appears fully engaged, continually providing compliments and encouragement. At the end of the cooking demonstration, Obama compliments the children who helped: "All of our sous chefs – well done, well done." And when reading to a group of young children, she pulls her chair closer so they can see the pictures better, and intersperses her reading with comments designed to draw them into the story: "Oh, oh, what's he going to do?" she says about a mouse in the story, then comments: "You can't guard your strawberry from the big, hungry bear. I know – I'm worried… That's a big strawberry for a little, bitty mouse." At the conclusion of the book reading, she compliments her young audience: "You guys are amazing, amazing."

While most of the Egg Roll videos were posted by the White House, some appeared repackaged by news organizations. For example, CBS News posted a clip in which the president is shown reading to children, with the first lady and their two girls seated beside him. In content and tone, it did not differ significantly from video posted by the White House.

In addition to the Egg Roll videos, the "Let's Move" program was promoted in a video posted by letsmove.gov, the program's website, which featured a rap song encouraging children to be active and eat healthy foods. The clip included a photo of Michelle Obama with a hula hoop. The White House also posted clips supporting the "Let's Move" campaign that showed Obama surrounded by children as they planted a vegetable garden on the South Lawn. One version of the spring planting – produced by the White House with the title "West Wing Week: 3/30/2012 or 'I've Got Seoul'" – showcased the activities of both the president and the first lady that week, which underscored the contrast between the public, professional role of the president and the domestic and maternal role of the first lady. While the president is shown traveling to the Republic of Korea to attend a nuclear security summit, where he also visited the DMZ, held a series of bilateral (and one trilateral) meetings and gave a major address to students at Hankuk University, back home, the first lady is shown surrounded by children, working in the garden.

The "Let's Move" initiative also was mentioned in a user-generated post by a young African American male who provided a humorous commentary on singer Mary J. Blige's commercial for Burger King. After telling Blige, "You don't need to be doing no Burger King commercials," he notes that Michelle Obama has the "Let's Move" campaign: "They trying to talk about being healthy – you [Blige] talking about chicken. You setting us back… I don't ever remember Salina endorsing Taco Bell." Although Michelle Obama and "Let's Move" are not the focus of this video, Obama is clearly represented as an advocate for healthy food choices. In this, she is not simply the First Mom to her own and the nation's children, but to all Americans.

The First Wife

Michelle Obama also appeared in a number of video clips as a supportive and loving wife who, at times, gently teases her husband as she asserts her dominance in the realm of the domestic. In the video clips posted by the White House, the relationship between the president and first lady appears to be that of a typical, professional and upper-middle-class, modern, married couple with two young children and a dog – Bo, their Portuguese water dog. If not for the husband's occupation, the Obama family could be the (admittedly upscale) family next door, with the roles of the husband/father and wife/mother delineated within updated although still gendered spheres – and with the same problems and concerns as other married couples with young children. In a CNN news clip,[11] the president speaks admiringly of his wife, first half-joking that he married her because she gave him good advice when they were both working at a Chicago law firm, then turning serious as he described the difficulties she faced balancing work and family – a difficulty most, if not all, mothers who work outside the home encounter. "Once Michelle and I had our girls, she gave it her all," he said, noting that she felt guilty that she wasn't giving enough time to the girls when she was at work but also, when she was with the girls, felt guilty that she wasn't giving enough time to her work. "And we didn't have the luxury for Michelle not to work," he added. "And so she had to constantly juggle it, and carried an extraordinary burden for a long period of time."

In another example of the public normalization of their relationship as a married couple, the Obamas are shown on a "date night" with other couples. "Date night" is both a fundraiser for the Barack Obama campaign, with the other couples chosen in a lottery of online campaign contributors, as well as an opportunity to portray the president and first lady much like any other American couple, with the same worries, hopes and dreams. When the Obamas arrive at the restaurant where three other couples are already seated, he introduces himself and the first lady: "I'm Barack Obama, and this is my wife, Michelle." The first lady smiles and, with a slight wave of her hand, says, "Hey.[12] I'm his date."

The portrayal of the Obamas as the "couple next door" also was evident in speeches at a state dinner in honor of British Prime Minister David Cameron and his wife, Samantha. The president's opening remarks included a self-deprecating joke about classic husbandly incompetence: "So far, the evening has been successful because I have not stepped on Michelle's train – my main goal this evening." He also joked that his and Cameron's wives marvel at their ability to do things like barbecue on a grill. Prime Minister David Cameron, in turn, muses aloud about whether Michelle wants to know what he and the president did the night before. He then says: "The truth is, we have to have a guys' night out because so often we find we are completely overshadowed by our beautiful wives." The implication is that the president of the United States and the prime minister of Great Britain are typical husbands in need of a boys' night out.

Although the president of the United States is ostensibly the leader of the "free world," Michelle Obama appears to be in full command of the first family's household in a way that is reflective of and yet transcends traditional domestic roles. Her dominance in familial matters is both acknowledged by her husband and asserted by the first lady in public comments. For example, the annual Easter Egg Roll on the White House lawn began with the president announcing that his job that day is "very simple – to introduce the powerhouse of the White House, the one truly in charge, as Malia, Sasha and Bo all know – the first lady of the United States, Michelle Obama." The first lady then takes the microphone and says, pointedly, "Thank you, honey." When describing that day's activities, she teases the president about his well-known competitiveness: "We're going to be over there doing a little egg roll. I think the president is going to try to beat a 3-year-old, which I *hope* he does not." In this public exchange, addressed to the families gathered on the South Lawn of the White House, the first couple also are playfully directing their comments to each other. When the president calls his wife the real power in the White House, Michelle Obama, standing beside him with her arm around their youngest daughter, smiles. When she intentionally refers to him as "honey" in a public acknowledgment of their private relationship, both she and the president smile and their audience laughs. When she suggests the president may be plotting to beat a 3-year-old, he raises his arm, pointing his finger toward the audience – seemingly as a warning to the 3-year-olds out there – and smiles. Theirs is a private joke turned public, the first lady teasing her husband about his competitiveness in a display of both affection and her agreed-upon dominance in the family's domestic affairs.

In addition, whether addressing parents, attendees at a conference or a gathering of military personnel and their families, the first lady never fails to speak with competence, conviction and eloquence – and, often, humor. Her comments frequently advocate support for her husband's policies, and she routinely discusses policy in terms of their effects on children and families – her own and others. In the 2012 Obama campaign video "The Road We've Traveled," which runs just over an hour and purports to provide "an inside look at some of the tough calls President Obama made to get our country back on track," the first lady appears only briefly. But when she does, it is to talk about the cost to families of waiting for Congress to pass the president's health care reform bill, the Affordable Care Act,[13] which she links to the death of her husband's mother: "She developed ovarian cancer. Never really had good, consistent insurance. That's a tough thing to deal with, watching your mother die of something that could have been prevented. And I don't think he [the president] wants to see anyone go through that."

The role of the first lady as wife also was invoked by the president in extending holiday greetings or welcoming people to the White House. For example, on the Islamic holiday of Nowruz, the president is shown in a headshot that opens with him saying, "Today, Michelle and I extend our best wishes to all those who are celebrating Nowruz around the world." In the same way, in receiving guests to the state dinner in honor of the British prime minister, the president states: "Michelle and I could not be more honored that you could join us as we host our great friends" – an affirmation of the first lady's role as both wife and hostess.

The First Hostess

In keeping with the domestic responsibilities of the first lady, Michelle Obama also is portrayed as an exemplary, gracious hostess – both in the realms of the virtual and the real. In a clip that introduced "A New Way to Tour the White House," she directs her remarks to the online viewer while introducing a 360-degree tour of the White House's public rooms (http://www.youtube.com/watch?v=TSQkaD_mXGo), welcoming viewers to a digital tour of "the 'people's house' – a place that should be open to everyone" – and inviting them to "enjoy the view because, after all, this is your house, too." Likewise, in another clip, the first lady welcomes high school girls to the White House and explains what goes on at a state dinner.

Her hostess skills also were noted in a "Wong Fu Weekend" clip, in which three Asian American young men excitedly recount their visit to a White House holiday reception as representatives of the Asian Pacific Islanders community. After shaking hands with the president and first lady, one of the men commented that Michelle Obama urged him to "Keep up the good work."

Advocate

In addition to the traditional domestic roles of wife, mother and hostess, the first lady appeared as an advocate for families – military families, in particular – and women. Indeed, she appears to be the administration's liaison for all manner of female-related issues and events. For example, she delivered remarks during a ship commissioning ceremony for the Stratton, the first ship in its class named for a woman.[14] Michelle Obama also spoke at a State Department ceremony honoring 10 women from around the world who had, the first lady explained, endured hardships and "daunting physical obstacles" to improve the lives of girls and women in their countries. One of the honorees, she said, had "risen through the ranks, commanding more than 100 male officers" in the Rio de Janeiro police force. "We love that," the first lady added, indicating her support for women in positions of power and authority. Obama also noted that young people had been invited to the ceremony to "encourage and inspire them."

Similarly, in a speech marking the two-year anniversary of the Affordable Care Act with "a women's week of action," the first lady spoke to other women as both a woman and a mother when she explained that health care reform has benefited millions of Americans and will provide a healthier future for her children and other children:

> This law also pays special attention to women's health, making sure we have preventative services we need – things like mammograms, wellness visits and prenatal screenings. Believe it or not, before my husband signed the Affordable Care Act into law, insurance companies could actually charge women up to 50 percent more than men for their health care premiums simply because of their gender. The new law will end that unfair practice. And as a mom, I know that the legacy of health care reform will be a healthier future for my daughters and for all our sons and daughters. And that's why we need to keep fighting to protect and to build on the progress we have made.

Several clips also featured the first lady's activities with the "Joining Forces" initiative. In a ceremony with an audience of military families, Jill Biden, the wife of the vice president, characterized her own and the first lady's commitment to serve veterans and military families as "our most sacred obligation." In a different clip of that ceremony, the first lady mentioned her appearance on the Nickelodeon channel's tween TV show *iCarly* in support of military families. "That episode really got the message out about our military families," she stated. And in still another video, the first lady described the president's actions in support of the troops and veterans. "We all have an obligation" to help veterans and their families, she concluded. "I hope you will join me in standing up for all those who have served." In this clip and others, Obama not only voices support for military families, but also for her husband and his policies.

Celebrity

While Michelle Obama is a celebrity in her own right by virtue of her status as first lady, her public engagements with celebrities in the entertainment world highlight the connections – and permeable boundaries – between political and Hollywood-style fame. A number of videos showed or mentioned the first lady in celebrity entertainment and gossip news – particularly those targeting a teenage or younger audience. Her appearances at events for children, shown in clips posted by entertainment and gossip news organizations, served to downplay and minimize any potential threat her popularity could present – political or otherwise – given the context of entertainment/gossip news as well as the age of its audience.

Several clips involved Michelle Obama's appearance at the televised Nickelodeon channel's Kids Choice Awards, where she presented singer/ songwriter Taylor Swift with a public service award. HollyscoopTV's host announced the upcoming awards show in a YouTube clip by stating: "Taylor Swift is one pretty amazing chick, and even the first lady thinks so!!" Obama and Swift are shown in several of the videos hugging on stage after Obama presents her with the award. In one video, Swift gushes: "I've always wanted to meet you. This is amazing. I'm so honored to be receiving this award from the first lady!"

In a clip from ClevverTV, an entertainment and gossip website for teenagers, the "teen heart-throb band" One Direction was said to have turned down a request from Michelle Obama to perform at the White House Easter Egg Roll because of a previous commitment. According to the announcer, "the invite went down after the first lady witnessed how One Direction brought the house down at the Kids Choice Awards, which she and her daughters, Sasha and Malia, attended." The announcer concluded by telling viewers: "Listen – it doesn't get any bigger than getting an invite to perform for the president and his family – particularly here in the States." Not only do stars like Taylor Swift want to meet the first lady, but an invitation from her is one of the most coveted in the U.S. In addition, Obama's celebrity status is such that, according to one YouTube clip, she also serves as a fashion icon: toymaker Mattel was said to be creating a Barbie doll that is running for political office, with Barbie's clothes patterned after an outfit worn by Obama.

Other video mentioned Michelle Obama only briefly within the context of celebrities who were the real focus of the story. For example, in a ClevverNews report about what celebrities are doing for Easter and Passover, the show's host notes, within a long list of celebrity activities, that actress Reese Witherspoon and her children were "seen in their Sunday best, celebrating at the White House Easter Egg Roll in Washington D.C.," and that actress Jada Pinkett Smith "rocked out there last year with her son Jaden and first lady Michelle Obama, while her daughter Willow performed for the crowd." Teen heart-throb Justin Bieber also was said to be "a veteran performer when it comes to this high profile affair."

Obama similarly was mentioned in a few video clips that focused on Beyoncé's post-childbirth figure. These clips, which briefly showed Beyoncé and husband Jay-Z leaving a building in New York, noted that they had just attended a fundraiser hosted by Michelle Obama. For example, one clip, which described Beyoncé's "curve-hugging dress" that "proves she is the hottest new mom" in New York City, asked: "So who could inspire Beyoncé to step out looking so stunning? None other than the first lady herself! Beyoncé attended a fundraiser dinner hosted by Michelle Obama." In these celebrity-focused stories, Michelle Obama is portrayed as having the same or more star power than Hollywood celebrities. However, the context of these clips as entertainment and gossip news, particularly in regard to children's news, confines Obama to the trivial and unimportant.

Authentic Voice

The few videos clips in which Michelle Obama appeared as a guest on late-night TV talk shows disclosed a side of the first lady only glimpsed in other YouTube clips. The talk show format provided an opportunity for the first lady to go off-script, to speak in an authentic voice that was smart, engaging and funny, able to deliver anecdotes and clever one-liners that sometimes outdid the show's host and demonstrated her intelligence as well as her independence. These appearances often included discussion of the "Joining Forces" initiative or her children, but the representation of the first lady went beyond the traditional roles of First Mom, First Wife or advocate for women and military families. The late-night format offered the first lady, particularly in response to questions by the show's host, the space to be more spontaneous than other formats allowed. For example, when Dave Letterman, host of *The Letterman Show*, asked if her husband has ever come home at the end of the day and said, "Oh, that John Boehner[15] – what an idiot," she replies, ostensibly tongue-in-cheek: "It has never happened. He is always upbeat, particularly about Congress." In this interview, Obama also revealed that she had sneaked out of the White House incognito to shop at Target, and also has taken Bo, the family dog, to Petco. "He is really a good dog – he is very well mannered," she added, then noted that Bo has a very busy schedule. "I'm thinking about getting him an agent," she joked. "He's very smart." When the talk turned to parenting, Obama said, again apparently tongue-in-cheek: "My children are perfect angels. I'm sure it's because I'm such a good parent." And when Letterman sought her advice about a childrearing problem he had with his 8-year-old, Obama asked: "Have you tried being the alpha?" to which Letterman responded: "No. Do I look like an alpha?" In this exchange, the first lady's banter is clever and funny – she appears as an interesting, intelligent and independent woman who refuses to be confined by White House protocol or convention, instead sneaking out to shop at big box retail stores where the middle class shops. In her advice to Letterman, she also reinforces her image as a no-nonsense, childrearing expert.

The anecdote of the first lady shopping at Target while in disguise was reposted from *The Letterman Show* by CNN, which included how she thought her cover was blown when a woman approached her: "A woman actually walked up to me... she said, 'Can you reach up on that shelf and hand me that detergent?'" The anchor ended the news story by stating: "In a more serious moment, Mrs. Obama told Letterman about her father, who had multiple sclerosis. She said she learned absolute, complete unconditional love from him." Besides reinforcing Obama's "everywoman" credentials – after all, she shops at Target – the CNN clip underscores her role as a beloved daughter, further humanizing her while adding another facet to the previously established familial framework of wife and mother.

Obama's appearance on the Comedy Central channel's *Colbert Report* similarly appears in several YouTube clips, including one from *ABC World News* in which host Stephen Colbert asks her, "Do you ever lord over the president the fact that you're more popular than he is? Do you ever say, like, 'Hey, watch it or I might not campaign for you?'" To this, the first lady replies: "I might try that when I get home." In a different video of that show, Colbert asks Obama: "As someone who has appeared on both my show and has also appeared on *iCarly*, which do you think has more gravitas?" Without missing a beat, Obama replies: "iCarly is about 16 [years old], and she's real deep" – implying, to the audience's laughter, that Colbert is not similarly "deep."

In another video that again demonstrates Obama's propensity for cheeky repartee, this one with day-time talk show host Ellen DeGeneres, DeGeneres airs a clip from a previous program in which the two of them are doing push-ups. After viewing this clip, the first lady quips that she could have done 35: "I stopped because I felt bad for you," she says. This clip, like others within the talk show genre, includes a reminder of Obama's role as a mother, but that is not the primary focus. This reminder occurred when DeGeneres showed the audience a photo of Obama in her prom dress – a fitted gold gown with a very high slit up her thigh. Obama's response was that she didn't think she would let Sasha and Malia out of the house with a slit like that.

While the White House and campaign clips confine her to the familial and domestic, her spontaneous responses on talk shows are conversational, impromptu and unscripted, and Obama is able to more fully reveal her sense of humor, wit, intelligence and self. Her authentic voice is often irreverent – as when she suggests she might go home and tell the president she may not campaign for him if he doesn't watch himself – as well as self-deprecating, as when she suggests, clearly tongue-in-cheek, that her children are angels because she is such a good mother.

The Black Woman

The first lady also inadvertently was at both the center and periphery of a political controversy that reduced her to – and solely characterized her by – the color of her skin and her gender. The controversy, recounted in clips from CNN as well as from conservative and progressive commentators, occurred during the 2012 presidential primaries when actor Robert De Niro, while introducing Michelle Obama at a fundraiser, jokingly referred to the wives of the Republican presidential primary candidates: "Callista Gingrich. Karen Santorum. Ann Romney. Now do you really think our country is ready for a White first lady?" When the crowd yelled "no," he added: "Too soon, right?" Former Congressman Newt Gingrich, badly trailing behind other candidates for the Republican party's nomination, blasted De Niro's comment as "inexcusable" and called for President Obama to apologize for De Niro's remarks. The first lady's spokesperson then released a statement calling De Niro's comments "inappropriate."

The liberal clips charged Gingrich with using De Niro's comment to gain airtime for his floundering campaign, while the conservative ones were critical of President Obama and sometimes De Niro. In a clip posted by the right-wing "Daily Worldwide News," a woman's robotic voice intones – against a static image of De Niro's face with the words "thrown under the bus" – that the actor was "going to learn what it is like to be publicly ridiculed and thrown under the bus by the Obama administration" because of his comment at the fundraising event. RT America's post asked whether De Niro's apology and the first lady's office calling the joke inappropriate is "yet another example that political incorrectness will be shunned." On the political left, "The Young Turks" posted a video in which one of the show's hosts says of De Niro's remarks: "Anybody who doesn't understand that's a joke is not bright." Claiming that Republicans had turned De Niro's humor into a "political slight," one of the hosts proclaimed that "It's way beneath the president and first lady to respond" to Gingrich.

While the appeal to racism inherent in Gingrich's comments and the ensuing controversy is unstated, it is clearly apparent in a user-generated clip from an unidentified White male who uses the incident to proclaim himself oppressed as a White person. Speaking to the camera, he began by stating that what De Niro had said was "uncool," and that the following was his "candid response to the situation, my personal feelings conveyed in the proper domain, YouTube, where almost everything is fair game." He then asked: "Do you ever feel like you're a White person being persecuted by society? Are you going to vote for Obama because you're not ready for another White woman in the White House?" He later states: "You don't feel totally received and respected as a White person in society anymore. White people, their ways are being looked down upon… The oppression in society is against us."

Gingrich's comments, while seen by some as merely an attempt to exploit De Niro's remarks for political gain, provided an opening for racist proclamations that positioned White people as oppressed by African Americans while simultaneously putting the White House on the defensive. Within this context, Michelle Obama was not the nation's first lady, but a Black first lady – her Blackness signified as both her defining and only salient characteristic. Although not the focus of the De Niro controversy, Michelle Obama's reduction to skin color is evidence of the difficulty Black women – even first ladies – face in attempting to stand straight in what Harris-Perry (2011) calls the crooked room of racism and sexism.

The Powerful Black Bitch

Included among the YouTube videos are those – often produced by White males – in which the political or ideological message may be libertarian or conservative but is not always coherent or clear. Nonetheless, the loathing for the first lady and president is palpable. These images draw on the classed stereotypes of the angry Black bitch, the welfare queen and the emasculating Sapphire, but they do not account for the power that Obama is represented as wielding in these YouTube clips. The working-class and middle-class stereotypes of Black women assumed their relative powerlessness, for within a racist and sexist worldview, it is unimaginable that a Black woman could, in fact, be powerful enough to represent a threat to White society. The power of the working-class bitch and Sapphire is limited to their community and the men in their lives; the former she is responsible for destroying, the latter for emasculating and driving away. Even Collins's (2005) middle-class educated Black bitch and Black lady have limitations to their power, for they are beholden to their boss for their employment and to the White establishment for recognition and status. Obama's representation in these video clips ushers in a new stereotype, that of the Powerful Black Bitch who is not beholden to anyone. The Powerful Black Bitch has free rein to exercise her power to serve her own selfish interests, and she is able to extend her control beyond the Black community to affect the lives of White people. She is dangerous, evil and in need of containment.

In a clip that represents Michelle Obama as a Powerful Black Bitch, Gerald Celente, a middle-aged, White male, is discussing a *New York Times* article, which he terms propaganda, about the first lady's support for the inclusion of more vegetables in the military's menus. He states, in a mocking voice dripping with contempt, "'Thank you for eating your vegetables... Eat your broccoli, boys.' This is disgusting. And it gets worse." He then holds up a photo of the coffin of a soldier being returned to an air base, and his voice becomes more agitated. "As Mrs. Obama is talking about those troops eating their vegetables, they don't show this picture, do they? As Mrs. Obama goes around the country, telling soldiers to eat their broccoli – war trials, tribunals, that's what I'd like to see! Why are we in Iraq? The Middle East is about to explode, but," he sarcastically adds, "don't forget to eat your broccoli!" In Celente's view, the first lady is complicit in the war – and the death of soldiers – by encouraging soldiers to eat vegetables.

Another clip, produced by "Obama Files," purports to explain how the Obama administration has become a dictatorship whose goal is to nullify Congress and the U.S. Supreme Court. It opens with an image of President Obama, ominous music and, at the bottom of the clip, a crawl that says: "Breaking News: The dictatorship has begun," and then proceeds to outline purportedly unconstitutional acts committed by the administration that have led to a dictatorship. The video, which calls for Barack Obama's immediate impeachment and imprisonment, includes video of Michelle Obama. Within the context of this clip, the first lady is an accomplice to the dictatorship, a partner to evil.

Some of the YouTube videos posted by conservatives contain footage taken from clips uploaded by the White House or the Barack Obama campaign, retitled to produce a different frame than initially intended. For example, "Breitbartnews" uploaded a clip in which President Obama discusses the difficulties his wife faced as a working mother balancing work and family. The title was changed to: "Obama: 'We Didn't Have the Luxury For Michelle Not To Work.'" While there are a number of ways this could be interpreted, it was likely meant to suggest a self-indulgent desire for luxury. It also undercuts the White House frame of Michelle Obama as a dedicated and attentive mother, for she appears to put a craving for material goods above caring for her children.

An additional clip, with the provocative caption "Michelle Obama: I am now more popular than the president," similarly suggests greed and a desire for power. In this clip, which provides footage from a "Joining Forces" ceremony, Obama states, tongue-in-cheek: "And then there's the episode that made me a fan favorite in every household. I am now more popular than the president – because I was on *iCarly*. There are kids who probably didn't know I was first lady, but they know I was on *iCarly*." The title of this clip suggests hubris if not outright megalomania, for the first lady appears to be reveling in her popularity and power.

In one of the few animated clips, which contained avatar-like figures of the first family, the White House is said to have pressured the media to eliminate stories from the internet about Malia traveling to Mexico during her spring break from school. The clip contends that Malia was accompanied by "25 Secret Service agents, which has drawn the ire of Internet commentators who see the entourage as excessive government spending." The focus of this clip is not on the first lady, but she is represented as a conspirator in this plot to muzzle the media and waste the public's money on her daughter's trip abroad. The concept of the first lady as self-indulgently squandering taxpayer money, a throwback to the stereotype of the welfare mother who prefers public handouts to work, was also apparent in a clip uploaded by Bernard Chapin in which he reviews a book by conservative activist and author Jason Mattera. Providing the viewer with "a flavor of what his writing is like," he says: "There's Michelle 'never been proud of America until I got to take $350,000 Spanish vacations on your tax dollars' Obama." This statement relies on the characterization of Obama as an unpatriotic, disgruntled and angry Black woman – albeit with the power to spend (White) taxpayers' money for her own enjoyment.

In a clip posted by *The Brad and Britt Show*, the voice of conservative radio talk show host Rush Limbaugh is heard over a photo of Limbaugh, clearly taken in his younger years, sitting in front of a microphone in his studio. Limbaugh claims that Barack Obama has "sold out" the Hispanic community by choosing to side with African Americans in comments about the Trayvon Martin case,[16] so he will have to make amends to win the Hispanic vote. Limbaugh continues: "I would expect you would see some photo ops of Obama in a taco truck... and by the way, once he eats one of those, then Michelle can fuss at him and scream at him for eating stuff that's bad for him." This characterizes the first lady as a stereotypical angry Black bitch, but Limbaugh is not finished; he then notes that Michelle Obama will be the commencement speaker at a university in North Carolina. At this point, the static image of Limbaugh at the microphone is replaced with a back shot of Michelle Obama in a red, form-fitting skirt, her rear accentuated by the angle of the photo. Over this photo, Limbaugh states: "I've got some sources up in North Carolina tell me they have already started work at the North Carolina A and T [Agricultural and Technical] State University campus to widen some of the doorways to make way for Michelle's rear end. So I believe those are some jobs Obama can claim credit for." In the space of a few sentences, Limbaugh has cast the first lady as an emasculating harpie, a Sapphire, as well as drawn on the popular image of the big-bottomed Black woman that is rooted in the commodification of and European fascination with Saartjie Baartman's buttocks (Collins, 2005). This illustrates another aspect of the Powerful Black Bitch: despite the veneer of power, she can still be reduced to and remains an angry Black bitch.

Discussion

This study of the representation of Michelle Obama on YouTube clearly demonstrates the video-sharing site's role as contested ground in the attempt to represent the first lady in ways that both reinforce and reject existing stereotypes. This struggle over the meaning and definition of Michelle Obama as the U.S.'s first Black first lady reflects society's discomfort with issues related to race, gender and class. Although traditional news also reflects this battle, it does not reflect the depth and breadth of views on public display via YouTube, where anyone with the desire and a video camera can upload thoughtful analysis as well as unsubstantiated conspiracy theories and hate-filled diatribes because, in the words of one of the posters, "almost everything is fair game" on YouTube. As such, YouTube provides a wider spectrum of ideological views – and extremes – than mainstream news.

Attempts by the White House and Obama campaign to confine Michelle Obama to the domestic sphere, within the traditionally feminine roles of mother, wife, hostess and advocate, reflect and reproduce the stereotypic Black lady. Even video connecting the first lady to celebrities, while reaffirming her own celebrity status, appeared within the context of children's activities, thereby blunting any threat her popularity might pose as a source of power.

The danger seemingly inherent in the prospect of a Black woman with power is encapsulated in the image of the Powerful Black Bitch, which was used by conservatives to cast Michelle Obama as selfish, self-indulgent and a threat to society. Because previous stereotypes did not anticipate Black women having power beyond their presumed ability to emasculate Black men and wreak havoc on Black communities, this depiction transcends earlier stereotypes. As more African American women gain access to political, economic and social power, the image of the Powerful Black Bitch is likely to become more prevalent within popular culture. It also is likely to be used to justify the denial of real power to African American women. In addition, the De Niro flap underscores the degree to which a Black woman as first lady remains untenable to many. Within this controversy, used as a pretext for both subtle and blatant racist appeals, Michelle Obama was reduced to the color of her skin, a reminder that all African American women can be thus diminished.

Within the limited space allocated to the first lady for self-presentation, Michelle Obama's authentic voice was most audible when spoken within the format of televised late-night talk shows. This provided her with the unscripted space to display a cheeky and, at times, self-deprecating sense of humor, quick wit and intelligence, as well as a refreshing lack of deference to her husband and the conventional expectations of a first lady. As an alternative to the stereotypic images of African American women in popular culture, Obama's image on late-night talk shows appears closer to that of the strong Black woman –

independent, unassailable and tough. This image, Harris-Perry (2011) points out, is nurtured in Black communities and is a rejection of the myths used by a White society to both define and confine African American women. Obama's authentic voice also could be heard, albeit *sotto voce*, in moments that highlighted her relationship with her husband. She does not defer to him, and she will publicly tease him about his competitiveness and other human foibles. While the teasing serves to humanize the president, it also normalizes their marriage. Theirs is a relationship to which other married women can relate. The public image of Michelle Obama as a wife who can more than hold her own with her husband and at the same time is supportive and loving also serves as an important corrective to the emasculating Sapphire stereotype.

Harris-Perry (2011) reminds us that, as an African American woman, Michelle Obama "is constrained by different stereotypes from those that inhibit white women," and that the public space for her to express a more independent and authentic voice during the 2008 presidential election shrank with her depiction as an angry and unpatriotic Black woman: "As First Lady, Michelle has crafted a more traditional role for herself. She is highly visible, but she has taken on relatively safe issues like childhood literacy, ending childhood obesity, advocacy for women and girls, and support for military families" (p. 289). Harris-Perry views Obama's self-proclaimed position as "Mom-in-Chief" as an act of resistance against the stereotypes used against Black women – her insistence on focusing on her children is both a rejection of and an important corrective to images of the bad Black mother and the mammy who would ignore her own children and family to ensure order in the White world.

Given the constraints of stereotypes, the strictures of the mythic first ladyship, and the White House's desire to "soften" the first lady's image, that Michelle Obama was able to resist stereotypic expectations and assert her independence and authentic voice – however limited the space for that voice may be – is no small matter. In addition, in her resistance, Michelle Obama has created more room for other African American women to both resist and further claim their space and authenticity within a White society. This space, however, is threatened by the new image of the Powerful Black Bitch who, selfish and self-indulgent, cannot be entrusted with power. As Black women work to disentangle themselves from the binds of the old, destructive and shaming stereotypes, it seems that new ones await.

YouTube Videos with Michelle Obama

- Justin Bieber & Taylor Lautner Get Slimed Kids' Choice Awards 2012 Show Highlights: http://www.youtube.com/watch?v=sk28NhenfiM
- Holleywood ft. Semi Duce – Michelle Obama: http://www.youtube.com/watch?v=qySZ8pNWNuY

- WFW 73 – We met President Obama! http://www.youtube.com/watch?v=Wz N0FfKne7o
- Dinner with Barack and Michelle: http://www.youtube.com/watch?v=dwBZ 5hKFkkw
- Sneak Peek: Ellen and Michelle Obama Reunite: http://www.youtube.com/ watch?v=9quMBGfVvm4
- Michelle Obama Letterman Show Appearance – 3/19/2012 part 1: http:// www.youtube.com/watch?v=L5w4FShx-s8
- The Road We've Traveled – Live Stream with David Axelrod and Mitch Stewart: http://www.youtube.com/watch?v=we2bpLWEjtc
- On Nowruz, President Obama Speaks to the Iranian People: http://www. youtube.com/watch?v=vBtkSa6RiPg
- A New Way to Tour the White House: http://www.youtube.com/ watch?v=TSQkaD_mXGo
- Obama's dramatic "Where the Wild Things Are" reading: http://www. youtube.com/watch?v=gwbHrewGg8s
- State Dinner for Prime Minister Cameron http://www.youtube.com/ watch?v=mX6mT0kpoyQ
- Michelle Obama honors Taylor Swift with Big Help award: http://www. youtube.com/watch?v=N8gHAm0eIb8
- First Lady Michelle Obama: Women's Week of Action Starts March 23rd: http://www.youtube.com/watch?v=Yi-2ES_-1FM
- De Niro Joke – Gingrich Demands Apology From President Obama: http:// www.youtube.com/watch?v=jWJHjXCPRXM
- Opening the 2012 White House Easter Egg Roll: http://www.youtube.com/ watch?v=mJylq0rsWKM
- Mary J. Blige Burger King Commercial: http://www.youtube.com/watch?v= t6VW5S47K0g
- West Wing Week: 3/30/2012 or "I've Got Seoul": http://www.youtube.com/ watch?v=dpi1LGEwlUs
- Beyoncé's Baby Weight – GONE!: http://www.youtube.com/watch?v=BVh9 OstLaaE
- One Direction (boy band) Turns Down White House Invite: http://www. youtube.com/watch?v=JSpE2ZJh4JA
- One Year of Joining Forces: http://www.youtube.com/watch?v=RF-Y2DbzCTQ
- Evolution of an Obama Dictatorship: Nullifying Congress to Nullifying the Supreme Court: http://www.youtube.com/watch?v=EQtkQ6Yz1ok
- First Lady Michelle Obama: "Join me in standing up for all those who have served": http://www.youtube.com/watch?v=uvc5yLipFWs
- First Lady Michelle Obama Hosts 2012 Spring Garden Planting: http://www. youtube.com/watch?v=Y3BsH6pxUa4

- Obama: 'We Didn't Have the Luxury For Michelle Not To Work': http://www.youtube.com/watch?v=rEKzFst5jgg
- Michelle Obama: I am now more popular than the president: http://www.youtube.com/watch?v=TcBCkMeMa60
- Are Americans scared to speak their mind? http://www.youtube.com/watch?v=ZDceTyKCbmw
- 2012 White House Easter Egg Roll – Yoga Garden: http://www.youtube.com/watch?v=h7nTvdyQaDc
- Taylor Swift, Selena Gomez, Victoria Justice & More Interviews Backstage & Red Carpet – 2012 KCA: http://www.youtube.com/watch?v=FHGlQTY4jCI
- ABC World News Now: Michelle Obama Appears on The Colbert Report: http://www.youtube.com/watch?v=EUqPhlE7cCs
- The Daily Show: 04/05/12: http://www.youtube.com/watch?v=OnvqrRi_IF4
- Obama does some press-ups and gets rejected by high-five: http://www.youtube.com/watch?v=9Itsmxq9WaU
- Taylor Swift To Be Awarded By Michelle Obama: http://www.youtube.com/watch?v=12NRdBMHIgk
- Robert De Niro's "White First Lady" Joke Draws Gingrich Demand for Apology: http://www.youtube.com/watch?v=IAh3Wm8kVxo
- Malia Obama Mexico spring break story disappears from Internet: http://www.youtube.com/watch?v=50Iu_UcKNqs
- A Newroz Message from President Obama 2012: http://www.youtube.com/watch?v=4on9jakrOj0
- 2012 White House Easter Egg Roll: Play with Your Food@ http://www.youtube.com/watch?v=UtFGoWCoi4w
- Michelle Obama on Letterman: "This Isn't Oprah!": http://www.youtube.com/watch?v=GXLnjlYMViM
- The First Lady and Dr. Biden Speak on the Joining Forces Anniversary: http://www.youtube.com/watch?v=rxhLTUtmHnM
- Champions of Change: Let's Move: http://www.youtube.com/watch?v=hBj4LBwJHm0
- Obama Describes Difficulties First Lady Faced in Balancing Career and Family: http://www.youtube.com/watch?v=PfcRtPhzBus
- Michelle Obama Previews the UK State Dinner (2012): http://www.youtube.com/watch?v=9nGKxSCtxxo
- How Celebrities Celebrate Easter: http://www.youtube.com/watch?v=67OXGkEXVF8
- 2012 Kids Choice Awards Pictures: http://www.youtube.com/watch?v=ujjVtmkHhZA
- Presidential Barbie Dresses like Michelle Obama?! Political Fashion! Chris Benz: http://www.youtube.com/watch?v=UKvVO2oyfDo

- Robert De Niro White Racial Joke – First Lady Joke: http://www.youtube.com/watch?v=jHU-4wqqhMI
- 2012 White House Easter Egg Roll: The First Lady Reads to Kids: http://www.youtube.com/watch?v=CR_sAAC_4rc
- Nick kids choice tonight. Michelle Obama there with Taylor Swift: http://www.youtube.com/watch?v=yf6EtBBkwmM
- Taylor Swift Wins in White, Twice! http://www.youtube.com/watch?v=U1TLlXqJ7BU
- Beyoncé Shows Off Her Tiny Waist: http://www.youtube.com/watch?v=b6h3NJN0UqQ
- 123 Lets Go – Let's Move: http://www.youtube.com/watch?v=TTpIiZveLJM
- Gingrich blasts Robert De Niro for 'white First Lady' joke at Obama fundraiser: http://www.youtube.com/watch?v=02eebW3SPH4
- The Colbert Report: 04/11/12 Recap: http://www.youtube.com/watch?v=fvo6DXw7bfU
- White House Easter Egg Roll 2012: Cutest Moments, Obama Shoots Hoops with Harlem Globe Trotters: http://www.youtube.com/watch?v=kTvIjxGxHR8
- Coast Guard Cutter Stratton Commissioning: http://www.youtube.com/watch?v=_t3DrVcYjQk
- Robert De Niro's racist statement during Obama fundraiser is a joke? http://www.youtube.com/watch?v=2_FI3MzRA-Y
- Gerald Celente – Michelle Obama Propaganda: http://www.youtube.com/watch?v=efGUcoy2Ykk
- Robert De Niro tossed under Obama bus: http://www.youtube.com/watch?v=uM1v6GY240w
- Michelle Obama Honors International Women of Courage: http://www.youtube.com/watch?v=3rLzVE0b104
- Lil' Rush on Trayvon Martin Case: http://www.youtube.com/watch?v=6Kk290-JWr0
- First lady's incognito trip to Target: http://www.youtube.com/watch?v=NMum2dInBdU
- Hollywood Hypocrites: http://www.youtube.com/watch?v=KzBn-k2pHfI

5

JUANITA BYNUM IN BLACK AND WHITE (NEWS)

On Aug. 22, 2007, Juanita Bynum, "the most prominent black female preacher in the country" (Dewan, 2007, p. A1), was attacked by her estranged husband, the Rev. Thomas W. Weeks III, in the parking lot of an Atlanta hotel where, according to witnesses, Weeks attempted to choke Bynum, then pushed her to the ground, where he proceeded to kick and "stomp" on her, and threatened to kill her. A hotel employee pulled Weeks off Bynum, who was taken to a hospital.

Bynum's reputation as a Pentecostal evangelist with a coast-to-coast ministry she shared with her husband virtually guaranteed that the assault would become national news, particularly within the African American community, where the attack forced the generally proscribed issue of domestic violence into the open. Although African American women are more likely than women of any other race to be victims of intimate partner violence (Violence Against Women Survey, National Institute of Justice and the Centers for Disease Control and Prevention, 2000), this violence, for the most part, has not been addressed by either the African American community at large (hooks, 1981; Richie, 1985; Smith, 1992; Love, 2008) or by its press.

In generating news nationwide, the Bynum assault offers a unique opportunity to compare coverage in Black and mainstream newspapers. How the news represents violence against women shapes both public discourse and public policy, as well as how we understand and view this violence (Kitzinger, 2004; Meyers, 1997; Weaver and Carter, 2006). A comparative study of news coverage of the assault also contributes to our understanding of the differences between the Black and White presses as institutions serving their respective communities.

This study compares news coverage of the Bynum assault through an analysis of the African American and mainstream newspapers in six cities with large Black populations. It attempts to ascertain: (1) how the violence was represented; (2) how Bynum and Weeks were portrayed; and (3) what are the differences and similarities in the coverage provided by the Black and White presses. This study is informed by Black feminist theory not only in recognizing the interconnected nature of gender, race and class but also in viewing violence against African American women within the context of White supremacy and patriarchy.

The study's findings indicate that, for the most part, the Black press avoided hard news[1] coverage of the assault and depended on "briefs" – short news often within a column – and feature stories. By providing an outlet for Weeks's accusations, particularly those reported in briefs, the Black press at times blamed Bynum for her own victimization. In addition, feature articles often portrayed both Bynum and Weeks as equally responsible for the violence. Conservative leaders within the Black church served as primary news sources who defined the attack within the context of mutual responsibility and failings, as well as causing harm to the church and the institution of marriage. The White press, on the other hand, was more likely to report the assault as a hard news story in which Weeks was portrayed as the perpetrator. Unlike the Black press, the mainstream press often highlighted what it saw as an ironic contradiction between Bynum's message of empowerment for women and her own life as the victim of spousal abuse. The White press was somewhat more likely than the Black press to view the assault within the broader context of patriarchy and male supremacy, but those instances were few and far between.

The Black Church, the Press and Violence Against Women

Juanita Bynum grew up attending a Pentecostal Church in Chicago and entered the ministry after a failed marriage, followed by what she acknowledges as a period of sexual promiscuity (Burford, 2001; Millner, 2007; Kellner, Ruether and Cantlon, 2006). In 1996, her big break occurred when evangelist T.D. Jakes invited her to speak to thousands of women at a singles conference in Dallas, where the response to her sermon was overwhelming (Burford, 2001, p. 185). Two years later, Jakes invited Bynum to address his "Woman, Thou Art Loosed" conference in Atlanta, which "propelled her into the high-energy world of auditorium and media evangelism" (Kellner, Ruether and Cantlon, 2006, p. 446). Bynum, who refers to herself as a prophetess, is known for sermons about women's empowerment that draw on her own experiences and urge women to forego premarital sex while turning to God for fulfillment and the promise of a worthy husband.

Bynum's message of empowerment and freedom from unhealthy relationships is rooted in the tradition of Black evangelism, with its promise of deliverance from slavery (Lincoln and Mamiya, 1990; June and Parker, 1999).

The institutional basis of Black church life, Harris-Perry (2011) points out, is formed by "the experiences of faith, celebration, worship, and resistance" (p. 223). According to Dyson (2003), the Black church's influence on African Americans cannot be overestimated; it shapes the ideas and values even of those who eschew church-going and do not consider themselves religious. That influence, he adds, includes the perpetuation of gendered inequities: "75 percent of the Black Church is made up of women, and yet they rarely have access to the central symbol of power – the pulpit" (p. 160). Collins (2005) explains that Black churches have "historically preached a politics of respectability, especially regarding marriage and sexuality because they recognized how claims of Black promiscuity and immorality fueled racism" (p. 108). Harris-Perry (2011) similarly states that, while faith may be a resistance strategy for Black women, that faith is often rooted in the patriarchal teachings of African American protestant churches. "In many ways," she explains, "these black churches create new forms of subjugation for black women through their promotion of inequitable gender leadership and their teachings about male domination in the home" (p. 223). She adds:

> Black liberation theology's silence on gender is a stunning omission, made possible by the long history of gender inequality in Christian churches of all racial compositions. Women were expected to sit in the pews, receiving messages from men in the pulpit. Their role was to recognize God in their pastor, not to expect or demand that he recognize God in them.
>
> (pp. 226–227)

Harris-Perry (2011) also points out that because "black American Christianity contains both oppressive and liberating aspects for black women," their expressions of faith are constrained by both White supremacy and patriarchy. Even as Black Christianity has resisted racial domination, it has supported and maintained sexism and gender inequality (p. 231).

Like the Black church, the Black press historically has concerned itself with deliverance from slavery and racial inequality. Jacobs (2000) states that the Black press's goals were: (1) providing a forum for debate and self-improvement; (2) monitoring the mainstream press; and (3) increasing Black visibility in White civil society. As Strother (1978) notes, "the white press have largely ignored the existence of Blacks or have presented a negative image of them" and, as a result, the Black press have "developed a race-consciousness designed to present Blacks' viewpoints, aspirations and struggles in a positive way" (p. 92). For the most part, Black people are portrayed in Black newspapers either as heroes whose accomplishments are to be lauded or as victims of a racist and unfair system (Shipp, 1994).

The White Press and African Americans

As noted in previous chapters, the White news media reflect racist coverage in over-representing African Americans as criminals, under-representing them as victims (Dixon and Linz, 2000) and portraying them as more threatening and self-serving than their White counterparts (Entman and Rojecki, 2000). These studies also have concluded that the news reflects modern racism, which assumes discrimination is no longer a hindrance to Black mobility and therefore asserts that African Americans are to blame for their lack of success (Campbell, 1995; Campbell, LeDuff, Jenkins and Brown, 2012; Entman, 1990, 1992).

In reflecting the interlocking race, class and gender biases of society, mainstream news organizations have largely ignored instances of violence against Black women by Black men, although extraordinary coverage is often provided when the victim is a White woman and the perpetrator a Black man (Benedict, 1992; Meyers, 1997). The news also tends to blame both African American and White women when they are the victims of male violence, implying that they are somehow at fault, while absolving the perpetrator of responsibility for his actions (Benedict, 1992; Meyers, 1997, 2004a).

However, news scholars have largely avoided examining news coverage of violence against Black women by Black men. The few studies to have looked at this have been limited to the mainstream media. For example, Lule (1995) found that mainstream coverage of boxer Mike Tyson's rape of an African American woman portrayed his victim as either a "gold digger" or a woman who should have known better. To date, no studies have examined how the physical abuse of an African American woman by an African American man is covered by the Black press, nor have any studies looked at whether this coverage differs from that in the White press.

African American Women and Violence

The lack of attention by news scholars to coverage of violence against African American women stands in contrast to the fact that African American women are more often the victims of intimate partner violence (IPV)[2] than women of any other race. One survey found that 26 percent of Black women experienced IPV, as opposed to 21 percent of White women (Violence against Women Survey, National Institute of Justice and the Centers for Disease Control and Prevention, 2000). The Bureau of Justice Statistics (2005) National Crime Victimization Survey's findings are even more disconcerting: in 2004, 6.6 Black women per 1,000 were IPV victims, compared with 3.4 White women – almost twice as many.[3] A more recent survey from the U.S. Centers for Disease Control and Prevention (Black et al., 2011) found that 4 out of 10 non-Hispanic Black women have been the victim of IPV, and half of all multiracial non-Hispanic women have been similarly abused.

Mama (2000) claims Black women have a more difficult time leaving abusive men than do White women "partly because the agencies that have moral and legal obligations to assist them are often staffed by people who hold racist views" (p. 49). African American women who are physically abused by African American men are victimized not only by the assault but also by a society that may not believe them and often does not provide them with the services and resources they need (West, 2000). Within Black communities, African American female victims of violence are often silenced while their abusers are supported (hooks, 1981; Lorde, 1992; Richie, 1985; Smith, 1992). Bent-Goodley (2006) notes that in the African American community, women are encouraged by family, friends and the church "to stay silent about the abuse so that negative stereotypes of African Americans are not reinforced" (p. 110). In addition, Black women who accuse Black men of violence and/or harassment often are considered "race traitors" by their communities (James, 1996, p. 143).[4] As an often-cited example, Anita Hill, whose televised testimony accusing U.S. Supreme Court nominee Clarence Thomas of sexual harassment riveted the nation in 1991, "was regularly maligned as a race-traitor who allowed her story of sexual harassment to be used by powerful white opponents to harm the credibility of an African American man. Many wondered what she had done to provoke or encourage the harassment" (Harris-Perry, 2011, p. 54). In addition, boxer Mike Tyson was "hailed as a returning hero by many African American political and social leaders" after his release from jail for the rape of an African American woman (Harris-Perry, 2011, p. 54). In both instances, according to Harris-Perry (2011), the response within African American communities was linked to the "continuing power of a common stereotype of black women as particularly promiscuous and sexually immoral" (p. 54). This myth of Black women's hypersexuality, embodied in the stereotype of the Jezebel, was created and perpetuated by White society and its institutions, but it also appears in "the internal politics of African American communities" (Harris-Perry, 2011, p. 55). Often, Harris-Perry (2011) adds, "the ideas, beliefs, concerns and viewpoints of black men are assumed to represent the entire race" (p. 231), while African American women are forced to bear the burden of misrecognition imposed on them "both by the structural constraints of white racism and by the intimate and often violent restrictions of black sexism" (p. 52).

Analytic Approach

In analyzing news coverage of the attack on Juanita Bynum by her husband, the constant comparative method was used to look for themes and patterns in coverage of the Bynum assault within the Black and White newspapers in six U.S. cities. The questions asked are: How is the violence portrayed? How are Bynum and

Weeks represented? And what are the differences and similarities in the coverage in Black and White newspapers?

The initial goal was to compare the Black and White newspapers in the five cities with the largest African American populations based on 2010 U.S. census figures, which are – in order of Black population size – New York, Atlanta, Chicago, Washington, DC and Philadelphia. However, Atlanta's Black newspaper – the *Atlanta Daily World* – did not mention the assault, despite the facts that: (1) the assault occurred in Atlanta; (2) the city has the second largest African American population in the nation; and (3) Bynum and Weeks maintain a ministry there. The decision was then made to include two additional cities from among the top 12 cities with the largest Black populations which also had both Black and White newspapers that covered the assault. In this way, Detroit, with the 9th largest African American population, and Memphis, in 12th place, were included in this study. New York's *Amsterdam News*, which is the largest circulation Black newspaper in the country, did not cover the assault,[5] although another African American newspaper in that city, the *New York Beacon*, did and is therefore included.

All news items – including feature stories, hard news, briefs and opinion pieces – that mentioned Bynum or Weeks between Aug. 22, 2007, when the assault occurred, and nine months later, on May 22, 2008, were analyzed.[6] This timeframe allowed for the inclusion of follow-up stories six weeks after Weeks's March 11 guilty plea. Ethnic NewsWatch was used to locate articles in Black newspapers, while Lexus-Nexus and ProQuest were used for the White press. Two competing White newspapers in both New York and Philadelphia were included because they both covered the assault. All news items were examined for themes and patterns. In many instances, news items contained multiple themes and are therefore represented in multiple thematic categories.

For the Black press, the newspapers included are the *New York Beacon*, *Chicago Defender*, *Afro-American Red Star* (Washington, DC), *Michigan Chronicle* (Detroit) and *Memphis Tri-State Defender*, all of which are published weekly. Also included in this study is the *Philadelphia Tribune*, which is published five days per week. The *Chicago Defender*, *Michigan Chronicle* and the *Tri-State Defender* in Memphis are all owned by Real Times, Inc.

For the White press, the newspapers are *The New York Times*, *Daily News* (New York), *Chicago Tribune*, *Washington Post*, *Detroit News*, *Philadelphia Inquirer*, *Philadelphia Daily News* and the *Memphis Commercial Appeal*. The analysis below begins first with a look at the Black press, and then at coverage in the White press, drawing on coverage within the categories to illustrate the relevant themes and patterns.

The Black Press

The Black press ran 25 news items, including 19 briefs, five articles and one opinion piece. The briefs in the Black press were short items in celebrity/gossip or entertainment/church news columns that were written by staff. Sixteen of the 19 briefs in the Black press were from the *Philadelphia Tribune*'s celebrity gossip column, one was in a celebrity/gossip column in the *Michigan Chronicle* and two ran in the *Chicago Defender* column, written by its entertainment and religion writer. These columns largely consisted of the staff writer's opinion or news of celebrities, or notices of local church events, sermons and concerts. The only hard news story, which appeared in the *New York Beacon* (2007, p. 4) was adapted from an Associated Press report that appeared a week earlier in the *Memphis Commercial Appeal*. The *Beacon* version contained a few slight alterations and no attribution to either the AP or the reporter.

Unlike the briefs, which primarily reiterated comments made by Weeks and Bynum or included news from other sources and the writers' own opinions, most of the articles relied on clergy and others within the faith community as primary news sources. These sources tended to view the violence and divorce as the inevitable result of stress related to co-pastoring or not putting God and family first. Within this context, both Bynum and Weeks appear equally responsible for the failure of the marriage – and, by implication, the assault.

With the exception of the *Beacon*'s slightly revised Associated Press story, the Black press's newspaper articles used the assault as a jumping-off point for features addressing violence within co-pastor relationships or, more generally, against women and other family members. For example, the lead paragraph in an article in the *Philadelphia Tribune* (Aug. 31, 2007) stated: "After Bishop Thomas Weeks III surrendered to charges of assaulting his wife, Juanita Bynum, last week, issues of domestic violence and emotional health among clergy are coming to the forefront of discussions in religious circles" (Phillips, 2007, p. 6D). This article, like others within this genre, quoted co-pastors and others who claimed "domestic violence among clergy is not a surprise" given their lack of outside support and the tensions that go with the job (Phillips, 2007, p. 6D). A few of the articles advised battered women to leave abusive relationships and provided the phone numbers for domestic violence hotlines and shelters. Some posited that a solution to domestic violence – among both pastors and the lay public – is to turn to God. The major themes within news coverage within both the briefs and other articles that appeared in the Black press were: assigning blame; harming the Black Church and marriage; naturalizing domestic violence; healing; and claiming irony.

Assigning Blame

A number of articles and briefs in the Black press sought to explain the cause of the assault, raising questions about who was responsible and what actions might have precipitated it. Depending largely on who was being quoted as a news source, as well as the format in which the news was presented, Bynum, Weeks or both were blamed.

Blaming Bynum

Both articles and briefs in the Black press questioned whether Bynum's actions were the cause of or contributed to the violence. This was particularly the case with the *Philadelphia Tribune*'s "What's the 411?," by writer Patty Jackson, who provided extensive coverage of Weeks's allegations against Bynum. Nine days after the assault, Jackson speculated about whether the cause was Weeks's jealousy of his wife's success or Bynum's "diva" behavior: "Did Weeks feel uncomfortable in her shadow?... Did her husband's jealousy lead him to beat her up, or was she an out-of-control Diva causing him to snap?" (2007a, p. 31E).

Jackson frequently reported what she called Weeks's "shocking allegations about the prophetess" (2008b, p. 31E) in subsequent "411" columns, giving him space to defend his behavior and discredit and blame Bynum: "Sources say he is ready to admit it was not easy being married to Bynum. He claims at one point, she threatened him with a rock, and she was known for her temper tantrums" (2007l, p. 31E). Jackson also reported Weeks's claim that Bynum "is the reason why the marriage fell apart" and that "she was never around to take care of him like a wife should" (2008a, p.31E). In addition, Jackson wrote that Weeks had said "Bynum wants him in jail so he can't marry another woman," and she "threw him under the bus because her ministry needs money," as well as that "the devil made him do it, and he was the one who was abused" (2008a, p. 31E).

Similar to Jackson's coverage, the *Chicago Defender*'s entertainment and church news columnist Effie Rolfe repeated Weeks's assertion that Bynum "wanted to emulate Oprah Winfrey in seeking fame as a television host because her ministry was suffering" (2008, p. 40). By repeating Weeks's allegations, as well as speculating about whether Bynum provoked the assault by her diva-like behavior, the briefs served to blame Bynum for her own victimization and obscure Weeks's responsibility for the assault.

Bynum as Victim

Although Jackson frequently reported Weeks's comments about Bynum and the assault in her *Philadelphia Tribune* column, in a few instances she challenges his assertion that he was, in fact, the victim. She states that Weeks "will not go away quietly" and that "Bynum says she is not surprised by his statements because he said if she ended the marriage, he would try to destroy her name" (Jackson, 2007d, p. 31E). And she clearly sympathizes with Bynum as she situates her as the victim of a violent man:

> She thought their routine blowups were normal (the shoving and the pushing). There was also the incident where a church member was physically attacked by Weeks. Bynum helped him cover it up to keep the

incident from going public. Now you see what happened to her. Bishop Weeks says Bynum was cruel and hard to live with, and he will prove it. Even if she was difficult, there is no excuse for stomping someone in the ground.

(Jackson, 2007j, p. 31E)

Blaming Weeks

Weeks is only held accountable for his actions in three articles. The *Memphis Tri-State Defender* briefly noted in a feature story that the National Black Church Initiative had urged Weeks[7] to step down as head of Global Destiny Ministries, with the National Black Church Initiative (NBCI) president calling Weeks's actions "morally wrong and reprehensible" (Edney, 2007, para. 10). In an opinion piece in the *New York Beacon* by Barbara Reynolds (2007), an adjunct professor at Howard University School of Divinity and the religion writer for the National Newspaper Publishers Association, Reynolds takes Weeks and other pastors to task for their un-Godly behavior. She states that Weeks "savagely choked, kicked in the stomach and stomped" Bynum, and she suggests that he should not "still [be] in his pulpit at Global Destiny Church" (p. 9). Reynolds holds Weeks and other pastors accountable not just for battering but also adultery, profanity, violence and the performance of "same-sex union ceremonies and preaching that 'homosexuality is not a sin'" (p. 9).

In addition, the *New York Beacon*'s version of the AP story clearly blames Weeks for the attack by quoting a police officer describing the assault. According to Officer Ronald Campbell, Bynum's "husband walked out to the parking lot area, turned back around and started to choke Miss Bynum... As he choked her, he pushed her down to the ground and started to kick her and also stomp on her" (*New York Beacon*, 2007, p. 4). Two paragraphs later, Bynum's publicist further clarifies what happened: "She was not in a fight with her husband: she was attacked by her husband" (p. 4). Unlike the other articles, this story focused on describing the assault and included statements that clearly represented Weeks as the perpetrator of the violence.

Both Parties are Responsible

A number of articles suggested that both the victim and assailant are responsible for ending domestic violence. This positions the victim as at least partially to blame for the abuse. The solution to the violence, the articles suggest, range from counseling to self-help books and turning to God – remedies for which both are responsible. For example, the *Memphis Tri-State Defender* quotes a psychologist, who also is an ordained minister, suggesting that "couples or individuals could turn to self-help methods by receiving instruction about their problems from credible books, tapes or by getting counseling or therapy if the problem persists" (Edney, 2007, para. 33).

The recommendation for self-help resources and therapy constructs domestic violence as a problem couples are equally responsible to "fix," which ignores the power dynamics within battering relationships and assumes both partners are at fault. In addition, advocates for battered women point out that couples counseling is often dangerous for women, who later may face their partner's rage for what was said in session (Kaufman, 1993). Like the other articles, this story lacks an understanding of the role male violence plays in sustaining patriarchy and male supremacy, as well as a more basic understanding of battering as the exercise of power, domination and control (Brownmiller, 1975; Meyers, 1997; Stoltenberg, 1989). In presenting both the recipient of the violence and the perpetrator as equally in pain and in need of help, these articles obscure the differential in power and present the violence as behavior over which the batterer has no control, as opposed to an attempt to exert power and control.

Harming the Black Church and Marriage

Some church leaders who were interviewed interpreted Weeks's assault as an attack on the church, God and marriage, although it is not always clear whether Weeks or the devil was responsible. For example, the *Philadelphia Tribune* reported that Pastor Deborah Parks was among those who view the incident between Bynum and Weeks as a "spiritual attack" on the church: "'It's definitely a spiritual thing because we know the adversary[8] wants to discredit God, church and people,' Parks said... 'Some folks are going to use this to unfortunately turn away from the church'" (Phillips, 2007, p. 6D). Within this context, the violence appears to be Satan's fault. In addition, Bynum is not the victim here; the church, God and others who may "turn away from the church" appear to be the true victims. In an opinion article in the *New York Beacon*, Barbara Reynolds suggests that if Jesus Christ showed up "in some of our churches," he might well "shed tears and walk out the door" (2007, p. 9). While once "church sanctuaries were treated as hallowed ground and the ordained clergy representing God," today, Reynolds states, "a demonic spirit of sexual perversion, prosperity, blindness and power-tripping is creating a sense of shame and cynicism among rank and file Christians that is actually driving some from the pews" (p. 9). Weeks's behavior, she claims, contributes to and is illustrative of this wider problem within the church.

In a similar vein, an article in the *Memphis Tri-State Defender* quotes Bishop T.D. Jakes – who helped launch Bynum's career within the Black evangelical movement – defending marriage and advising people not to give up on love. Jakes said he hoped the "recent separation and divorce announcements of Christian power couples, including the hotel parking lot beating of Prophetess Juanita Bynum-Weeks by her minister husband, won't deter marriages"

(Edney, 2007, para. 1). Jakes emphasized that marital problems among religious leaders is no reason to give up on marriage: "Don't give up on Love. Love works" (Edney, 2007, para. 4). The problem here appears not to be Weeks's attack on Bynum, or a society which naturalizes violence against women more generally, but that couples could give up on love and marriage as a result of the assault.

Naturalizing Domestic Violence

The Bynum assault also was mentioned in feature articles that attempted to educate the reader about domestic violence. These articles naturalized violence against women by presenting it as the inevitable outgrowth of life's many frustrations and stresses, to which anyone may fall prey. They also provided advice for "healing" the abuse, including counseling and self-help books. The articles tended to rely on clergy and Christian counselors to explain what might have gone wrong in Bynum's marriage and that of others who divorce. Among the causes cited are job stress, lack of outside support and shared values, past childhood trauma, superficiality in choosing a partner and not putting God first and home second.

The *Afro-American Red Star* published two feature articles about domestic violence in which the Bynum assault is used within the context of discussing family violence more generally. In the lead of the first article, spousal battering is mentioned along with other types of family abuse, which is said to be "as old as humankind's existence on earth" (Prince, 2007, p. A6). That article further asserts that: "Unguarded anger erupts first on those in closest proximity, physically and emotionally" due to "frustration gained from employment situations" or "pain gained in the public arena" (p. A6). These comments naturalize domestic violence, presenting it as the inevitable result of workplace frustrations or displaced pain. Emphasizing that domestic violence is as old as life on this planet – just the way things are – suggests the impossibility of eradication, for it appears to be a normal outgrowth of life's frustrations to which everyone is subjected and to which anyone may succumb. The *Afro-American Red Star* also states that: "Unbridled anger needs to be treated with physical outlets for stress, along with professional counseling and medication, if necessary" (Prince, 2007, p. A6). These prescribed remedies, however, further naturalize male violence by placing it within the context of other emotional or physical problems.

The other article in the *Afro-American Red Star*, based on an interview with the Rev. Dr. Unnia L. Pettus about her book *Nobody But God: A Journey of Faith from Tears to Triumph*, calls Pettus's book "timely because of recent press coverage regarding domestic violence between two ministers, Juanita Bynum and her estranged husband, Bishop Meeks (sic) that took place recently in Atlanta, GA" (*Afro-American Red Star*, 2007, p. C5). The book focuses, according to Pettus, on "the prevalence of domestic abuse among couples in the faith community" (p. C5). Again, domestic violence is presented as a common occurrence, even among clergy. And, as with the other article in the *Afro-American Red Star*, an understanding of the role that domestic violence plays in maintaining male power and control is missing.

Victimization as a Choice

In addition to presenting violence as the natural outcome of life's stresses, the *Afro-American Red Star* also presented victimhood as a choice by asserting that:

> It is difficult to get help for adults who've settled into the mode of victim in abusive relationships. The psyche often tells them pain is what they deserve or that they've in some way provoked the attack; especially if fists are familiar from their childhood.
>
> (Prince, 2007, p. A6)

This claim blames the victim for settling "into the mode of victim" (p. A6), thereby making victimhood appear to be a choice rather than the outcome of repeated and sustained abuse. In addition, the *Afro-American Red Star*'s interview with Unnia Pettus similarly suggests being a victim is a choice. Pettus, the article states, wants to "inspire and encourage the abused not to live as victims any longer" (*Afro-American Red Star*, 2007, p. C5). Thus, it is the victims who need to change – which, according to Pettus, is only possible through God's salvation.

Healing

News sources also expressed the need for healing for Bynum and Weeks, which sometimes came in the offer of prayer. In the case of Juanita Bynum, it also came within the context of her moving forward with her life.

Bynum Moving Forward

Although the Black newspaper briefs quoted Bynum far less frequently than they did Weeks, when they did, the focus was on her putting her husband and the past behind her and redefining herself for the future. Approximately six weeks after Weeks's guilty plea, the *Chicago Defender*'s Effie Rolfe observed that Bynum's "television career seems to be blossoming" with her appearance on the television show *Divorce Court* (2008, p. 40). The *Philadelphia Tribune*'s Jackson also reported that Bynum has "no bitterness" and is attempting to put the past behind her (2007k, p. 31E). Sympathetically noting that "the past year was very tough for the religious leader," Jackson states that "Bynum says she has a new outlook on life and a new focus. And, maybe one day, she will be able to love again" (2007c, p. 31E). Jackson later reported that despite Weeks's "begging," Bynum has decided to end the marriage and "is looking forward to new challenges in 2008" (2008c, p. 12).

Bynum also was reported in the *Philadelphia Tribune*'s "411" column to have said "she will dedicate her life to being an advocate against domestic violence," and that while she has forgiven her husband, "she feels she must end the marriage because... this is not the first incident" (Jackson, 2007i, p. 31E). Bynum was said to be releasing a new album and DVD, "Juanita Bynum Unplugged," with "a portion of the proceeds going to organizations fighting against domestic violence"[9] (Jackson, 2007f, p. 31E). Bynum not only appears to be moving forward, she is represented as taking the high road, identifying herself as a survivor of domestic violence and committing herself to helping other survivors.

Both Bynum and Weeks in Need of Healing

Articles also emphasized the need for forgiveness and understanding for either or both Weeks and Bynum, as well as others caught up in domestic violence. For example, the *Afro-American Red Star* noted in a feature article about family violence that it is not only the victim who needs help: "The abuser needs help too." The article states: "The bruise inflicted on another just serves up another unhealthy dose of anger for the batterers. It's an unending cycle of pain for everyone involved" (Prince, 2007, p. A6). A minister quoted in the *Memphis Tri-State Defender* also emphasizes forgiveness and understanding: "We just need to understand that except for the grace of God, there go I" (Edney, 2007, para. 35). And Serita Jakes, T.D. Jakes's wife, states in this article that people should not judge "Lady Bynum" harshly but instead should pray "that God would help heal the brokenness" inside (para. 8). The *Chicago Defender*'s Effie Rolfe, also offered "heartfelt prayers" (2007, p. 21).

Creating Irony

In what was unusual for the Black press, the *Michigan Chronicle*'s celebrity gossip writer, Steve Holsey, suggested that Bynum wasn't what she claimed to be. Holsey took Bynum to task for referring to herself as favored by God: "I hate it when certain church-goers say they are 'God's people,' 'the saints' or that they are 'highly favored.' Just how 'highly favored' was evangelist Juanita Bynum when her 'minister' husband Bishop Thomas W. Weeks III beat her up recently?" (Holsey, 2007, p. D1). While Holsey writes that he wishes Bynum "nothing (but) the best," he also states that it is "always a mistake" to suggest one is special to God (p. D1). The focus of this brief was not to condemn Weeks or the assault – or even to express sympathy for Bynum – but to use the attack as an occasion to denounce Bynum for hubris and deception.

The *New York Beacon*, in its adapted AP story, also highlighted the irony and contradiction between preaching women's empowerment and being the victim of spousal abuse. Its lead began: "Juanita Bynum, a televangelist with a national following for sermons about women's empowerment, pressed charges against her estranged husband Thursday after she was bruised in a confrontation with him during a meeting to reconcile, police said" (*New York Beacon*, 2007, p. 4). By including Bynum's sermons about women's empowerment in the same sentence as mention of the assault, the news draws on irony for impact.

The White Press

The White press ran 27 news items – 10 articles, which is twice as many as appeared in the Black press, 16 briefs and one op-ed piece. The Associated Press figured prominently in news articles within the White press, with AP reporter Errin Haines covering the story from Atlanta. The *Washington Post* provided the most extensive coverage of the assault and its aftermath, likely a result of the fact that Bynum and Weeks maintained a Global Destiny Ministries church in the *Post*'s coverage area. As was the case within the Black press, the White press often used Weeks's assault on Bynum as an opening to discuss domestic violence more generally.

The "briefs" in the White press most often contained factual updates about the case in columns such as the *Washington Post*'s "Nation in Brief," the *Chicago Tribune*'s "Across the Nation" or the *Philadelphia Inquirer*'s "In the Nation." The White newspapers' reliance on hard news briefs rather than the celebrity/gossip or entertainment and church news columns in the Black press is a reflection of the greater access White newspapers have to news services that include these briefs, as well as their status as dailies, which provided them with more frequent opportunities to run brief updates and stories than the weekly Black newspapers. In addition, the Black press's emphasis on providing an alternative to mainstream news is reflected in its reliance on local columnists and reporters as opposed to mainstream news services.

While the preponderance of briefs were in hard news columns, references to Bynum and Weeks occasionally appeared in the celebrity/gossip columns, which generally provided straightforward details of the assault and related developments but occasionally also offered editorial comments. For example, the *Philadelphia Daily News* "Tattle" column commented that details about the Bynum–Weeks marriage, to be discussed by Bynum on the televised show *Divorce Court*, "are sobering" (Conrad, 2008, para. 24). Another example of editorializing in celebrity/gossip columns appears in the *Philadelphia Inquirer*'s "Celebrity Watching" column which told readers not to "judge" Weeks "until you hear what he has to say, whenever his lawyers let him say it" (Holmes, 2007b). The major themes within news coverage were: creating irony; assigning blame; naturalizing domestic violence; healing; and leading through ministry.

Creating Irony

The White press, far more often than the Black press, questioned Bynum's legitimacy as a self-proclaimed "prophetess" and advocate for women's empowerment. This was done primarily through implication and the juxtaposition of details of the assault with mention of her advocacy of women's empowerment, although sometimes the news was more direct. For example, a *New York Times* article by Shaila Dewan challenged Bynum's credibility as a prophetess and spiritual leader, noting in the lead sentence the "remarkable" and "shocking" contradictions between Bynum's life and her message of empowerment:

> The attack in a hotel parking lot here last month was remarkable not only because the victim, Juanita Bynum, is the most prominent black female preacher in the country, a televangelist who is pals with Oprah, admired by Aretha, and who recently signed on to campaign for Obama. It was shocking, especially to legions of women who latched onto her message that only chastity and self-respect would bring true love, because the attacker who choked, stomped and kicked her, Bynum said, was her husband. The episode... raised questions about the trajectory of Bynum's career as a woman who called herself a prophetess.
>
> (Dewan, 2007, p. A1)

Dewan notes that Bynum seemed to have been rewarded by "a model marriage" (p. A1). Since the attack, the article states, Bynum "has tried to reinvent herself once more, announcing that she is 'the new face of domestic violence.' But Tom Joyner, the syndicated radio talk show host, did not let her off the hook so easily: 'If you're a prophet,' Joyner asked, 'didn't you see this coming?'" (p. A1).

The article also quotes a sociologist of the neo-Pentecostal movement who noted that the assault is a challenge to Bynum's credibility: "Maybe she's been living a lie all these years." This possibility is implied later in the article, where Bynum is said to have "publicly focused on the duties of a Christian wife, counseling women to give their husbands plenty of sex and to ask them, 'Do I please you?'" In her seminars, the article stated, she told women: "I don't care what kind of husband you got, that's your covenant vow, and you have a responsibility to make him feel like he's a wonder when you know he ain't" (p. A1)

Bynum's credibility also was called into question when the *Philadelphia Inquirer*'s "Celebrity Watching" column reported that the "home of televangelist and 'prophetess' Juanita Bynum" was being auctioned after the assault. To this brief update, it added: "To paraphrase Tom Joyner, didn't she see this coming?" (Holmes, 2007a).

In addition, an article in the *Detroit News* also calls into question Bynum's professed ability to see into the future when it asks: "If Bynum – a woman who claims to hear from God – is beaten by her husband, how can the average person recognize an abuser?" (Taylor, 2007a, para. 5). And the *Washington Post* notes that while Bynum and Weeks were a "highly marketed dream team," Atlanta police responding to Piedmont Hospital "found a different story" (Harris, 2007b, p. B7) – implying a contradiction exists between the marketed image and the reality.

Assigning Blame

Frequent references to the details of the attack reinforced Weeks's responsibility, as did instances in which Bynum discussed the assault or previous instances of abuse. For example, a *New York Times* article quoted Bynum as acknowledging prior "pushing and shoving" and stating that she wanted to "take some classes" to find out why she is attracted to abusive men (Dewan, 2007, p. A1). That same article also drew on police reports of the assault and noted that a warrant had been issued for Weeks's arrest. In addition, an Associated Press article in the *Memphis Commercial Appeal*[10] began by stating that "Juanita Bynum, a televangelist with a national following for sermons about women's empowerment, pressed charges against her estranged husband Thursday after she was bruised in a confrontation with him during a meeting to reconcile, police said" (Associated Press, 2007, p. A8). Details of the confrontation and injuries are provided by a police spokesperson, and Bynum's publicist later establishes that Bynum "was not in a fight with her husband: she was attacked by her husband" (p. A8).

With few exceptions, the hard news briefs avoided editorial comments and provided short updates consisting of two or three sentences that reiterated details of the attack, the charges and more recent developments in the court case. These news briefs emphasized Weeks's actions and, in doing so, implied guilt. For example, the *Chicago Tribune* noted that Weeks, charged with aggravated assault and making terroristic threats, was free on $40,000 bond ("Televangelist's husband breaks silence," 2007, p. 17). A *Washington Post* brief similarly noted details of the assault, his not-guilty plea and $40,000 bond, and that Bynum has filed for divorce ("Religion briefing," 2007, p. B9). The same AP brief in *The New York Times* and *Memphis Commercial Appeal* reported that Weeks had pleaded guilty to assaulting Bynum, "was sentenced to three years' probation and then turned to her and apologized" (Associated Press, 2007, p. A8). That same brief also noted that Weeks must "undergo violence and anger counseling and complete 200 hours of community service" (p. A8). The *Philadelphia Inquirer*'s "In the Nation" column more concisely stated that Weeks had pleaded guilty to assault and "was sentenced to three years' probation and community service, and apologized to her" (*Philadelphia Inquirer*, 2008, para. 13), and in a previous brief pointed out that the National Black Church Initiative, a "national group of black and Hispanic churches," was calling for Weeks to be suspended from the ministry "because of allegations" he beat his wife (*Philadelphia Inquirer*, 2007, para. 5). That brief also contained details about the charges and assault.

Like the hard news briefs, the celebrity/gossip briefs also described details of the assault or, less frequently, quoted Bynum, both of which tended to portray Weeks as responsible for the violence. For example, the *Philadelphia Daily News*'s "Tattle" column described the assault and Weeks' sentence, then noted that Bynum said she was trying to make the marriage work, but things "just kept getting swept under the rug" and she began to "adapt to a very wrong and very unhealthy" marriage (Conrad, 2008, para. 32).

Weeks is Not a Criminal

Only rarely was Weeks absolved of responsibility in the White press, and in those instances it was Bynum herself or church leaders who raised questions about his culpability or the criminality of his actions. In an update that appeared in both the *Philadelphia Inquirer* and the *Washington Post*, Associated Press reporter Errin Haines (2008) reported that Weeks "was sentenced to three years' probation and then turned to her [Bynum] and apologized" (para. 1). The article included comments from a press conference held by District Attorney Paul Howard, who noted that "a personal plea from Bynum… convinced prosecutors not to pursue jail time for Weeks" (para. 10). "Many people in her situation would've been asking for him to be put in jail," said Howard, who called Bynum's request "courageous" (para. 11). Bynum also is reported to have said: "I don't believe my husband is a criminal" (para. 13). In the article, Bynum denies that Weeks's abuse was criminal – and therefore, by extension, that Weeks and other men who physically assault women are criminals. The message that men who abuse women are not criminals, and that to not press charges is "courageous," denies the criminal and potentially lethal nature of violence against women; the emphasis on forgiveness over justice serves the interests of the perpetrators at the expense of the abused.[11]

In addition, a *Washington Post* article (Harris, 2007b) noted that the leaders of the Prophets' House, Bynum's and Weeks's "Global Destiny Church in the District" had "launched a three-day fast and urged the flock to focus on God" (p. B7) in the wake of news of the assault. That article quoted evangelist Azizah Morrison, exhorting congregants: "Get off the phone. Now is not the time to gossip. Now is the time to seek the Lord… You wasn't there. You don't know what happened" (p. B7). While his statement condemns gossip, it also challenges the veracity of accounts in the press. The article concludes with a quotation from Morrison urging the congregation to "ask God to vindicate the name of our pastor" (p. B7). By not including details of the assault from reputable authorities, such as the police, the assault itself is called into question, and Weeks is not held accountable for his actions.

Patriarchy is the Problem

A feminist analysis of the assault briefly appeared toward the end of articles appearing in the *Detroit News* and the *New York Times*. In both cases, comments made by a female pastor and a female seminary professor reflect a feminist understanding of the role of violence against women in maintaining patriarchy. Near the close of the article in the *Detroit News*, Valerie Davis, a seminary professor in Memphis, notes the difficulty women who are "gifted, strong and powerful" have in "any relationship" due to "a sexist culture" in which "women are under pressure to prove they were really called" and men "are always under pressure to prove they are not being run by some woman" (Taylor, 2007b, para. 16). Women pastors, she adds, work to "stroke or protect their [husband's] ego" (para. 17) as well as being "under pressure to be demure and cute and not appear to be less than feminine to people, so they will not be accused of being less than a woman" (para. 18).

The New York Times article by Shaila Dewan (2007) includes comments by a female pastor who teaches seminary classes on domestic violence and notes that some mega-churches "perpetuate a conservative message that can lead to abuse" (p. A1). The pastor also states that she didn't consider Bynum a "liberation preacher," but an "empowerment preacher" whose audience is "interested in self growth, how good they can be and how God loves them, but not in how to do the kind of things that stop abuse, that fight oppression, that fight hunger and incarceration and ask the reason why'" (p. A1).

Black Family in Crisis

The one opinion article in the White press, written by Harvard University sociologist Orlando Patterson (2007), appeared in the *New York Times* and briefly mentioned the assault within the context of other instances of woman-abuse by Black men to illustrate "the crisis in relations between men and women of all classes and, as a result, the catastrophic state of black family life, especially among the poor" (p. 13). It argued that addressing racial bias in the judicial and prison system is not enough:

> Disproportionate numbers of young, black men will continue to be incarcerated until we view this social calamity in its entirety – by also acknowledging the central role of unstable relations among the sexes and within poor families, by placing a far higher priority on moral and social reform within troubled black communities, and by greatly expanding social services for infants and children.
>
> (p. 13)

As with other articles, the author fails to place violence against women within the context of systemic male supremacy and a patriarchal social order which grants men control and power over women.

Naturalizing Violence

As with the Black press, some articles in mainstream newspapers used the Bynum assault as a lead-in to a story more generally about domestic violence. In these cases, the press described the warning signs of abuse and emphasized the ubiquity of violence against women, presenting violence as an inevitable result of life's stresses or failure to put God first. Although the intent of these articles presumably was to educate the reader about the danger signs of domestic violence, they failed to address the role of systemic misogyny and patriarchy. In a *Detroit News* article with the headline "Domestic Violence Can Happen to Anyone," information about domestic violence, including a description of "warning signs" that women and young girls should be aware of, was provided, along with details of Bynum's assault (Taylor, 2007a, para. 13).

A second article in the *Detroit News* used the Bynum assault to more broadly address the stresses and difficulties that married co-pastors encounter in maintaining a marriage while working alongside each other in the church (Taylor, 2007b, para. 6). The problem, the article's sources emphasize, is the co-pastoring relationship itself – not misogyny, male supremacy or the need for the male co-pastor to remain in charge. The solution is to "maintain balance in their lives by always keeping God first and their marriage and family second" (2007b, para. 6). If they don't, "pressure mounts, tempers flare and good judgment is lost, causing damage to themselves and their congregations" (2007b, para. 6). Several co-pastoring ministers are quoted discussing the need for pastors to work on their marriages – for example, for the "preacher" to "make it right with your wife" before going to bed (which assumes the preacher is the husband and not the wife) and the "wife" to "not let the sun go down on your wrath" (2007b, para. 6). The gist of this line of thinking is that the woman's anger is the problem; it assumes that within the co-pastoring relationship, the male is the dominant minister and the wife's anger is what endangers the marriage.

Healing

The only occasion in the White press in which Weeks is said to be in need of healing was in an article in the *Washington Post* in which Bishop T.D. Jakes urged people not to "lose their faith every time a minister gets into trouble" (Harris, 2007a, p. T3). Jakes also called for more options to rehabilitate ministers: "We need a place where fallen ministers can be restored… some of them have medical issues… People have personality disorders and need professional help" (p. T3). With these statements, Jakes attributes Weeks's violence to a personality disorder that can perhaps be fixed with "professional help" (p. T3). Through his comments as quoted in the article, Jakes elides issues of power and control that are at the heart of domestic violence, instead presenting the abuse as something that Weeks had no power over, just as one does not have power over a personality disorder.

Leading through Ministry

Two articles in the *Washington Post* (Harris, 2007b, p. B7; Thomas-Lester, 2007, p. B5) were about attempts by the Black church to address the issue of domestic violence, establishing a role and vision for the church as a key to its eradication within Black communities. These articles focused on Project Safe Sunday, an annual church-sponsored event designed to address violence against women in the State of Maryland. The first article, which announced the upcoming event in local Prince George's County churches, noted that more domestic violence cases are filed in Prince George's than anywhere else in Maryland (Harris, 2007b, p. B7). This year's observance of Project Safe Sunday, the article stated, "comes in the wake of the highly publicized case of Juanita Bynum, a popular evangelist who was beaten in the parking lot of an Atlanta church[12] by her husband Bishop Thomas Weeks, with whom she shared a huge international ministry that at one time was based in Prince George's" (p. B7). The article states that Project Safe Sunday was established "as a way to involve one of the most influential institutions in people's lives in battling the problem" of domestic violence (p. B7). The pastor, acknowledging that violence occurs within the church community, noted that the church previously has not been willing to talk about domestic violence: "The church is not a haven for saints, but a hospital. For the longest time, talking about domestic violence has been off-limits, but it is a vexing problem plaguing our community" (p. B7).

The second *Washington Post* article about Prince George's County's fifth annual observance of Project Safe Sunday contained a "special message" for the congregation at Kettering Baptist Church: "If you are in an abusive relationship, you should get help, whether you are the victim or the victimizer" (Thomas-Lester, 2007, p. B5). The article, as with the previous one, noted the prevalence of domestic violence in the county and that the focus of this year's annual event was on the perpetrators. According to State's Attorney Glenn Ivey, one of the founders of the annual event, "If you don't deal with the batterers, they just find somebody else to batter, so we have to get ahead of that… It's not enough to get help for the victims. We've got to focus more attention on the perpetrators" (p. B5). The article also noted the cases of women who had been murdered by their partners or ex-partners, as well as the difficulties Ivey faced in getting pastors on board: "I had some ministers tell me, 'Brother Ivey, I'm not touching that. That's too hot'" (p. B5).

Both articles include testimony from former batterers who credit God with delivering them from their abusive behavior. A minister quoted in an article in the *Washington Post* also urges congregants who are abusive to "seek help and admit their abuse to help others": "We need to testify," he said. "We need to tell the story that 'I was in it, but I've been set free. I have been delivered from it, and I'm never going back again'" (Thomas-Lester, 2007, p. B5). In this article God is the redeemer. But both articles affirm the necessary and central role of Black churches in eradicating domestic violence within their communities.

Discussion

Although the White and Black presses had some themes in common, the differences in how they framed the violence, as well as Bynum and Weeks, are significant in emphasis as well as content. Both presses questioned Bynum's legitimacy as an advocate for women's empowerment given her status as a victim of her husband's abuse, but for the Black press, this was limited to one snide comment by a celebrity/gossip columnist and one AP article, which not coincidentally appeared in two mainstream papers. However, the suggestion that Bynum might be a fraud was a recurring theme in the White press. And while the *Philadelphia Tribune*'s gossip column gave considerable space to Weeks's accusations that Bynum was at fault, the theme of "blaming the victim" was entirely absent from the White press, which instead implicated Weeks as the perpetrator of the violence by recounting details of the assault and subsequent criminal proceedings. In addition, relegating the assault to gossip columns in the Black press undercuts the seriousness of domestic violence, placing it on a voyeuristic par with details and criticisms of celebrities' lives.

Other than the gossip columns and the AP coverage, the Black press largely ignored the assault itself and used it as a heuristic device to talk about violence against women in general or within co-pastor marriages in particular. These feature stories turned to church leaders to contextualize and explain the violence, which was often portrayed as the result of not putting God first in their lives. Church leaders urged readers not to give up on love and marriage, emphasized the pressures inherent in co-pastor marriages and blamed Weeks's attack on job stress or even the devil. The majority of these church leaders chose not to condemn the assault; rather, they advocated compassion and understanding for victim and assailant, both of whom were seen as equally responsible for the violence and the disintegration of their marriage. For a number of sources in the Black press, victimization was a choice, Bynum and Weeks were both in need of healing and the main concern was that the assault was bad for the church and marriage. At no time did these newspapers demonstrate any understanding of the dynamics of battering as they relate to male power, privilege and control.

The White press, on the other hand, covered the assault primarily within the context of hard news briefs and stories. The frequent reiteration of details of the attack resulted in news that much more clearly placed the blame on

Weeks, although an opinion piece citing the violence as symptomatic – and the product – of the crisis within Black families, as well as Bynum's own denials that her husband is a criminal, provided a counterweight to this argument. In addition, the White press quoted sources who unambiguously – albeit briefly – placed the violence within the context of patriarchy, and it ran two feature stories, both appearing in the *Washington Post,* dealing with the Black church's attempt to halt domestic violence within their communities through Project Safe Sunday. These feature articles articulated a role for the church in stopping the violence – a role that was missing from coverage in the Black press.

The Rev. Aubra Love (2008), founder of the national Black Church and Domestic Violence Institute, has argued that Weeks's sentence and the response of church leaders does a disservice to African American women who are victims of domestic violence, as well as to all Black churchwomen: "Domestic violence is a crime against not only the victimized, but also against the county, state and/ or federal government. There exists a moral obligation to send a swift and strong message that beating a woman, especially an intimate, will not be tolerated" (p. 3). For Love, at issue is accountability to "the congregation and community for anyone serving in leadership at the predominantly female institution of the Black church" (p. 5).

What is clear from this study is that the type of news formats – whether gossip/ celebrity briefs, feature articles or hard news stories – as well as the choice of news sources played significant roles in shaping news coverage of the assault on Juanita Bynum – for better or for worse. What also is clear is that both the Black press and the White press were responsible for perpetuating representations that ultimately do a disservice to African American women who are the victims of violence. The Black press could have interviewed progressive African American women within the church who, like Love, would have been able to frame the violence not simply as a matter of individual psychopathology, job stress or not putting God first in a marriage, but as the crime that it is. In failing to hold Weeks accountable for his actions, the Black press reflected the combination of White racism and Black sexism that fosters the misrecognition and oppression of Black women within African American communities (Harris-Perry, 2011). For its part, the White press used the story to question the legitimacy of Bynum's ministry and her role as an advocate for women's empowerment. In doing so, it similarly missed the opportunity to unequivocally condemn violence against women, draw on news sources that could have framed the violence within the context of male dominance and control and send the message that, as Rev. Love (2008) states: "Beating a woman, especially an intimate, will not be tolerated" (p. 3).

6

VIOLENCE AGAINST AFRICAN AMERICAN WOMEN IN LOCAL NEWS

Freaknik as a Case Study

Throughout the 1990s, Freaknik was an annual rite of spring in Atlanta. The pre-final exams weekend of street parties and cruising[1] drew African American college students from across the U.S. Begun in 1982 as a "modest picnic in the park for a couple of hundred students" from historically Black Morehouse and Spelman colleges, the event attracted, at its peak in 1994, up to 200,000 student and non-student participants (Helton, 1996, p. H4). It unofficially ended in 2000 after the city decided to strictly enforce traffic and curfew laws, crack down on lewd public behavior and spread the word that Freaknik was not welcome (Suggs, 2000). A 1998 editorial in the *Atlanta Journal and Constitution* explains: Freaknik had "turned into a destructive, chaotic and abusive affair years ago. Its main focus became sexual harassment and sexual attacks on women" ("Resolution for Atlanta," 1998, p. 12A).

As noted in the previous chapter, the problem of Black men's violence against Black women raises sensitive issues of gender and race. While Chapter 5 looked at coverage of the domestic violence assault on televangelist Juanita Bynum in African American and mainstream newspapers, this chapter explores violence against African American women in local Atlanta TV news coverage of Freaknik during 1996. Although this study was conducted a number of years ago and appeared in its original version in *Critical Studies in Media Communication*, it is included in this book because it provides a foundational look at violence against African American women by African American men in the news, as well as a baseline for the earlier chapters in this book in terms of its use of intersectionality to explore stereotypes and representation. This chapter argues that in news coverage of violence against African American women, the convergence of gender, race and class oppressions worked to minimize the seriousness of the violence and portrays its victims primarily as stereotypic Jezebels who provoke male violence through their own behavior. Male perpetrators are invisible and passive within this discourse. The news also reinforces race and class stereotypes by positioning locals as inner-city troublemakers and students as middle-class, good citizens. I conclude that the news's juxtaposition of locals and students works ideologically to affirm middle-class values and norms as a remedy for poverty and racism while supporting the modern racism belief that success and failure depend upon individual initiative.

African American Women, Violence and Class

Studies of news coverage of violence against women indicate the news tends to blame women for their own victimization while absolving their assailants of responsibility (Benedict, 1992; Bumiller, 1990; Chancer, 1987; Cuklanz, 1997; Meyers, 1994, 1997; Steeves, 1997), thereby perpetuating a good girl/bad girl or virgin/whore dichotomy (Benedict, 1992; Meyers, 1994, 1997). Media coverage of violence against women supports the interests of the state (Edwards, 1987; Finn, 1989–1990; Steeves, 1997), with the news rarely covering violence against African American women unless it is sensationalistic or highly unusual (Benedict, 1992; Meyers, 1997).

Black feminist theorists emphasize that the nature of sexual assault can only be understood within its social and political context, which reflects the "complex interconnectedness of race, gender, and class oppression which characterize that society" (Davis, 1985, p. 10). Angela Y. Davis (1998) notes that Black women "have always suffered in far greater proportion and intensity the effects of institutionalized male supremacy" (p. 186). The experience of violence against Black women, according to James (1996), is "magnified by racism and classism" (p. 142).

This socialization is not limited to a White public. African American feminist scholars and activists have criticized the tendency within Black communities to silence female victims of male violence while rallying around the men who abused them (hooks, 1981; Lorde, 1992; Richie, 1985; Smith, 1992). Lorde (1992) notes that the need for racial unity has made Black women "particularly vulnerable to the false accusation that anti-sexist is anti-Black" (p. 500). Black women and men who support patriarchy, explains hooks (1981), "have a tremendous investment in presenting the social situation of Black people in such a way that it seems we are only oppressed and victimized by racism" (p. 115). Indeed, D.E. Davis (1997) notes that African American men, like White men, engage in street harassment because they "have been socialized to exercise their male status to oppress women" (p. 197). Defining street harassment as a form of sexual terrorism that includes verbal and non-verbal markers that frighten women and reinforce fears of rape, she claims that this harassment is "genderized and racialized for every woman": its racial aspect relates to the woman's background, and its gendered nature maintains male supremacy and female subordination (p. 195).

A Black feminist perspective "doesn't require the shortchanging of any aspect of Black women's experience and... doesn't assume that racial oppression is more important than sexual oppression or vice versa" (Smith, 1992, p. 185). While feminist standpoint theory more generally "advocates that knowledge production and validation should be grounded in one's everyday life, and especially the everyday lives of the oppressed" (Griffin, 1996, p. 181), the self-defined standpoint of Black women provides the foundation of Black feminist thought (Collins, 1991).

This perspective differs markedly from Weberian or Marxian approaches, which traditionally have been applied to the analysis of class structure and identity. Unlike Black feminist theory, they have not been able to address the interconnection of class, gender and race. Weber saw class identity relying not on "an infallible list of occupations for each class" but on "overall, gross differences in the real economic rewards" received by those in different occupations (Landry, 1987, p. 11). Education was a means to provide workers with different levels of skills that could be bartered in the marketplace. From a Weberian point of view:

> education is a *cause* or *source* of an individual's class position, rather than a defining characteristic, and income is *one* of the many rewards resulting from one's class position. Neither income nor education, therefore, are part of the definition of class.
>
> (Landry, 1987, p. 5)

Early Marxism viewed class consciousness as arising from the experiences of wage laborers under capitalism, with class position determined by occupation and the individual's relationship to the means of production. Contemporary social theorists have come to view class identity as complex and contradictory, reflecting "multiple class positions that individuals can occupy at different moments in their lives" (Gandy, 1998, p. 26). Boxill (1992) points out that Marx's characterization of the lumpenproletariat is similar to contemporary descriptions of the underclass, but without the appeal to racism.

Despite their contributions to the theorizing of class, neither Weberian nor Marxian perspectives have successfully combined the concept of class with an understanding of both gender and race oppression. Barrett (1988) notes the difficulty traditional schools of social and economic thought have had in integrating race into the already stressed analysis of gender and class:

> existing theories of social structure, already taxed by attempting to think about the inter-relations of class and gender, have been quite unable to

integrate a third axis of systematic inequality into their conceptual maps. Theoretical perspectives using the more flexible vocabulary of subjectivity and discourse have made it possible to explore these issues without being constrained by the need to assign rank in what is effectively a zero-sum game of structural determination.

(p. x)

Socialist feminists have debated the relationship between gender and class, particularly whether women's oppression can be independent of class division and the capitalist mode of production. For example, German (1983, 1989) argues that women's oppression is a function not of patriarchy but of class society and the role of the family in reproducing labor power. However, as Barrett (1988) points out, the most effective voices "addressing questions of class, inequality, poverty and exploitation... are those of black women, not white socialist-feminists" (p. xxiv).

Methodology

In drawing upon a Black feminist paradigm that includes gender, race and class in the analysis of violence against African American women in Freaknik news, this study asks how, in what ways, and to what effect these signifiers of exclusion and domination work within representation. I employ discourse analysis to explore the representation of: (1) the women, (2) the acts of violence against them, and (3) the perpetrators of this violence. The concern here is not with the effect of representation on audiences, but of the effect of class, race and gender on representation.

Local television news coverage of Freaknik was chosen for analysis because, given the paucity of news involving violence against African American women (Meyers, 1997) and Freaknik's propensity for anti-female violence, the event seemed to guarantee that at least some reporting of this violence would be inevitable. Exact numbers are impossible to come by because rape and other acts of physical assault are infrequently reported to police – and African American women are less likely to report such abuse than White women (Davis, 1985; Wright, 1998). However, rape statistics gathered by the city's rape crisis center from the Grady Memorial Hospital emergency room provide some indication of the magnitude of the problem. In the Friday through Monday *prior to* Freaknik 1996, four rape victims were seen in Grady's emergency room, and in the Friday through Monday *following* Freaknik, eight women were treated. In four days *during* Freaknik, from April 19 to 22, the number skyrocketed to 20.[2] The number of rapes during Freaknik represents a 400 percent increase over the weekend before and a 150 percent increase over the weekend after Freaknik.

For two weeks, from April 12 to 25, 1996, the 11 p.m, half-hour newscasts from the ABC, NBC and CBS network affiliates in Atlanta (WSB, WXIA and WGNX, respectively) were taped.[3] Although Freaknik was primarily a weekend event – beginning the afternoon of Friday, April 19, and continuing through Sunday, April 21 – this study includes news stories before, during and after Freaknik so as to evaluate the pre-Freaknik framing of violence as well as any post-Freaknik follow-up stories about violence against women.

All stories that mentioned Freaknik were transcribed. Those that did not involve violence against women were examined for underlying themes and patterns to provide a context for understanding the stories of violence. The discursive analysis of these stories was a necessary first step to providing a framework for the analysis of stories involving violence against women. News stories specifically involving or referring to violence against women during Freaknik in any way were isolated from the other stories for in-depth analysis of the representation of the victims, the violence itself and the perpetrators. In addition, news stories and editorials about Freaknik in the *Atlanta Journal and Constitution* for the years 1994, 1995 and 1996 were examined less formally to enlarge the framework for understanding.[4]

TV news coverage of Freaknik appeared as "packages" in which related topics were segued together into one, relatively seamless story. For example, two days before Freaknik, WXIA aired a package with three topics: the city's denial of a park permit for Freaknik events, hiring extra security for Freaknik and Freaknik's effect on baseball ticket sales. Although different topics were covered, they were presented as aspects of one story, with Freaknik the central theme.

Discourse is closely associated with ideology and the reproduction of social hierarchies, and its analysis provides a way to examine ideologies as expressed in written, spoken and visual texts. Discourse is not simply a linguistic practice: it refers to and constructs knowledge about a particular topic. As noted previously, the analysis of discourse examines not only how language and representation produce meaning, but also the relationship between representation, meaning and power, and the construction of identities and subjectivities (Hall, 1997).

In news studies, van Dijk (1991) explains, discourse analysis looks at the following: the topics as they are expressed in headlines and story leads; overall schematic structures, which express the meaning of the text through conventional categories that include headlines, leads, layout and sentence structure; local meanings or "local coherence," which make sense of a story by relying on a community's "knowledge and beliefs about society" (p. 178); semantic strategies, which are goal-directed properties of discourse; and implicitness, which is the "implied or indirect meanings or functions of news reports" (p. 17).

Implicitness resides at the microlevel of news discourse, where rhetoric and style can be systematically analyzed for underlying meanings and ideologies. Microlevel rhetorical devices include: (a) *vagueness*, which conceals responsibility for negative actions; (b) *over-completeness*, which adds irrelevant details that may, in fact, be "relevant within a more general negative portrayal of a person or group" (p. 185); (c) *presupposition*, "a special case of implications" in which the news media "may indirectly and sometimes rather subtly state things that are not 'known' by the readers at all, but which are simply suggested to be common knowledge" (p. 183); and (d) *implication*, through which information inferred from "previous knowledge and beliefs is combined with information actually expressed in the text" (p. 181). An example of implication, van Dijk (1991) notes, is when a news report states a person "claims" she is being discriminated against, which may suggest the person is lying.

Semantic strategies, which are "goal-directed properties of discourse" (van Dijk, 1991, p. 187) include: (a) *blaming the victim*, a strategy which faults the victim for "acting in such a way that prejudice or unequal treatment is justified" (p. 193); (b) *admission*, commonly used by the news media to avoid charges that they are discriminatory and which involves the occasional assertion that most members of a particular minority group are law-abiding citizens (pp. 197–198); (c) *comparisons*, "not only between 'us' and 'them,' but also between different ethnic groups or different situations" (p. 195); and (d) *contrast and division*, which include "the implicit contrast between (good) 'us' and (bad) 'them'" (p. 197). These rhetorical devices and semantic strategies, along with topics and structures, are examined within this study. In the sections that follow, I provide a brief overview of Freaknik coverage in the *Atlanta Journal and Constitution* from 1994 to 1996 and then examine the major themes and frames in television coverage of Freaknik 1996 in the week prior to the event. Finally, I examine the incidences of violence against women in Freaknik reporting.

Freaknik Coverage

Freaknik coverage in the *Atlanta Journal and Constitution* from 1994 to 1996 placed the event within a racialized context that blamed locals rather than students for any acts of violence and initially failed to recognize sexual harassment as an issue. In 1994, traffic congestion and gridlock – which caused financial hardship for businesses – as well as trash and public urination in residents' yards were cited as the primary problems caused by Freaknik. Mayor Bill Campbell noted "relatively few acts of violence" that year, adding that those who committed them were all Atlanta residents (Scruggs and Blackmon, 1994, p. 1A). Post-Freaknik articles in 1994 noted the dilemma Campbell faced in reversing his prior policy of welcoming students to Freaknik. While White residents primarily opposed the event, Black residents supported it. The heated debate between supporters and opponents prior to the event that year was played out in the city council, where "members exchanged harsh words, tinged with racial overtones" (Vickers and Helton, 1994, p. 1A).

In 1995, articles dealt with Campbell's efforts to discourage students from coming to Atlanta for Freaknik. Sexual assaults, along with looting, were newly identified as problems during Freaknik 1995. Ten rapes were reported between Saturday night and Sunday afternoon during Freaknik, and Police Chief Beverly Harvard was quoted as being "mad as hell" because some of the women at Freaknik "stripped and permitted men to grope them" (Scruggs and McDonald, 1995, p. 5B). While residents expressed shock at the sexual undercurrent Freaknik had taken on (Harrison, 1995), Atlanta gangs were blamed for taking advantage of Freaknik and causing most of the looting (McDonald and Cowles, 1995). Articles also noted the racial divide among Atlanta residents: a poll conducted by the newspaper found that 69 percent of African American residents thought Freaknik was good for the city, while 62 percent of Whites considered the event harmful and cited traffic, sexual harassment and looting as problems (Fears, 1995a). The city council also was split over the issue along racial lines (Fears, 1995b).

The newspaper's 1996 coverage noted that Campbell had softened his opposition to Freaknik, ostensibly to placate the city's African American community (*Atlanta Journal and Constitution*, 1996). Other articles concerned the city's traffic plan, the business community's response to the event and police efforts to arrest potential and real troublemakers. These issues were echoed in Freaknik television coverage before and during the event that year.

The TV stations aired a Freaknik-related story or news package almost every day during the period of study, from April 12 to 25.[5] The stories became longer and their placement within the program earlier the closer to Freaknik they ran, with the most time and attention occurring during the event. By April 24, the only Freaknik stories were follow-ups to a murder.

Even before Freaknik began, the news represented the event as a threat to law and order and a potential descent into crime and chaos. Pre-Freaknik stories utilized videotape from the previous year of unmanageable traffic jams and gridlock; they showed long lines of stalled traffic with young African Americans hanging out of their car windows, walking among cars, dancing inside, on top of and beside cars. Other pre-Freaknik stories dealt with organizations preparing for Freaknik by training volunteers "to help maintain order and register a lot of voters," or, in the case of a group of lawyers, assisting students who had been arrested for non-violent crimes. One pre-Freaknik story reported that volunteers were being trained to mediate confrontations and "set examples for those people that may have hostile attitudes." An organization of local Black ministers, another story reported, called for a day of fasting and prayer "to ask for calmness, to ask for peace, to welcome these young people that are coming to the city." The emphasis on the need to maintain calm and order in the face of anticipated "hostile attitudes" and crime served to emphasize the danger and threat Freaknik posed to the city.

During Freaknik, reporters in helicopters pinpointed the most congested roads while reporters on the ground interviewed participants and chronicled events. Coverage centered on the tension between police trying to keep traffic moving and efforts by participants to literally party in the streets. WXIA's Bruce Erion, reporting live on Saturday night from the "sky cam" helicopter, noted that: "Kids have gotten things figured out, out there. What they've been doing, believe it or not, is... They're just getting out of their cars until a police officer arrives and says, 'Hey, no party here on the interstate, please.'"

News stories before and during Freaknik frequently referred to looting and vandalism the previous year. The stations showed videotape of young, Black males, en masse, rushing into shops whose front doors had been forced open. Other videotape showed streets littered with the aftermath of looting, as well as baton-wielding police walking through streets strewn with rubble. Looting footage from Freaknik 1995 was also shown on the Friday of Freaknik 1996, as WGNX anchor John McKnight reported that: "All 1,500 Atlanta police officers will be working the streets. The plan is to avoid the traffic gridlock and sporadic looting connected with the event last year." Other pre-Freaknik stories dealt with Atlanta businesses hiring extra security during Freaknik, "just in case things get out of hand," or attempting in other ways to prevent looting. These stories invariably included file footage of looting from the previous year. A continuing story throughout Freaknik and the week following was the shooting death on Thursday night or early Friday morning (stories were inconsistent) of a 23-year-old Ohio man who had driven to Atlanta for Freaknik. With one exception, the investigation and arrests were the only Freaknik news after the event.[6]

References to the previous year's looting routinely mentioned that those involved were local, and this distinction was continued in the 1996 coverage. On the Thursday before Freaknik, for instance, WGNX covered a pre-Freaknik party that mentioned "a few arrests – these, young men for attempted robbery," over videotape of two men handcuffed by police. Reporter Leigh Green later in the broadcast referred back to the videotape: "Now, I need to add one other point to all of this. Many of the people you saw in the piece that we just showed you are, of course, not visiting students at all. That includes the two men who are under arrest. They are locals simply out taking part in the Freaknik festivities." While the locals Green is referring to *could* be local students, they were not described as such, and the context of other stories which contrasted locals with students implicated locals as criminally inclined non-students. The distinction between locals and visiting students ignores the presence at Freaknik of the many African American students attending area colleges.[7] Disregarding local students ideologically serves to simplify and emphasize the distinction between locals as inner-city thugs and out-of-towners as well-behaved students. In addition, as a semantic strategy, the admission or assertion that students, as opposed to locals, are generally law-abiding citizens allows the news to deflect charges that its coverage may be racist.

Reporters kept a running tally of Freaknik arrest statistics, with the figures broken down by in-state (local) and out-of-state figures. The frequent tallying of arrests attested not so much to the criminal nature of Freaknik, but to the dangers of giving locals an opportunity to create trouble. It also reinforced the contrast and division between locals and students. WGNX reported:

> Atlanta police have made dozens of arrests this Freaknik weekend, but they tell us the majority of them were not out-of-towners, and a large number of those arrested were children – 228, to be exact, some as young as 12 years old. The charge, violating the city's curfew law – children under 16 can't be out alone past midnight.

WXIA's arrest breakdown for Saturday night's newscast was 195 Georgia residents and 164 from out-of-state. By Sunday night, the numbers were 846 people arrested or charged, of which "the majority were from Georgia – 461; 364 were from out-of-state; 307 cars have been impounded and 14 weapons seized." WGNX anchor John McKnight reported on Sunday night that police "arrested 846 people over the weekend, most of them locals using Freaknik as a chance to cause trouble." The contrast and division of Freaknik participants into problem-causing locals and law-abiding out-of-state students was class-based, with the locals linked to inner-city crime, a hallmark of White public perceptions of the underclass. The police's treatment of these two groups also highlights the differences between them. While transgression by the locals resulted in their arrest, that of the students merely warranted a polite request to not "party here on the interstate, please."

Much of the police department's crime prevention plan during Freaknik centered on local youths under 16 years of age at home under a curfew. As WGNX's Leigh Green reported: "The latest police technique for avoiding trouble is to round up local juveniles, mostly for minor offenses and mostly to try and keep large groups of young locals from spoiling the party." The implication is that the locals – particularly young locals – had best be rounded up to prevent them from ruining Freaknik. The rhetorical device of over-completeness was used to stigmatize these youths as coming from dysfunctional homes with little adult supervision or caring. For example, on Saturday night, WXIA's Jim Shuler reported that 228 juveniles were detained the night before for breaking curfew. Of that number, he said, 111 were still in jail Saturday morning "because their parents didn't want to come and pick them up." By Saturday afternoon, he added, only 21 juveniles remained at detention centers, and "they were being escorted home personally by Atlanta police." Claiming that their parents didn't want to come and pick them up may seem superfluous within the context of a story about crime prevention, but its relevance exists within the negative portrayal of these youths and their families. By emphasizing the number of youths arrested for breaking curfew, and that many of their parents would not get them from jail, the news reinforces popular notions of inner-city families as consisting of dysfunctional, negligent parents unable or unwilling to discipline or control their lawbreaking children. This echoed a major theme of Freaknik coverage – that the locals are underclass troublemakers prone to crime and out to spoil the party for the primarily law-abiding students who are Freaknik's only legitimate participants.

Freaknik Violence Against Women

The news media's Freaknik coverage plan focused on traffic and potential property damage – as evidenced by the use of helicopters to spot gridlock, repeated references to the previous year's looting and the presence of reporters at shopping malls and other areas that had been the site of past looting. Significantly, the news did not warn women that attending Freaknik might put them at risk of physical harm, nor did it actively seek out stories that dealt with violence toward women. Only when the cameras just happened to be where a woman was being or had just been physically assaulted did the violence become news. This occurred three times during Freaknik coverage. In addition, two other stories referred to attacks on women. In almost all cases, the news minimized the seriousness of the violence, blamed the victims and absolved the perpetrators of responsibility. This section examines in chronological order these five instances.

Instance #1

WXIA opened its newscast on Friday night with footage of three women trying to walk past a gauntlet of men reaching out to grope and grab them. As a man attempts to grab the last woman around the waist, she pulls away and keeps walking. This scene is shown with a voice-over by anchor Angela Robinson, who is African American: "Short skirts draw a crowd tonight at Underground Atlanta. Freaknik '96 is underway." Her comment about short skirts implies the women's clothing – and, by extension, the women – are to blame for the street harassment shown. Co-anchor Mike Landess then introduces himself and continues the story: "Now those young girls had to ask police for escorts to be able to get back to their cars. We have team coverage of the first day of Freaknik, beginning with Nina Jimenez at Underground Atlanta. A big crowd already?"

Jimenez moves the story's focus to the crowd size and interviews with students before returning to the incident that opened the newscast. In a voice-over, she says:

> Down Peachtree Street, it's like a parade – and at times quite a show. But for Madeema Jones and her friends who drove in from Little Rock, this is not the kind of Freaknik fun they expected. The group needed the police to help them get away from a mob of young men.

When Jimenez states that Freaknik is at times quite a show, a woman in a bikini top is shown dancing provocatively out of a car window. Cheering men surround her car and attempt to grab her, but she glides into the car and out of reach. The combination of the verbal and visual texts implies that the woman's actions are the show to which Jimenez refers.

As Jimenez mentions Madeema Jones and her friends, the camera cuts to Dana Patterson, identified in caption as a "Little Rock visitor." Patterson is with two other women in a parking deck. She describes what happened: "Guys came from everywhere, overwhelming, grabbing your purse, grabbing your butt. And you couldn't, you can't do nothing, cause it's just from all, just all of them, just come in a huddle. And it's ridiculous – you can't even walk up the street." The camera then turns to Madeema Jones, also identified as a "Little Rock visitor." She is wearing a sheer, white shirt (a bra is visible underneath). She tells the reporter: "It's really not safe, you know, and I really do think that if they can't control, they just need to cut it out, you know. Because I did not come here to expect, you know, my clothes being half-way torn off." The video cuts to a long shot of the women being escorted down the street by a police officer on motorcycle. The camera focuses on Jones, who is wearing a very short, white skirt. This appears to support the opening statement that short skirts provoked the men to action. The camera cuts back to the parking deck, to Maleesha Medlock, another "Little Rock visitor." She says: "It's scary. I was scared. I never experienced anything like this before."

The story then cuts to officers running through a parking lot while Jimenez provides the closing voice-over: "Atlanta police are here in full force trying to control the few troublemakers who usually turn out not to be college students." This again implies that non-students are troublemakers, and students are law-abiding. The camera focuses on Jimenez: "Now, other than those problems that the young women were having walking through the crowds, police report that they've had no official arrests related to Freaknik. And right now, it's just a matter of keeping traffic moving – something they seem to be doing pretty well right now."

This story reinforces several themes that were repeated in various forms throughout Freaknik coverage. By positioning the harassment of these women against the gyrations of a woman who appears to be welcoming and encouraging male attention and desire, the story suggests violence against women is the result of female provocation. Indeed, the opening of the story – "Short skirts draw a crowd at Underground Atlanta" – places the Little Rock visitors in an active role, for they chose their clothing as well as to walk through Underground Atlanta. This reflects the myths that what a woman wears and where she goes are the cause of sexual assault.

Robinson's comment is vague in not specifying the type of crowd being drawn by short skirts – that is, leering, groping men. Nor does she attribute any action to them, other than being passively drawn to short skirts. The men are invisible and passive in the spoken text, although the video clearly shows them groping, leering, and reaching out to grab the women. The spoken text – which is privileged in the newscast because it makes sense of, contextualizes and explains the visual – establishes the harassment as the women's fault and responsibility. It also is constructed as a matter of minor consequence. Robinson initially denies the seriousness of the harassment, and this denial is emphasized when Jimenez focuses first on the size of the crowds and interviews with students. Co-anchor Landess's account of how "those young girls had to ask police for escorts to be able to get back to their cars" also suggests that nothing serious happened to the "girls," for had a crime been committed, arrests would have been made. Landess's reporting reflects the lack of concern on the part of both the police and the news about sexual assault. Indeed, a very different picture would have emerged had the story represented the men as attacking the women.

The use of the term "young girls" further implies the real problem may be their youth. Had they been older, the discourse suggests, they might have known how to avoid this situation – or how to get out of it on their own. Because the situation was resolved by returning the women to their car, the issue appears to be not one of sexual assault and harassment, but of the women being in the wrong place at the wrong time, and perhaps too young and inexperienced to control the crowd. Jimenez's characterization of what occurred as a "kind of Freaknik fun" trivializes the harassment, as does her closing reference to "those problems that the young women were having walking through the crowds." By not specifying what the problems were, this statement implies the difficulty was the women's inability to navigate the crowds, rather than that the men were sexually harassing them.

This news segment also underscored another theme in Freaknik coverage – that there were, in the words of Nina Jimenez, "few troublemakers, who usually turn out not to be college students." This denies the pervasiveness of violence against women during Freaknik while reinforcing the contrast and division between troublemaking non-students and law-abiding students. This division draws on class and race stereotypes that link Black college students to middle-class aspirations and behaviors (Landry, 1987) and local, Black non-students with inner-city poverty and crime associated with the underclass (Abramovitz, 1995; Lawson, 1992). Within the context of Freaknik coverage, "local" becomes code for inner-city, non-student Black youth who engage in crime and may be seen as part of an underclass with deviant values and behaviors.

Instance #2

That same Friday night, WSB reporter Pam Martin introduced a segment within a larger story of Freaknik coverage: "As we've said before, there have been few problems. But there have been some tense moments tonight." From the beginning, then, this story is constructed as an incident of tense moments rather than a serious problem. Footage from WSB's Chopper 2 showed two women crawling on the trunk of a car as a group of men around the car attempt to grab them. Martin's voice-over describes the scene:

> Two young women were seemingly trapped by scores of young men. Some of the men, it appeared, touched and groped the women as they tried to get off the trunk of the car. Soon after, a police patrolman rode by and dispersed the crowd. No one was cited in the incident.

This story was rare in directly attributing abuse to "scores of young men" rather than blaming the women: the men "trapped" the women; some men "touched and groped" as the women tried to escape. However, the criminality and seriousness of the assault is undercut by the fact that "no one was cited in the incident," for it appears that no crime occurred. This supports Martin's comment that what occurred was tense, but nothing more.

Instance #3

On Sunday night, WGNX opened its newscast with a voice-over by anchor John McKnight and videotape of a crowd of Freaknik participants, followed by footage of Police Chief Beverly Harvard and other police officers talking to two women. The caption "Freaknik Dies Hard" appears upon the screen. McKnight states: "Freaknik dies hard on the streets of Atlanta with parties and gridlock running into the night. The city's police chief herself has to step in when one street party gets out of hand." The story continues with reporter Tiffini Diaz who "has our look at last-minute parties and one case that got out of hand."

Diaz opens live from Auburn Avenue, in the heart of Atlanta's historic Black district,[8] with a general wrap-up of Freaknik, including a positive evaluation by students, before she returns to the party that "got out of hand." Diaz states:

> Here on Auburn Avenue, it's gone from partying in the streets to street sweepers. Everyone says they had a pretty good time. With the exception of a few problems, Freaknik '96 turned out fairly well. Young people enjoyed themselves, cut loose, liked to party. In fact, they were having such a good time this afternoon that instead of heading home and back to school, a lot of them brought their partying here to Auburn Avenue and the Sweet Auburn Festival. It was here on Auburn Avenue, though, this evening, that some of the fun got out of hand.

The camera focuses on a street crowd and then zooms in on what appears to be a light blue cloth crumpled in the street while Diaz's voice-over explains that she "stumbled upon this crowd moments after two young ladies are attacked dancing in the street. One woman's underpants torn off, thrown to the ground."

The screen cuts to a student identified as "Kenya Smith, Witness." She says: "As everyone dispersed, you saw two women coming out, holding their clothes up to their bodies because they had almost gotten raped." Diaz then states, over footage of Smith talking to Police Chief Harvard:

> That attack terrified college student Kenya Smith. She shared her concerns with Atlanta's Police Chief Beverly Harvard. Harvard spent today out with Freaknik partyers and arrived here just seconds after the attack ended. Harvard told us she worries about the lewd behavior taking place during the Black college spring break.

The camera then turns to Harvard, who states: "It shows disrespect as it relates to women disrespecting themselves. But it also causes problems for other women who don't want to be groped, who don't want to be fondled. And so it's a very serious concern." With these two sentences, Harvard constructs the near-rape as a problem created by the women not simply for themselves, but for other, "innocent," women, as well. The contrast between lewd and innocent women not only positions the former as bad and the latter as good, but also leaves no room for the men who stripped the women of their clothing and almost raped them. Because the men are neither mentioned nor blamed, the news implies the fault lies solely with the women.

Harvard's comments are legitimated by both her office as the chief of police and her social location as a Black woman. As police chief, she speaks both for the law and the City of Atlanta. As a Black woman, Harvard's contrasting of the stereotypic good girl/virgin with the bad girl/whore bears the authority of one speaking from knowledge of her own gender and race.

From the beginning of this story, the news denies that the near-rape of two women is anything more than fun that got out of hand. What transformed it into something "out of hand" is vague. The only clue is that the women were attacked while dancing in the street, which implicates their dancing as the lewd behavior that is the probable cause of the assault.

After Harvard, the footage shows a scantily-clad woman dancing suggestively, her legs around a man's waist and arms around his neck, in what can be considered a representation of Harvard's bad girl. Diaz intones over this video: "Some young people argue that it's all part of Freaknik fun. They dance in traffic jams for all to see, and a few say they think they can handle the crowds." The camera then cuts to an unidentified female, in short shorts, dancing with several men around her and a large stick in her hand. The camera focuses on her as she shimmies and explains: "See, when I shake, see, they like the way I shake. And I'm gonna have to bust on 'em, you see what I'm saying, if they touch," she adds as she brandishes her stick.

This woman appears to be dancing for male attention – "see, they like the way I shake." But, unlike the women who were disrobed and almost raped by the mob of men, she appears prepared to defend herself from the inevitable result of that attention. The message to viewers may well be: "If you are going to tease, you had better be prepared for the consequences."

Diaz then says: "Aside from some complaints about the city's traffic diversion plan, Freaknik '96 is getting overall good reviews." Later in the newscast, Chief Harvard states: "Overall, I am very pleased. We have not had any significant problems at all." At the end of the Sunday night newscast, anchor John McKnight summarizes events on the final day of Freaknik:

> To sum up for now our coverage of Freaknik '96: Freaknik dies hard on Atlanta streets with partying and traffic congestion continuing into the night. One incident on Auburn Avenue started to get out of control, where a group of men were observed by Atlanta Police Chief Beverly Harvard assaulting two women. But overall, the chief says smaller crowds and increased police force kept Freaknik '96 under control with fewer arrests than last year.

Thus, the news agrees with Harvard that no significant problems arose. The attacks on women are trivialized and considered minor – certainly not as important as the city's traffic congestion. Indeed, Diaz states that the Auburn Avenue "incident... *started* to get out of control," implying that it never got beyond the initial stages. This story also contains a contradiction. Early in the report, Diaz notes that Harvard "arrived here just seconds after the attack ended." By the end of the report, the anchor claims "a group of men were observed by Atlanta Police Chief Beverly Harvard assaulting two women." The presence and role of Harvard and other officers remain unclear. What is clear but unstated is that no arrests were made, despite the fact that numerous witnesses were present and the police either witnessed or were present "seconds" after the assault. The lack of arrests denies the criminality and seriousness of the assault. The guilty party remains the "lewd" women.

Instance #4

WXIA's coverage of a news conference with Chief Harvard on the Monday after Freaknik indicated the police's traffic control plan had worked well. "All in all," reporter Paul Crawley states, "she gives her troops and most Freaknikers high marks for good behavior." Crawley continues:

> Another thing she said was better this year was the not so much lewd conduct on the part of women being groped and fondled here in the middle of Freaknik here. Last year, a couple of rapes. As of this evening, apparently one possible rape on Stewart Avenue – still not sure it was

Freaknik connected – that, only a few hours ago. But all in all, the police chief gives her troops, those from 20 other departments that helped – including the GBI, state patrol, Dekalb County, surrounding areas – and the students, pretty much of an "A."

The comment about not as much "lewd conduct on the part of women being groped and fondled" clearly blames women for encouraging men to sexually assault them. Although the story failed to identify the form this lewd conduct took, the context of Freaknik coverage implies it may have been their short skirts, dancing or other sexually "provocative" behavior.

By claiming a "possible" rape occurred, Crawley legitimates speculation that this could be a woman's false accusation. The news also suggests that the exact number of rapes last year – and, by extension, the rapes themselves – are insignificant, for statistics could have been obtained. (Many would argue that the 10 rapes reported the previous year hardly constitute "a couple.") This lack of specificity stands in marked contrast to the frequent updates in the number of arrests and criminal charges, and their classification by local and out-of-state offenders.

Instance #5

A follow-up Freaknik story on WXIA Monday night opened with video of an unidentified, White male, seemingly college-age, seated in a car and displaying through his rolled-down side window what appears to be his driver's license. He complains: "We're not happy with Freaknik. We don't want it back." In a voice-over, reporter Keith Whitney states: "From the motorists who were stripped of their rights," a clear reference to the unhappy motorist. The video cuts to a woman walking past a group of men. She is holding a silver, sleeveless dress or shirt against her chest. Over this video, Whitney adds: "To the women who were stripped of their clothes, the fallout from Freaknik '96 still hangs like a mushroom cloud of anger over the city." The story then moves to a classroom of criminal justice students at Georgia State University, located in downtown Atlanta, where students, who had studied the city's response to Freaknik, charged city government and the police with racism, including the practice of "red-lining" to keep Freaknik traffic out of White neighborhoods while letting it over-run Black neighborhoods. A student also states that police attempts to keep students away from a mall "reeked of racism."

This story equates motorists caught in gridlock with women who have had their clothes ripped from their bodies – an equation which denies the criminality and seriousness of this violence. And while the story opens with an angered motorist and a physically assaulted woman, it does not deal with their anger, as suggested by the introduction. Instead, Whitney's reference to women stripped of their clothes, along with footage of the woman holding her clothes against her body, is a gratuitous introduction to a story about racism in Freaknik policing. Racism, the real focus of the story, is positioned as far more important than the sexual abuse of Black women. The assault is, after all, only accorded a fleeting image and a clause in the story's lead.

Conclusions and Implications

News coverage of violence against African American women during Freaknik blamed them for their own victimization and minimized the seriousness of the violence. The news implied these women were either naives, such as the Little Rock visitors who unwittingly placed themselves in harm's way, or, more commonly, oversexed Jezebels whose lewd behavior provokes men to grope, fondle and even rape. The naifs were identified as out-of-staters, code for law-abiding students. Their representation was gendered as victims of sexual harassment, class-based in terms of their association with middle-class behavior and values and racialized within the context of their background and the event. Their comparison to the Jezebels who – unlike the naifs, according to the news – *do* want to be "fondled and groped" also reflects the racialization of gender.

The naive student may be forgiven her transgressions by virtue of her inexperience, but not so the Jezebel. By casting her in the role of the sexually aggressive Black woman, the news justifies her abuse. The news also largely denies that men actually raped or attacked women. With one exception, men who assaulted women were rendered both invisible and passive: unnamed when women were stripped of their clothing, they were involuntarily drawn to short skirts, and enticed by shaking, dancing female bodies to touch or even rape.

The Jezebels' lewd conduct links them to the bad behavior and moral lapses associated with Black women and poverty. Portraying women as "the Jezebel, whore, or sexually aggressive woman" (Collins, 1991, p. 77) implies a lack of socially appropriate values that corresponds not to popular perceptions of White, middle-class, female behavior but to cultural presuppositions and stereotypes of Black, underclass women. As Painter (1992) points out, sex is the "main theme associated with poverty and with blackness" (p. 206). Moreover, skin color, sexuality and class are connected within popular iconography, such that the sexually active "bad girl" is linked to dark hair and dark skin, as well as the "wrong side of the tracks"; "her willingness or desire to be sexually active could be dismissed as the allegedly hypersexualized, unrestrained behavior of the lower classes" (Douglas, 1995, p. 66).

Black and poor are often conflated within cultural understandings of race (Lawson, 1992), so that all African Americans – male and female – are presumed within the popular (White) imagination to be poor unless qualified in a way that indicates middle or upper class. The classification of African Americans as college students is just such a qualification, moving them out of the presumed category of poor into that of the middle class. Bourdieu and Passeron (1977) emphasize that the educational system contributes to the reproduction of class relations by legitimating and certifying class privilege. As Landry (1987) states, the significance of a college education as a means of moving into the middle class "cannot be overstated" (p. 104).

Within TV news coverage of Freaknik, education appears as central to representation and serves, *in the absence of other class signifiers* (the lewd behavior of the Jezebel being such a signifier), as a primary definer of class identity and belonging. The news, lacking other class markers, appears to link both male and female African American students to the middle class because a college degree is perceived to be a middle-class aspiration as well as a form of social mobility that enables the poor and working class to move into the middle class.

While the news identified male troublemakers as non-student locals, the Jezebels are not similarly identified, thereby leaving open the possibility that, while their lewd behavior may be that of the lower classes, at least some of them might, in fact, be students. Rather than undermining the role of education as a class signifier, this may instead serve to reinforce gendered, racial and class stereotypes about Black women. In short, it may suggest to some that even a college education is not sufficient to dampen the unrestrained hypersexuality of Black women.

Barring displays of lewd conduct and other markers associated with the poor and working class, the presumed middle-class status of the students distances them from the "codes of crime, drugs, and social problems activated by the urban underclass" (Gray, 1989, p. 383). Classifying African Americans as responsible students or crime-prone locals supports cultural beliefs and stereotypes about race and class that uphold and justify the inequitable distribution of material resources. As Gray argues:

> Media representations of Black success and failure are ideological precisely to the extent that they provide a way of seeing underclass failure through representations of middle-class success. Implicitly operating in this way of viewing the underclass (and the middle class) is the assumption that since America is an open racial and class order, then people who succeed (and fail) do so because of their individual abilities rather than their position in the social structure.
>
> (p. 382)

Drawing on Bhabha's (1983) theory of the ambivalent nature of the stereotype, Cloud (1992) notes that images of racial differences are "ambivalent," contained in a binary meaning system in which "apparently oppositional representations of racial identity participate in a conservative, multistructured yet hegemonic social totality" (p. 314). The image of crime-prone or lewd underclass youth gains salience and has meaning within the context of its inverse – educated, well-behaved, middle-class Black youth. Of course, middle-class White youths also serve as a type of inverse, but with different implications. Comparing White college students with Black non-students may elicit charges of racism as an explanation of social inequities. But comparing Black students with Black non-students ties success or failure to individual responsibility and initiative.

This racial and class-based binary system is complicated by the addition of gender, which is similarly ambivalent. To say that gender, class and race are linked in social consciousness and popular imagery, and must be understood and analyzed as such, is not to deny that commonalities exist among those within a particular race, class or gender. However, the meaning and representation of class status is both gendered and racialized: racialized through historical background, and gendered within a system of male supremacy and female subordination. The news's representation of the Jezebels' lewd behavior reflects a gendered, racialized and class-based understanding of trouble-making which differs from that of the male locals, who were arrested for having weapons, looting and fighting – but, significantly, not for sexual assault and other forms of anti-woman violence.

In essence, the news criminalized Black men primarily with respect to property damage while decriminalizing them concerning their abuse of Black women. The safety of Black women appears of less consequence than that of property. In addition, by blaming the victim, by turning the abuse against her so that she appears responsible for it, the news establishes and reinforces the parameters of appropriate public behavior for women, providing all women with a warning about the dangers of transgression while reaffirming middle-class values and behaviors as the antidote for male violence against women.

Smith (1992) and hooks (1981) have criticized the African American community for its reluctance to hold Black men accountable for violence against Black women. The news appears similarly reluctant. This may be a function of the news's general tendency to blame most women who are the victims of violence for their own abuse (Benedict, 1992; Meyers, 1997). It also may be reflective of an "extra sensitivity" Atlanta reporters profess to have concerning issues of race given the city's predominantly Black population (Meyers, 1997, p. 95). Any extra sensitivity, however, apparently does not extend to gender issues. Instead, the news seems to mirror society's interest in protecting men at the expense of the women they abuse.

The characterization of Black women as Jezebels also reflects the role of age in representation. While older women may still be portrayed as Jezebels, their depiction within the news will differ from that of the Freaknik participants because of their years, as well as the context of news coverage. Frequent references to under-age, curfew-breaking locals as troublemakers, and the depiction of young adult African American women as Jezebels who entice men to sexual assault, emphasize the presumed threat young African Americans pose to society.

This study also found that although the spoken text blamed women for their own victimization, the visual text at times contradicted this. While the words may work to recuperate any challenge to a patriarchal understanding of women "leading men on," the images potentially provide an alternative perspective that holds men accountable for their violence. Whether and how various audiences perceive this contradiction are areas for further investigation. In addition, comparison of news coverage of spring break for Black and White students is likely to disclose race-related differences that this study could not address.[9]

Applying a theoretical model that conceptualizes the inseparable and interlapping nature of gender, race and class to violence against women in the news points to the poverty of news studies that have singly explored race or gender as if they were unaffected by the other or by class. For, as Smith notes, political analysis and strategies that address how multiple oppressions "dovetail and interlock provide the clearest and most revolutionary agendas for change" (1992, p. 185).

7

CRACK MOMS AND THE NARRATIVE OF PATERNALISTIC RACISM

Crack cocaine, a smokeable form of cocaine hydrochloride, has been linked by the news media to inner-city Blacks and Latinos, while the use of powdered cocaine by affluent Whites has been largely ignored (Potter and Kappeler, 1998; Reinarman and Duskin, 1996; Reeves and Campbell, 1994). For the most part, crack addicts are depicted within the media as males, although Reeves and Campbell (1994) also note the stereotype of the "she-devil" crack mother (p. 213), the aggressively sexual Black Jezebel who threatens the lives and safety of her born and unborn children and is responsible for an "epidemic" of crack babies as well as the "poverty of values" crippling the inner city (pp. 208–209). However, the narrative of the "crack mother" and the story it tells us about African American women, motherhood and addiction remain largely unexplored.

This chapter, based on an article that previously appeared in the *Journal of Communication Inquiry*, is included in this book because it established the theoretical groundwork to articulate the existence of a gendered form of racism within the news – paternalistic racism – which has been noted in the book's earlier chapters. Given the news's tendency to support the status quo (Hall, 1982; Hartley, 1982), as well as its role in shaping social and political policy (Potter and Kappeler, 1998; Reeves and Campbell, 1994; Shah et al., 2002), a narrative of paternalistic racism within the news can impact public discourse on the adoption of laws, the development and availability of social programs and services, whether women who are addicts receive incarceration or treatment, and to a large extent, the welfare of their children. As Shah, Watts, Domke and Fan (2002) pointed out: "News constructions, emphasizing certain details while omitting others, help to shape citizens' political perceptions and preferences by encouraging certain avenues of thought and action" (p. 340). An examination of the narrative of crack mothers in the news can tell us something about the dominant social discourse about these women and their children, as well as its implications for shaping public perceptions and policy.

This study combines critical cultural studies with feminist media studies and Black feminist theory to conceptualize the interconnection between gender, race and class in representation within a hierarchy structured in dominance linked to White supremacy and patriarchy. It also draws on a feminist perspective on women and addiction. Van Zoonen (1994) points out that cultural studies is the dominant theoretical approach underlying the field of feminist media studies. These two theoretical perspectives have much in common: both grew out of Marxist theory, leftist politics and progressive political movements; and both engage in representational studies of popular culture to illuminate relations of power.

This study provides a narrative analysis of a seven-part newspaper series titled "Growing Up with Crack," which appeared in the *Atlanta Journal-Constitution* at a time when the City of Atlanta had one of the highest crack cocaine addiction rates for women in the nation. An analysis of the series provides a look at the story told about female crack addicts and their children. In exploring the narrative's major themes and character types, this study found four themes dominant within an overarching narrative of redemption: (1) redemption from addiction is possible for the few who are dedicated and hard working; (2) the state's child protective services and politicians are largely to blame for the plight of crack babies; (3) crack addicts are the victims of a "demon drug" over which they have no control; and (4) the dedication and compassion of exceptional individuals is necessary to redeem the mothers and save the children. Five character types – the victim, the addict, the hero, the villain and the foot soldier – carried out these themes within the narrative of a White, professional middle class working to save women and children of the Black underclass. The underlying paternalistic racism of this narrative reflects the intersecting, multiple oppressions of gender, race and class.

A Feminist Perspective on Women and Crack

Feminist scholars argue that acknowledging the interconnection of race, gender and class is essential to understanding the female addict. A feminist perspective on women and substance abuse is "grounded in recognition of the vital role played by societal inequities, especially as related to power or lack of power, and accompanying variations in self-esteem and vulnerability to substance use and abuse" (Abbott, 1995, p. 258). Cultural factors such as gender role expectations, developmental issues such as childhood abuse, and structural forces such as poverty and racism are essential to understanding women's crack cocaine use, addiction and possible remedies. Sterk (1999), in her ethnographic study of female crack users in Atlanta, pointed out that they meet with harsher social disapproval than do male users because drug use is seen as incompatible with being a woman. She notes that the lives of the female crack users in her study exemplified the interconnectedness of gender, class and race: most were African American or Hispanic women raised in poverty or White women treated as "White trash" (p. 6), and violence was common in their lives – many had been sexually and/or physically abused as children and were living in violent homes and/or experiencing violence in drug-use settings and their communities. "In general, much of the violence in the lives of the women in this study was related to issues of gender as well as to their crack use" (p. 174).

While many female crack addicts resort to prostitution to support their habits, others pay for crack by "participating in the drug business or through 'hustles' such as shoplifting, credit card fraud, and thefts from motor vehicles" (Sterk, 1999, p. 3). Sterk (1999) classified female crack users into four types: (1) "queens of the scene," who finance their habit by dealing crack or preparing crack "rocks" for high-level dealers; (2) "hustlers," who support their habits through illegal activities other than prostitution; (3) "hookers," who support their habit through prostitution; and (4) "older struggling rookies," who started using drugs in their thirties and exchange their bodies for crack (pp. 24–25).

Ratner (1993), in an ethnographic study of sex-for-crack exchanges, divided these transactions into three types: (1) the "casual" exchange, in which the same individuals are involved, sometimes in a "sugar daddy" relationship that is often a transitional stage preceding the need for more frequent exchanges; (2) the "sex-for-money-for-crack" exchange, in which prostitution is usually the addict's sole source of income; and (3) the "sex-for-money-or-crack" exchange, typified by desperation, in which women and men provide sexual services, most frequently oral sex, "in exchange for a small amount of crack or for almost any sum of money" (pp. 11–13). According to Ratner, those directly trading sex for crack overwhelmingly come from impoverished, dysfunctional families, have low self-esteem and feel they have no control over their lives. The sex-for-money-for-crack exchanges increased their feelings of self-disgust and frequently were tied to attempts on the part of the person with the crack to humiliate and demonstrate their control over them (pp. 18–19).

Koester and Schwartz (1993) pointed out that a power imbalance between the sexes ensures that men dominate the exchanges, so that women who exchange sex for crack are "among the most marginal and vulnerable members of the crack scene" (p. 193). The low status of these women reflects their powerlessness, sense of hopelessness and lack of control over their lives:

> Poor women with limited marketable skills trade sex for crack because they are addicted and because they have no other means of supporting their habit. Their powerlessness and marginality fuel the sex-for-crack phenomenon.
>
> (p. 192)

Educational and treatment approaches must be tied to a "holistic framework" that addresses the material circumstances of their lives and the problems they face on a daily basis: "The danger of contracting HIV may not be the chief worry of these women; poverty, addiction, abusive relationships, the risk of incarceration, and the loss of their children may be of more immediate concern" (Koester and Schwartz, 1993, p. 202).

Sterk (1999) noted that the addicts in her study who were mothers "tended to view their caregiving role as their most salient role, but when they were smoking crack this role was often overshadowed by their role as drug users" (pp. 22–23). A central theme was the ongoing conflict between their roles as mothers and drug users: "On the one hand, most women experienced difficulties controlling their crack cocaine use, while on the other they sought to demonstrate that they were worthy mothers" (p. 11).

Among the strategies women used to balance these roles was to use drugs when the children were at school, asleep or out of their view. Some purchased groceries and other necessities before buying drugs or worked overtime to provide for their children. Sterk (1999) reported, however, that few women acknowledged the extent to which their crack use affected their roles as mothers. Nevertheless, as Ratner (1993) pointed out: "The strongest internal force for positive change in many of these women is their desire to be more responsible and effective as mothers" (p. 29). Sterk (1999) stated:

> Those women who wanted to be "good" mothers believed they would have to be free of drugs to do so and they often viewed drug treatment as an effective means to achieve this goal. For a substantial number of women who wanted to be mothers, the discovery of their pregnancies served as a positive turning point.
>
> (p. 131)

Although pregnancies motivated some women to seek treatment, "the treatment seldom prepared them to remain drug free or for their parenting responsibilities" (Sterk, 1999, p. 132). Few programs for women also accommodate their children, and "aggressive, confrontational" treatment approaches that may be effective for men may increase women's feelings of guilt and shame rather than addressing their negative self-images and low self-worth, according to Sterk (1999, p. 136). She said treatment programs for women must be holistic and address not only their addiction but their social roles, as well as vocational and interpersonal skills, because their "primary needs centered around survival in a world that offered them little in terms of housing, employment, and personal happiness" (p. 141).

Crack in the News

This depiction of the female crack addict does not often appear in the news. Rather, according to Reeves and Campbell (1994), she has appeared within the context of an antifeminist and anti-social-welfare backlash that targets out-of-work people of color in the inner city and draws upon the myth of the Black matriarch "as the irrational nurturer of chaos" and the welfare mother as too dependent (p. 99). The journalistic view of crack mothers, they claimed, "often reduced women to their reproductive identities" (p. 192) while drawing on a hybrid of Collins's (1991) four controlling images of women – the mammy, matriarch, welfare mother and Jezebel. The result is "a composite 'she-devil'" fusing the image of the welfare mother with the sexually aggressive Jezebel who presents a particularly menacing image of Black fertility personified by out-of-control sexuality (Reeves and Campbell, 1994, p. 213). Berated "as an enemy to the innocent life within," the crack mother was demonized as a monster while her children, the crack babies, were demonized as future delinquents and a burden on society (Reeves and Campbell, 1994, p. 208). The news linked a so-called "epidemic" of crack babies to a "'poverty of values' crippling America's largely black inner cities" (Reeves and Campbell, 1994, p. 209).

This view is consistent with that of critical cultural studies scholars, who emphasize that the news represents the interests of a ruling elite within a hierarchy of competing social formations. By presenting the views, values and opinions of those in power as natural, commonsensical and inevitable, the news builds consensus around this "dominant ideology" so that it appears grounded in everyday reality. For example, Hall et al. (1978) found that media portrayals of racial violence tend to legitimate the criminal justice system, building support for a law-and-order state while simultaneously portraying Black youth as a threat to social order.

The representation of African Americans – adults as well as youths – as criminals, a common theme within the news, does the ideological work of supporting the dominant power structure (Campbell, 1995; Campbell, LeDuff, Jenkins and Brown, 2012; Dixon, 2006a, 2006b, 2008b, 2011; Entman, 1990, 1992, 1994; Entman and Rojecki, 2000; Ferguson, 1998). As part of this work, the news creates and sustains "moral panics" through the portrayal of certain groups and activities as tearing at the fabric of an orderly and lawful society. Moral panics are characterized by copious news coverage of the group or activity in question, followed by public outcry, increased law enforcement activity, political posturing and policy formation. Cohen (1972), who pioneered the concept of moral panics in his study of British Mods and Rockers during the 1960s, found they were portrayed in the news as folk devils whose activities inevitably would lead to disaster. Young Black males also have been targeted for moral panics (Hall et al., 1978), as have "sex fiends" and "drug scares," the latter of which involves a period during which numerous social problems, such as crime, illness and educational failure, are blamed on a chemical substance (Reinarman and Levine, 1997).

Crack surfaced as a drug scare in the 1980s. According to Potter and Kappeler (1998) news magazines, television and newspapers, in particular, worked with the state to create a moral panic around crack use as a means of continuing and extending the Reagan administration's "war on drugs" (pp. 8–9). Reeves and Campbell (1994) similarly claimed news coverage of the war on drugs was co-opted by the Reagan administration. While they blamed TV journalism "for its role in legitimating a reactionary political agenda in its knee-jerk support of the war on drugs," they concluded that the primary culprit was "the New Right operating under the banner of Reaganism" (p. 2). Drug experts and journalists:

> benefited personally and professionally from producing a series of moral panics that centered on "controlling" crack and its users: journalistic recruitment in the anticocaine crusade was absolutely crucial to converting the war on drugs into a political spectacle that depicted social problems grounded on economic transformations as individual moral or behavioral problems that could be remedied by simply embracing family values, modifying bad habits, policing mean streets, and incarcerating the fiendish enemies within.
>
> (p. 3)

The construction of the crack scare linked crack cocaine use to inner-city Blacks, Hispanics and youths, all of whom had been the previous targets of moral panics. Potter and Kappeler (1998) pointed out that during the 1970s, when an expensive form of powdered cocaine was popular among affluent Whites, "both the media and the state focused their attention on heroin, seen as the drug of the inner-city poor" (p. 9). It was only when cocaine became available in the inexpensive form of crack, they added, that "the scapegoating common to drug scares" began, starting in 1986 with media hype that contained highly inflated estimates of crack use and dire warnings of impending disaster from a crack epidemic (p. 9). In fact, crack use, having peaked four years earlier, was declining at the time, and media reports about its highly addictive nature and related health dangers were widely exaggerated. Nevertheless, new laws were created to increase prison sentences for crack use and sale.

Potter and Kappeler (1998) claimed that this link between race and cocaine is not accidental: "Starting with the crack panic of the 1980s, both the state and the media have gone to extraordinary lengths to tie illicit drug use to African Americans while ignoring heavy drug use among affluent whites" (p. 13). They add that false beliefs about crime "play a disproportionate role in the formulation of government and law enforcement policies" (p. 12), diverting "attention away from the social and cultural forces that cause crime to individual pathologies: they reinforce stereotypes of minorities, poor people, and people who are 'different'" (p. 15).

However, even when the news attempts to present a compassionate, positive portrayal of minority communities, it is unable to evade the negative stereotypes that accompany "'dysfunctional' social activities, such as crime, drugs and out-of-wedlock births" (Parisi, 1998b, p. 239). Particularly problematic is the narrative convention of personalization, which draws on individual profiles and anecdotes. As Parisi (1998b) noted, when the fragmented stories of individuals are presented as sufficient to explain life, society becomes defined as "an aggregate of separate individualities" divorced from social, political and economic realities (p. 242). When combined with social problems such as drugs and crime, personalization encourages racist stereotyping by treating individuals "as objects, who embody social problems, rather than subjects and centers for consciousness" (p. 242).

In constructing cocaine use as either a criminal pathology or moral disease, the user becomes a "super deviant" whose demographic profile on the evening news is "predominantly black or Latino, young, male, poor, and isolated in the inner city" (Reeves and Campbell, 1994, p. 26). The news created and legitimated Reagan's war on drugs from 1981 to 1988 as a political spectacle in three phases of coverage, during which the cocaine narrative told by the news changed "from a white, upper- and middle-class addiction tale to a black, inner-city horror story" (Reeves and Campbell, 1994, p. 64) and from a therapeutic narrative to a pathologic/criminal narrative as it shifted emphasis from class to race and from White people to people of color. During the first phase, which centered on the drug's use by the White middle class, these offenders were offered therapeutic intercession. The second phase focused on race and class to evoke images of urban chaos. During the third phase, the war on drugs became a major issue in the 1988 presidential campaign.

Reeves and Campbell (1994) also found that the cocaine narrative involved four major social types: (1) primary definers of the problem – the experts and authorities in law enforcement or drug recovery; (2) transgressors, consisting of private citizens, who can be rehabilitated, and delinquents, who are beyond redemption; (3) representatives of common sense – the private citizens' or on-the-street voice of consensus; and (4) well-informed journalists. Over the course of the three phases of their study, the chief definers changed from the treatment industry to law enforcement and politics; increasingly, transgressors were defined as people of color. In addition, Reeves and Campbell pointed out that the narrative was created by reporters and news sources who were "overwhelmingly male" (p. 64).

Beginning in 1987, Reeves and Campbell (1994) noted, a kind of revisionist coverage drawing on a fatalistic "discourse of doom" rehumanized cocaine transgressors as tragic victims "of the 'slings and arrows of outrageous fortune' whose 'fate' is to make bad choices and pay the consequences" (p. 233). This discourse ignores the inequality of material and social resources that provide a breeding ground for the desperate conditions that encourage drug use.

Analyzing News Coverage

This study provides a narrative analysis of a series called "Growing Up with Crack" that ran for seven days, September 27 through 30 and October 1, 2 and 4, 1998, in the *Atlanta Journal-Constitution*. It looks at the story the news tells about crack mothers and their children, examining the major themes and what Reeves and Campbell called the major social types, or characters, from a theoretical perspective informed by critical cultural studies and Black feminist theory that emphasizes the role of gender, race and class in the narrative, as well as a feminist understanding of women and addiction. The series, written by reporter Jane O. Hansen, was featured prominently on the front pages and, on the last day, was complemented by an editorial.[1] At the time of the study, Atlanta had one of the highest rates of women smoking crack cocaine in the country.[2]

Narrative analysis is particularly useful in exploring "how media representations of gender, race, class and sexuality have functioned to naturalize and legitimize systemic social inequalities" (Soderlund, 2002, p. 442). Parisi (1998b) notes that it is an important analytical tool in addressing "social and ethical values in reporting, including questions of racism in the process" (p. 240). For example, he has used it to uncover aspects of modern racism in an eight-part series in the *Washington Post* (1998a) and a three-part series in the *New York Times* (1998b). Narration, as he has pointed out, "inevitably involves political assumptions, ideology, social values, cultural and racial stereotypes and assumptions as well as specific textual strategies" that are aligned with particular social and economic interests (1998b, pp. 239–240).

Reeves and Campbell (1994) stated that contemporary narrative theory distinguishes between "story" and "discourse" – story being "concerned with 'what happens to whom' while discourse asks 'how the story is told'" (p. 50). Form, or how the narrative is related, is revealed in the structure of the plot, the sequencing of events, the coherence and complexity of a narrative and the choice of metaphors or language which may not be evident in the analysis of content (Leiblich, Tuval-Mashiach and Zilber, 1998, p. 13). Riessman (1993) has noted that the emphasis in narrative analysis is not on why a particular story is being told but on how it is told through both form and content (p. 2).

Leiblich, Tuval-Mashiach and Zilber (1998) identified four approaches to narrative analysis: (1) a holistic-content reading, which looks at the meanings provided by the whole narrative, focusing on the one or two particular themes that emerge from throughout the narrative or focusing on specific sections of the text within the context of the entire narrative; (2) a holistic-form reading, which focuses on how the plot is structured, how the story is developed and how it ascends or descends toward a specific event; (3) a categorical-content reading, also known as content analysis, which defines specific categories within the narrative and organizes sections into those categories; and (4) a categorical-form reading, which focuses on stylistic or linguistic characteristics of specific parts of the narrative.

This study employs a holistic-content reading, which requires that specific sections of the text be analyzed for emergent themes that occur within the context of the entire seven-part series. This is done, as Reissman (1993) stated, by identifying similarities or patterns "across the moments into an aggregate, a summation" (p. 13).

The Series

The series title, "Growing Up with Crack," is ambiguous in not defining who is growing up with crack – the children of crack mothers, young addicts or both. However, a headshot of a different African American baby or toddler ran each day as part of the logo, suggesting the children of crack mothers, in particular the "crack babies," are of primary concern. In addition, the photos cast the problem as one of race, of Black babies raised by their addicted mothers.

At the end of each day's installment, a "How to Help" column listed various agencies and programs, tied to the day's topic, and what donations and volunteer work are needed. For example, two drug treatment programs were listed with a story about a counselor whose job is to get addicted women into treatment. With the exception of the first day, the main stories revolved around a specific character. The articles are presented chronologically below with their headline. This section is primarily descriptive, a necessary first step when looking for patterns and themes across a series of articles.

Story 1: "A Forsaken Generation"

The series introduction promises to explore the plight of "a hidden generation of motherless children," "orphans rearing themselves" and "teenagers having babies of their own" by presenting "their stories and those of the committed individuals trying to help." The page one story and three related articles establish the problems facing "Atlanta's first generation of crack babies" coming of age, outlining the topics and themes to come as well as the major characters.

The primary story introduces S., the 16-year-old daughter of a crack mother and the mother of a 5-month-old son. Growing up, S. watched her mother "shoot-up" and was sold for sex by her mother to a dope dealer. She left school in seventh grade and wanted a baby so she could give it the love she never had. S. is African American and is shown in a photo holding her son.

The article also introduces Donna Carson, a social worker who has "devoted her life to working with pregnant addicts." Carson explains: "I don't know that we can help some of these 15-year-olds. They're like orphaned teens. They're too much like wild animals. But we know their babies could have a better chance." Carson, a White woman with blonde hair, appears in a photo sitting cross-legged on the floor, kissing the head of the African American baby in her lap.

Another article, "Looking for Mom," describes 13-year-old Reginald Shannon's search for and troubled relationship with his crack-addicted mother, who was 15 when he was born. A thin, African American youth, Shannon is shown in four photos walking through deserted, desolate streets. He lived until recently with his grandmother and four younger siblings in a single-bedroom apartment.

Two other articles share a separate page. "The Damage" details the harm to children when they have an addicted mother. It notes that the majority of pregnant women who smoke crack are African American. A photo of a researcher shows a White woman; in the cutline below, she says: "The drug is not good, but the environment is worse."

The other article, "Motherless Children: Orphans of Crack Raising Themselves," describes the problem in the United States and Atlanta, citing cocaine as "a primary force behind the growth in child abuse and neglect reports, which tripled from 1 million in 1980 to more than 3 million in 1996." In Atlanta, an estimated 80 percent of abuse and neglect cases are drug related, with crack the primary culprit. The article concludes that missing fathers "is nothing new" among "poor, urban families," a term that signifies a Black underclass. But the lack of mothers due to crack cocaine is a recent and particularly devastating development – a "pretty hard pill to swallow," in the words of an addiction counselor.

Story 2: "A World That Breeds Despair"

This story is not simply about the hopelessness and desperation implied by the title. It also is the story of Demetria Walls, a 33-year-old former crack addict who is an addiction counselor for Project Prevent, a program developed in response to the growing number of newborns abandoned at Grady Hospital by crack-addicted mothers. In a headshot at the top of page one, Walls appears as an attractive, heavyset African American woman with dreadlocks.

Walls is described as:

> often a colorful sight. One day she wears gold shoes, yellow-tinted glasses, huge gold hoop earrings and tight black pants, her hair tucked under a broad-rimmed red straw hat with a gold bow... Another day she wears denim shorts, low-heeled black pumps and a low-cut purple T-shirt that

matches her purple nail polish, her hair in loose curls. But the flamboyant dress belies a serious, streetwise woman…

The extensive detail describing her "colorful," "flamboyant" attire codes her as poor, for her tastes are not those of the middle class. In addition, the description of her clothing, in particular the tight pants and low-cut T-shirt, sexualizes her body so that it may be viewed as that of a (former) prostitute and/ or drug addict.

The story is told as a day-in-the-(work)-life of Walls, who "spends several days each week cruising Atlanta neighborhoods looking for crack-addicted women she can get into drug treatment and off the streets so they can properly raise their kids." The goal of drug rehabilitation is presented as a way to save the children – to get the mothers off drugs so they can be responsible parents. This particular day, Walls's mission is "to convince a 23-year-old woman with three children [L.] to go into treatment." L. admits she may not feed or bathe her children right away when using crack, but she says she loves her children and denies she is ever gone from them for more than a few hours: "I be wondering who's watching my children." Later, Walls admits she "has little hope that L. will show up in the morning at the detox center, as she's promised." But Walls "doesn't judge these women" because she has "been there" herself. Although she "can't help but feel disappointed," Walls "knows that until they hit bottom, there's little she can do."

The story implicitly contrasts Walls's life with that of the addicts. Walls lives with her two children – one of whom had been taken away from her because of her addiction and later returned – in her own home in a safe community far from Atlanta's drug scene. The women she attempts to get into treatment are often homeless and unable to properly care for their children.

Story 3: "When They Can't Go Home"

This story focuses on 15-year-old A., the daughter of a crack addict who desperately wants to bring her medically fragile son, Baby M., home from the hospital despite her lack of familial support and resources. A. is not an addict, and her child's condition is not the result of her crack use. Nevertheless, the story implies that problems facing Baby M. are similar to those of crack babies, just as the problems facing A. – lack of structure, parental supporter supervision – are common to the children of crack addicts.

The article chronicles the progress of Baby M. and the concerns of social workers and doctors as the day nears when he is healthy enough to leave the hospital. Phyllis Day, a seasoned social worker for Project Prevent, and Millie Gonzales, a 23-year-old "teen specialist," disagree about whether to bring in the Department of Family and Child Services. "'You're thinking about her [A.],' Day tells Gonzales. 'I'm thinking about the baby.'"

A. is presented as a tragic figure: "When she was a little girl, the family's money went toward her mother's crack habit" so that her home "eventually lost the gas, water and electricity." Her mother's drug use "frightened" A. and her younger brother; they "was scared she was going to die." A.'s life, the article states, "has been a chaotic existence devoid of the childhood experiences many Americans take for granted." At the time of the article, A. was living with her mother, who had stopped using drugs but "can't control her" and "recently had her picked up by juvenile authorities and placed on probation for unruliness." Day explains that A. is like many teens who have raised themselves: "Teenagers who don't have the supervision they need at home are wild things."

The poverty in which A. lives is evident in descriptions of her home: in the kitchen, "a pink towel with a hole covers the window"; in the bedroom, "a bare mattress lies on the floor, springs poking through the middle. A dirty sheet serves as a curtain, and an old baby carriage stuffed with trash and baby clothes sits in the corner." In a photo, Gonzales and Day appear outside A.'s apartment building, which has the bleak look of a public housing complex, its dirt lawn marked by scattered patches of grass. Both Gonzales and Day appear to be African American in this photo, as does Baby M. in a separate photo.

By the end of the story, the state Department of Family and Children Services has placed Baby M. with foster parents ill-equipped to deal with a medically fragile child and has restricted A.'s visits to one a month, which social workers fear will irreparably break the "bond between mother and child" so that "the baby will never have a permanent home." In this setting, the child's health declines, and he is returned to the hospital. If he recovers, the article states, he will be placed in another foster home rather than with the mother who wants him.

Interspersed with the account of Baby M.'s progress is an indictment of the lack of funding and resources for medically fragile children in Georgia. "Without enough special [foster] homes," the article states, the children "are being farmed out to places that often are more expensive and less humane alternatives" – or being sent home with their addicted mothers. A sidebar, "Saved for What?" notes that about 40 percent of the babies born to crack-addicted parents at Grady Hospital go home with them, which "can be excruciating for medical personnel, who perform near-miracles to save their lives, only to have to stand aside sometimes and watch them go home to potentially dangerous situations."

Story 4: "'Family First' System Puts Children Last"

The fourth installment further indicts the state for its lack of services and attention to children in need, pitting its incompetence and lack of caring against the compassion and dedication of social workers and medical personnel. The primary article presents a series of horror stories, beginning with Harriet Hawkins, a crack addict who had sold her 3- and 4-year-old nieces to a child molester for crack after the state finally took away her seven children, one of whom she also sold for crack. Hawkins, who is African American, is shown in what looks like a police lineup photo. Other horror stories include the 11-month-old "dumpster baby," whose mother threw her out with the trash when the child died after being left alone while her mother was in the hospital having another crack-addicted baby; and two premature, medically fragile twins first sent home to a crack-using father and brain-damaged mother, then to foster care with a couple who ran a day care center in their home, where the risk of infection was extremely high.

Medical and social workers, particularly Dr. Neal Simon, a neonatologist, and Donna Carson, head of neonatology social work at Grady Hospital, are portrayed as fighting valiantly, if unsuccessfully, with the state's uncaring and immovable child protective services agency. Simon recalls the "anguish" he and others at Grady felt, and how "angry and frustrated" he was, when the agency would not protect Harriet Hawkins's children. Carson fought for months with the county's children's services agency "over the fate of sick twins who were born prematurely to a crack-addicted mother." The agency's employees, Carson says, "don't get it. They say their philosophy is to keep these families together." The problem is presented as both a "broken child welfare system… bogged down by bureaucracy, too many complex cases and rules that endanger children's lives," and a philosophy that advocates keeping families together no matter what.

An accompanying story, "Last Chance: Baby Court," describes how juvenile court gives mothers whose babies are born with positive drug screens "one last chance to keep their babies" and not go to jail. This "tough-love" approach, the article states, is "designed to force women into drug treatment for the sake of their children." The story underscores what happens when the mother is unable to kick her habit but wants her child. A judge contrasts "the luckiest child in the state," born to a crack addict who gives birth under a false name in the hospital and then abandons her child, to "the most unlucky child," whose mother periodically expresses an interest in regaining custody. The abandoned child can be adopted by "a family who wants and loves the child," he says. The one whose mother comes in and out of the child's life is doomed to linger in foster care. The article also notes the dearth of residential treatment programs, particularly those that allow children, for women addicts.

Story 5: "Moms Again"

The fifth installment is about older women raising their grandchildren, as told through the life of Mary Shannon, a 55-year-old African American woman raising her crack-addicted daughter's five children, who range in age from four months to 13 years, in her two-bedroom apartment.[3] Her homeless, 28-year-old daughter is said to be involved in the sex-for-crack subculture. Shannon appears as a loving and devoted mother and grandmother. She coos at the 4-month-old, calling him "pookie-poo," "my baby," "my heart," her "lump of sugar." In a photo, she beams at the baby as he grasps her finger; in another, she holds the baby, giving him a kiss. She walks the streets looking for her daughter, "hoping to coax her back into drug treatment." While she condemns her daughter's lifestyle, she defends her "when her grandson speaks disparagingly about his mother," explaining that his mother is sick, "but it don't mean she don't love you." Shannon is represented as overburdened financially, physically and emotionally with the needs of her five grandchildren. Although she appears to be coping, the article states, at night, "when everyone's asleep," Mary Shannon "sits in the darkness and cries." In a caption beneath a photo of her slumped in a chair, she says, "I need a life preserver."

Story 6: "Babies Help Moms Stay 'Clean'"

This is the story of Tifiney Jones, a former crack addict in a residential recovery program who credits the birth of her son as the turning point in her addiction. She appears in a page one photo, a young, heavyset Black woman kissing the forehead of the child cradled in her arms. The article credits various social services with Jones's success: Project Prevent, whose addiction counselor got her into a treatment program; Family Links, which cares for infants up to 30 days a year while their mothers get drug treatment; and Gateway Cottage, the residential treatment program in rural Georgia where she is making a clean start for herself and her baby.

Jones, the article states, "is one of the lucky ones" and one of the hardest working and courageous:

> She's lucky because she got a slot in one of the few residential drug treatment programs in Georgia that takes addicted women and their babies. But she also fought hard to overcome her crack addiction, and unlike many addicts who quickly relapse and give up, she's pursued with passion every opportunity set before her.

She is described as an outstanding student and a devoted, loving mother. Her son is the reason she gave up crack: "'The only way I wanted to stop was so I could keep my baby,' she says. 'If I didn't have him, I'd be somewhere in Atlanta right now getting high. Or I'd be dead.'" The article briefly discusses Jones's past, how "crack became her reason for living," and how "in the dark of night, she would get into the cars of men she didn't know – young men, old men, faceless men who promised to give her crack in exchange for sex."

Dr. Toby Hill, the 53-year-old director of Gateway Cottage, is a retired school superintendent described as "quietly religious" and "an unlikely director of a drug treatment program" that is home to nine women and their thirteen children. While he "could have accepted a lucrative offer to become headmaster of a private school," he instead chose "shepherding women and children to school, advocating for them in court and trying to find enough money to keep the program afloat." He explains: "This is where I need to be." The story implies that it is through the efforts of Hill, and those like him, that Tifiney Jones and other crack-addicted women are able to craft drug-free lives. In a photo, Hill appears to be a White, middle-aged man.

A sidebar discusses a drug that may help cocaine addicts. It explains that the changes in the brain caused by cocaine, "the most addictive drug known," are "at the root of craving and key to explaining why relapse rates among crack addicts are so high."

Story 7: "Seeking Solutions"

The final feature presents solutions to the problems of children growing up with crack. It focuses on Donna Carson, who appeared in earlier articles and is the head of neonatology social work at Grady Hospital. She is represented as the embodiment of the creativity, compassion and dedication lacking among state and county child welfare agencies and personnel – a "beacon" at Grady. Described as having "blonde, curly hair and clear blue eyes," she founded Project Prevent, Family Links, a special nursery for abandoned newborns and a program for the homeless teenage daughters of addicts with babies.

Carson attempts to paint a human face on crack-addicted mothers so that her staff realizes what happened to the addicts is "pretty much what could happen to any of us." She "is devoted to" crack mothers: "She gets their heat turned on when it's cut off, food when they're hungry, medical treatment when they're sick. She listens to them, befriends them, threatens them and most of all coaxes them into drug treatment." She does this, the article emphasizes, "for one reason: Carson doesn't want the babies of crack-addicted women to grow up alone, addicted and lost like their mothers."

In contrast to Carson, state and county social service agencies are represented as uncaring and unresponsive, and Georgia politicians are described as punitive in their promotion of "short-sighted, politically popular policies that punish innocent children while incurring long-term costs for medical care, police and prisons, and child protective services." The article emphasizes that "drug treatment is the cheapest and most effective weapon in the government's war on drugs" and that residential programs "are the most effective kind of treatment for crack addicts." It enumerates the savings to taxpayers from treatment and criticizes the state and counties for lacking essential services and not enforcing the few existing laws to protect children.

The Narrative – Discussion and Conclusion

The focus of the series is the battle waged by medical personnel and social workers to save the innocent children of crack-addicted mothers. The mothers have no intrinsic value; drug rehabilitation is the means to get them off drugs so they can properly raise their children. This message is consistent throughout the narrative. The tough-love approach of juvenile court "is designed to force women into treatment, for the sake of their children." Even Donna Carson, Grady Hospital's "beacon," is "devoted to" these women "for one reason: Carson doesn't want the babies of crack-addicted women to grow up alone, addicted and lost like their mothers."

Within an overarching narrative of redemption, four themes predominate: (1) Recovery and redemption from crack addiction is possible for those few who are dedicated and hard workers – particularly if the right social services are in place. The lives of Demetria Walls and Tifiney Jones as recovered or recovering addicts attest to the possibility of redemption. Jones, in particular, embodies the hard work and commitment needed. But determination alone is not enough without social services and the programs she was "lucky" enough to get. (2) Georgia's child welfare agencies and services, as well as its politicians, are indifferent and uncaring at best and potentially deadly to the innocent children of addicts at worst. (3) Women who are crack addicts are the victims of both circumstance and a powerful demon drug and therefore responsible neither for their addiction nor for its effects on their children. (4) Only the dedication and compassion of exceptional individuals can redeem the mothers and save the children. As promised in the series introduction, the articles tell the stories of "the committed individuals trying to help." The series seeks to enlarge their ranks through the "How to Help" columns that accompany each installment.

To illustrate these themes, the narrative employs five major social types – that is, characters crucial to the telling of the story – constructed through the use of profiles and anecdotes to personalize the problems facing crack mothers and their children and the efforts of those trying to help. The social types are (1) the victim, who is the child of a crack mother; (2) the addict, whether still using crack, in recovery, or recovered; (3) the hero, who is selflessly devoted to saving the innocent victims; (4) the villain, who is part of the problem; and (5) the foot soldier, who takes orders from the hero and works on the frontlines with the addicts and/or their children. In the larger narrative of redemption, it is necessary to look at these types through the lens of gender, race and class to more fully understand who is in need of saving, who has been saved, and who is doing the saving. From this vantage point, the story becomes that of a White, professional middle class attempting to save women and children of the Black underclass, whether the women deserve it or not, because innocent children should not suffer for their mother's sins.

The heroes of this narrative are Dr. Neal Simon, the neonatologist at Grady Hospital who is described as anguished, frustrated and angry when his attempts to help the children of addicts are rebuffed by child welfare agencies; Donna Carson, the social worker who created a variety of programs to help the children of crack addicts; and Dr. Toby Hill, the "quietly religious" retired school superintendent who could be making considerably more money as a private school headmaster but instead is committed to the rehabilitation and recovery of crack mothers. Photos of Hill and Carson indicate they are White. And while no photo of Simon appears, he is likely to be considered White by readers based both on his name, which may be Jewish (as is that of the well-known Jewish playwright of the same name), and on cultural expectations and stereotypes concerning physicians and other highly trained professionals.

The foot soldiers in this war on drugs include former crack addicts who work for Project Prevent, such as Demetria Walls, and social workers like Phyllis Day and Millie Gonzales. They are neither the generals nor the visionaries in this war, as are Carson, Hill and Simon. Their job is to get pregnant addicts or crack mothers into treatment or to otherwise save the children. Mary Shannon, drafted into this war by a daughter who left her with five grandchildren, also can be considered a foot soldier. Overburdened and overwhelmed emotionally, financially and physically, she lovingly raises her grandchildren and combs the streets for her daughter. The foot soldiers in this series are African American.

The crack addicts themselves – whether still using crack, recovering or recovered – also are African American, in addition to female and, with the exception of Demetria Walls, impoverished. Walls and Jones represent the rewards of redemption. As a recovering addict, Jones presumably has a bright future if she stays the course. Walls has a job, a home and custody of her child. She serves in the narrative as both a foot soldier and a recovered addict.

Those who have not redeemed themselves through drug treatment and recovery are portrayed as a threat to their children and signify the dangers of drug abuse and addiction. While they are central to the narrative, they rarely speak for themselves. Most often, they are portrayed by social workers and doctors in horror stories of women who sell their children for crack to child molesters or leave their dead baby in a dumpster. While the active addict is seen as deviant and dangerous, perilous to her innocent children both in utero and outside the womb, she is condemned neither by the series nor by social workers and medical personnel. Instead, she is represented as being in the grip of a demon drug over which she has no control, "the most addictive drug known." As Carson points out, what happened to these women is "pretty much what could happen to any of us." Rather than the "she-devil" demonized and blamed for the plight of her children and the "'poverty of values' crippling America's largely black inner cities" (Reeves and Campbell, 1994, p. 209), the female crack mother is "alone, addicted and lost," deserving of treatment rather than prison, concern rather than condemnation – if only to help her children. In addition, her engagement in sex-for-crack exchanges, rather than the result of an innate "out-of-control black sexuality" (Reeves and Campbell, 1994, p. 213), stands as a testament to the power of crack cocaine.

The victims are the children, "crack babies" and older youth who at best are neglected and at worst may die as a result of both their mother's addiction and the state's apathy. The lucky ones find refuge in the recovery of a mother or the home of a grandmother. The youngest victims are voiceless, depicted as either medically fragile or as abandoned, neglected and sometimes sexually exploited by their crack-addicted mothers. Under the circumstances, it seems natural that doctors and social workers should speak for them, articulating their basic needs. The older children who raised themselves and have their own babies, like A. and S., are allowed a voice but are represented as the product of structureless households, "wild animals" who lack the resources to be good mothers. The narrative holds out little hope for them; the prospect of a better future belongs to their babies. As Donna Carson says, "I don't know that we can help some of these 15-year-olds… They're too much like wild animals. But we know their babies could have a better chance."

The villains here are the state's child welfare system and politicians. They are blamed for endangering the children of crack addicts and denying necessary treatment to their mothers. The series exposes a "broken child welfare system" that is "bogged down by bureaucracy" and wrongly committed to keeping families together at all costs. Politicians are said to promote "short-sighted, politically popular policies that punish innocent children while incurring long-term costs for medical care, police and prisons, and child protective services."

In narrative analysis, it is necessary to look at what is missing as well as what is included in the story. Missing from this series are the men responsible for addicting these women and/or impregnating them – the crack dealers and the men who exchanged crack for sex. The omission of these men, except as a rare footnote,[4] leaves the female crack addict solely responsible for her situation. By eliminating these men from the narrative, the news reinforces stereotypes of African American men as criminals and sexual predators while simultaneously not holding them accountable for their actions.

Parisi (1998b) noted that news coverage that combines personalization with a social problem such as drug abuse within a minority community inevitably reinforces negative stereotypes about that community and the individuals involved. While the series sought, like Donna Carson, to put a face on the female crack addict and to avoid blaming her, by presenting the problem within the context of the African American community, the series inevitably supports racist ideas about African American women as bad mothers, criminals, drug addicts and prostitutes. Parisi (1998a, 1998b) emphasized that even a journalistic commitment to compassion and understanding is not enough to counter racist stereotypes. Underlying such coverage, he concluded, is "the phenomenon of modern racism, which shrouds the continuation of stereotype in the appearance of interracial compassion and comprehension" (1998a, p. 188).

However, the racism within this series differs from that found by Parisi and others. It carries what Myrdal (1964) has called a "strong, paternalistic tinge inherited from the old plantation and slavery system" whereby Southern Whites took pride in their "benevolence toward Negro dependents but would resent vigorously their demanding this aid as a right" (p. 445). Paternalistic racism also was found in pro-integrationist news coverage of the 1948 decision to integrate the U.S. military (Meyers, 1996).

In the narrative of crack mothers, paternalistic racism reflects the interconnection of gender, race and class, for it is impoverished African American women who must be saved. Barrett (1988) has noted the difficulty Marxism and other theories of social structure have encountered in attempting to integrate multiple axes of oppression within their conceptual maps. However, to ignore the intersectionality of gender, race and class in representation is to obscure and distort the experiences and material conditions of those being studied – to erroneously conclude, for example, that modern racism describes the situation facing African American crack mothers as opposed to a gendered form of racism that is, at its core, paternalistic.

The narrative of the crack mother described here could have been different had the series gone beyond the traditional, institutional sources to include those within the African American community working to solve the problems of crack-addicted mothers and their children. The themes and social types also would have been different had the series addressed the relationship between poverty, racism, powerlessness, sexism, violence and drug abuse. But as Reinarman and Duskin (1996) noted, the news typically does not discuss how grinding poverty and racism can lead to despair that, in turn, can lead to drug abuse. Nor does the news typically consider the role of gender. The result is that the narrative of the crack mother denies that inequality of resources and power may be at the root of drug addiction. To admit this would threaten the legitimacy of the state as well as expose the futility of its "war on drugs." Indeed, by citing the failings of the system – the uncaring child welfare agencies and self-serving politicians – the series simultaneously legitimizes its role and authority. The answer, it seems, is not an end to poverty and inequality grounded in race and gender bias but for those in positions of power to be more compassionate and less punitive. By defining the problem facing the children of female addicts as one of an uncaring and unresponsive bureaucracy, the series further denies that the subordinate position of women within the drug culture and society at large, as well as the abusive relationships, poverty and violence they endure, are connected to the material conditions of their and their children's lives.

8

FINDING AFRICAN AMERICAN WOMEN IN THE NEWS

A Conclusion

The hypersexual Jezebel. The emasculating Sapphire. The respectable Black lady. The bad Black bitches for whom crime and illegal drug use constitute a lifestyle. And now the Powerful Black Bitch, a recognition of Black women's growing influence as well as a warning about the dangers of allowing them real power.

These stereotypes, some older than others, are evident in news coverage of African American women. However, the goal of *African American Women in the News* is not simply to ask whether their representation reflects stereotypes commonly depicted in popular culture. Nor is it just to determine whether the findings of previous news studies apply to Black women. Certainly, those were among the objectives. But, more broadly, the intent of this book is to explore the portrayal of African American women from an intersectional perspective in a variety of news formats, platforms and contexts. Who, in fact, are these women? How might they be characterized within different media formats and platforms? How does the intersectionality of gender, race and class affect representation? And what can their portrayal in a variety of news contexts tell us about the status of African American women in society and in their own communities?

The chapters in this book provide a view of African American women in the news that is complex and, at times, seemingly contradictory, reflecting both the interconnectedness of gender, race and class as well as the struggle over meaning that is inherent in popular culture. The findings also are the result of differences in format, platform, target audience, focus of inquiry and methodology. For example, in local news, African American women were portrayed both as victims of crime or natural disaster, and as bearers of middle-class respectability in their roles as commentators on events, experts or spokespersons. In national, cable network news, they were primarily voiceless, muted in background imagery that illustrated the news being reported. However, they also appeared in a network news feature as a hard-working mother trapped in a dangerous, crime-ridden neighborhood, in need of assistance from (White) outsiders to obtain the safety and better life for her children that are unattainable within her own (Black) community. And they appear as a rape victim, a kidnapper and a woman who is likely mentally ill. First Lady Michelle Obama was represented in YouTube video clips as a respectable Black lady (Collins, 2005) in her capacity as First Mom, First Wife, First Hostess, celebrity and advocate for families and women, but also as a Sapphire and a Powerful Black Bitch.

In African American newspapers, televangelist Juanita Bynum, a victim of domestic violence, was represented as partially responsible for her own victimization, but in White newspapers she was clearly the victim of her husband's physical attack. In local TV news, women who were assaulted during a college spring break were categorized within coverage by their presumed class status as either non-student Jezebels who provoked rape or as students who were naive, innocent victims. And in an Atlanta newspaper series about crack cocaine and the mothers who are addicted, African American "crack mothers" who were trying to get clean were seen as deserving and in need of assistance from a White professional, middle class – unless they were considered beyond the pale because of continued drug abuse and related criminal actions.

Taken together, these studies paint a multifaceted and more complete picture of African American women in the news than would be the case with fewer studies that had a similar focus. An overarching view of this research also provides us with several arguments and conclusions:

- An intersectional approach to the study of representation in the news is essential. The findings of previous news studies that failed to address the interrelation of gender, race and class are not necessarily applicable to African American women.
- The stereotypes and myths associated with African American women in popular culture continue to be present in the news. In addition, because popular culture is dynamic and readily adapts to cultural and social change, new stereotypes are formed to address societal transformation.
- Racism, like race itself, must be understood as gendered as well as classed. Paternalistic racism applies to news coverage of African American women under specific circumstances.
- Differences in the representation of African American women reflect not only variations in news format, platform, audience, focus of inquiry and social environment, but also the ideological struggle over the meaning of Black womanhood. Played out in the news as well as other forms of popular

culture, this struggle reflects the interests of competing ideologies and their constituencies, as well as the social status of Black women in the U.S. today.

The remainder of this chapter draws on and contextualizes the research in this book to elaborate on the above.

Themes, Stereotypes and Racism

While some of the findings of previous studies that did not address intersectionality and the gendered nature of news are nonetheless applicable to news coverage of African American women, other findings either are inaccurate, incomplete or only valid under specific circumstances. Of particular relevance here are themes, stereotypes and racism in the news.

Research in this book indicates that the dominant themes in news coverage of African American women are victimization, poverty, crime, dysfunction and violence. Dysfunction characterized not only individuals and families, but African American communities more generally, and it frequently underscored stories in which the other themes also were present. For example, family and individual dysfunction, as well as crime, violence and, by implication, poverty, were evident in the story involving the Tennessee mother attacked by a female relative who kidnapped her baby in order to sell the child. The Ohio woman who had offered to pay for the purchases of strangers but did not have the money to do so most likely was mentally ill, resulting in personal dysfunction. And in the CNN story about the 6-year-old boy who was shot on Chicago's South Side, the impoverished community itself can be seen as dysfunctional, with residents afraid to speak out to stop the crime and violence that literally cripples their lives. Similarly, the City of Atlanta appears dysfunctional when its water department can't figure out how to charge residents, with some receiving monthly water bills for $3,000 when the correct amount is closer to $30. The fact that the city has a majority Black population serves to reinforce (White) racist perceptions of African American incompetence in administrative and government functions.

Other news scholars have found the most salient themes in news coverage of African Americans to be crime, violence, chaos and poverty (see, for example, Dixon, 2004; Entman and Rojecki, 2000; Heider, 2004; McCormick, 2010; Stabile, 2006). But they did not similarly see dysfunction and victimization as relevant themes – most probably because they were not specifically looking at African American women. Their studies of local news, in particular, found that the predominant image of African Americans was as criminals. However, the research in this book indicates that African American women are far more likely to be portrayed in both local TV and cable network news as victims than as criminals. In local news, which devotes considerably more coverage to crime than does national news, they are the victims of burglary, theft, rape and murder, as well as natural disasters such as tornadoes. Furthermore, as victims, they are generally portrayed sympathetically, as innocent of any actions that might have precipitated their victimization. For example, coverage of the murder of Katherine Johnston, the elderly woman killed by Atlanta police in a drug raid gone wrong, included interviews with a young friend, who likened her to a grandmother and helped to frame the crime as inexcusable and the perpetrators as guilty. In weather-related stories, women who had lost their homes or their churches to tornadoes were "lucky to be alive" and deserving of the support of church members or others in their communities.

In addition to being portrayed as victims, African American women are sometimes represented as stereotypic in the news, and at other times in ways that challenge traditional ideas about African American women and their place in society. In local news, they often were commentators, spokespersons or experts, reflecting the professionalization of Atlanta's Black middle class as well as providing a contradiction to the negative images associated with Black poverty and crime. Furthermore, African American women in local news almost always seemed middle class in appearance, demeanor and speech. And while African American women were largely relegated to the background in cable network news, occasionally a positive depiction of an African American woman was shown, as was the case when FOX News paired its White, male medical correspondent with an African American woman who was a physician and bested him in a health care debate. In addition, Michelle Obama by-and-large was portrayed positively in YouTube clips uploaded by the White House and Obama campaigns, although she was confined to fairly traditional, gendered roles in which she could be characterized within the stereotype of the Black lady. As Collins (2005) explains, the middle-class or upper-middle-class Black lady is respectable and responsible, as well as "beautiful, smart and sensuous" with "no cornrows, gum chewing, cursing, miniskirts, or plunging necklines" to emphasize her sexuality, which is relegated to the safe confines of her marriage (pp. 139–140). The representation of First Lady Michelle Obama within the context of this stereotype, while obviously restrictive and limiting in authenticity, nevertheless was successfully orchestrated first by the Obama presidential campaign in 2008 and subsequently by the White House to counter and neutralize the image of the angry, militant Black woman that preceded Michelle Obama's entry into the White House. As such, the stereotyping of Michelle Obama as a Black lady occurred as an act of resistance to the more destructive and harmful stereotype of the angry Black woman. Significantly, within the format of late-night talk shows, Obama was able to break free of the restrictive confines of the domestic sphere and the public's expectations for a Black Lady to express a more authentic voice that was witty, intelligent and independent.

Nevertheless, some of the more traditional and negative stereotypes of African American women also were evident in the news. The working-class stereotype of the Black bitch, the Jezebel and the sexualized version of the bitch which "constitutes a modern version of the Jezebel, repackaged for contemporary mass media" (Collins, 2005, pp. 127–128) appeared in local stories involving arrests for gunfire or drugs, as well as a prostitution sting. The bad Black bitch was epitomized in cable network news by the woman who kidnapped a newborn from her mother, allegedly with the intent of selling the child. Keisha Williams, the aide to a police chief charged with providing her with a car and badge for which she was not authorized, also could be considered a sexualized bitch given the implication that they might have been involved in an illicit sexual relationship.

The Jezebel, although updated with the image of the sexualized bitch, has not been wholly replaced by her; they were both in evidence within news coverage. The Jezebel was prominent in Freaknik coverage, where the stigma of Black women's sexuality worked to blame rape victims for provoking their assault because, as James (1996) explains, "the public is not socialized to view black females sympathetically in rape cases, given their historical construction as whores" (p. 144). This coverage suggests that in cases of rape, African American women may still be viewed as old-fashioned Jezebels or the more modern bitch who provokes or even welcomes sexual assault. In the CNN story about the woman who recanted her charge of rape years later, she can be viewed as both a bitch and a liar whose cry of rape cannot be trusted.

Evidence of the emasculating Sapphire – sometimes referred to as the Black matriarch – was rare, although she was evoked by Rush Limbaugh in his pronouncement that Michelle Obama would "fuss… and scream at" the president "for eating stuff that's bad for him." Obama also could be viewed in the Sapphire role through her own and the president's comments, which situated her as "the real power within the White House." Although the president and first lady limited that power to the domestic sphere, conservatives invoked the controlling, power-hungry Sapphire to frame her quip about being "more popular than the president" because she was on the tween show *iCarly* as evidence of an out-of-control desire for dominance.

In addition to stereotypes, both modern and paternalistic racism were in news coverage involving African American women. Although previous studies had found that the news reflects modern racism (Campbell, 1995; Campbell, LeDuff, Jenkins and Brown, 2012; Dixon, 2008b; Entman, 1990), that body of research did not discover paternalistic racism in the news. Modern racism posits that racial bias and discrimination are no longer with us. From this perspective, African Americans who have not achieved social and economic equality have only themselves to blame and are, therefore, not deserving of help from the larger society. Paternalistic racism, on the other hand, sees some African Americans as deserving of assistance, a contradiction to the premise within modern racism that assigns blame and therefore sole responsibility to those who have not succeeded on their own. As a gendered form of racism – related to the paternalism under which some women are presumed to be helpless and thus in need of assistance from men – paternalistic racism may be applied to African American women but not, in most instances, to African American men. Originally applied to news coverage within a study about how the *Washington Post* reported on and supported the 1948 attempt to integrate the military (Meyers, 1996), paternalistic racism may no longer be applicable to African American men or even groups of both African American women and men. In our current "post-racist" society, with its presumption that we are beyond race and therefore past the need for remedial civil rights legislation, it may well be this form of racism is reserved for some African American women seen as particularly and uniquely deserving due to specific life circumstance over which they have little control. These women, as described in Chapters 3 and 7, include the devoted and hard-working mother of a 6-year-old shooting victim who hopes to someday move her children out of their crime-ridden neighborhood on Chicago's South Side, as well as mothers addicted to crack cocaine who are attempting to start new lives for themselves and their children.

Contextualizing Difference

The various and sometimes contradictory representations of African American women in the news reflects not only the intersectionality of gender, race and class, but also the ongoing ideological struggle within popular culture over what it means to be an African American woman. Popular imagery, stereotypes and cultural myths are never static; they adjust over time to accommodate cultural change as the dominant ideology works to maintain its supremacy. That Michelle Obama can, on the one hand, embody the characteristics of the perfect mother and, on the other hand, the emasculating Sapphire or the self-serving Powerful Black Bitch reflects the contest over meaning as well as the evolution of a stereotype. Up until fairly recently, it was inconceivable that an African American woman would, in fact, have sufficient social, economic and political power to be deemed a threat to White males, so there was no need for the existence of the Powerful Black Bitch to warn of the danger presented by empowered African American women who are not beholden to their bosses or White society. The foundation of the Powerful Black Bitch is the working-class bitch; the Powerful Black Bitch has neither the refinement nor respectability of the middle-class Black lady. The Powerful Black Bitch is, instead, selfish and self-serving, and her existence justifies the denial of economic, social and political power to African American women. As indicated in the YouTube video clips posted by right-wing individuals or organizations, the Powerful Black Bitch will inevitably use what power she has for evil.

The image of the Black lady, while more socially acceptable than the militant and angry Black woman, also has material and ideological consequences for African American women. As Collins (2005) has pointed out, the stereotypes of middle-class African American women as Black ladies, modern mammies and educated Black bitches justifies workplace discrimination against them and is "used to explain why so many African American women fail to find committed male partners – they allegedly work too hard, do not know how to support Black men, and/or have character traits that make them unappealing to middle-class Black men" (p. 146). In essence, they are blamed for the failings of their relationships and, consequently, the deterioration of Black communities. In the case of Juanita Bynum, the stereotype of the Black lady opened the door for the Black press to question whether she had driven her husband to abuse by her diva-like behavior and, as her husband claimed, lack of ability to support him as a wife should. Ultimately, the stereotype of the Black lady who does not know how to treat her man undermined Bynum's status as a survivor of domestic violence by raising questions about her culpability so that she was seen as equally at fault for the violence she experienced at the hands of her husband. In these ways, the stereotypes ascribed to African American women work to maintain the gender, race and class oppressions.

In addition to ideologically-driven cultural stereotypes, differences in news format and platform, as well as target audience and the social environment, contribute to shaping news content. For example, the emphasis within the local news format on crime and disaster resulted in coverage that highlighted stories in which African American women were victims. Cable network news, on the other hand, with its focus on national issues, policies and politics, primarily used African American women as background illustration for stories because few African American women other than celebrities and members of the president's family have the national prominence to warrant network coverage. As a result, African American women who were the story's focus, as opposed to the backdrop, in national TV news were most likely to be featured within in-depth stories that highlighted the themes of victimization, poverty, dysfunction, crime and violence. In addition, YouTube's user-distributor format provided an outlet for a wider range of representation than was permissible in more traditional and mainstream news outlets.

Differences in representation also are a consequence of dissimilar target audiences and social environments, as well as news format. For example, the role of the Black press has been to portray African Americans in a positive light given both the negative coverage often accorded them in the mainstream media and the expectations of its African American readership (Shipp, 1994; Strother, 1978). In addition, among the most influential institutions shaping the social environment of Black communities is the Black church (Dyson, 2009), whose leaders tend to preach a socially conservative "politics of respectability"

(Collins, 2005, p. 108) concerning gender and sexuality that maintains sexism and gender inequality (Harris-Perry, 2011, p. 231). Within this framework, and relying heavily on gossip/celebrity column briefs and features that drew on conservative voices within the Black church, coverage within Black newspapers of the assault on Juanita Bynum by her husband raised questions about her culpability and possible role in provoking the attack. On the other hand, the White newspapers, operating within a different social environment and serving a different (White) audience, mostly provided hard news coverage that provided details of the assault and clearly held Bynum's husband accountable. The *Washington Post* also provided two feature stories about an attempt within Black churches to address domestic violence in the communities they serve. Nevertheless, the White press missed the opportunity to frame domestic violence within the context of male supremacy and patriarchy by drawing on advocates for battered women as news sources, thereby perpetuating the idea that violence against women is a matter of individual psychopathology.

The social environment – at the micro-level of the newsroom and the meso-level of the city[1] – within which local TV news was produced also was responsible for the preponderance of middle-class African American women shown. As indicated in Chapter 2, these images normalized middle-class Black women, providing a contradiction to stereotypes associated with poverty, promiscuity and lack of education. The fact that a significant number of African American women who, in appearance and behavior, could be seen as middle-class professionals undoubtedly is a result of Atlanta's large, middle-class African American population. As such, the findings in Chapter 2 are not generalizable to other cities; they are uniquely related to the racial and socioeconomic demographics of Atlanta. In addition, White journalists working alongside Black colleagues in Atlanta's newsrooms have likely learned over the years to be sensitive to issues of race. In media markets with a smaller African American population and fewer African American journalists, that sensitivity may be missing. Nevertheless, the predominantly middle-class images of African American women in local TV news in Atlanta point to the possibility that local news programming in cities with similar demographics may also break with negative stereotypes to represent African American women as capable, attractive and educated professionals.

The potential danger within this scenario is that, in line with the concept of enlightened racism (Jhally and Lewis, 1992), images of professionally successful African American women may be used to deny the continuing existence of gender and race discrimination, thereby blaming those who are less successful for their lack of similar accomplishment. However, to assume this would be the case without engaging in further study risks misunderstanding the gendered nature of racism. We cannot presuppose that because a theory, stereotype, argument or conclusion is accurate for men that it will likewise fit women.

Gender has long been the glaring blind-spot in representational studies within the news, especially when the focus is on race. In studies which ignored the specificities of gender, African American women have been subsumed within the broader category of African Americans, or side-stepped completely when the focus is on African American men. The result is that they are – to borrow a term coined almost 50 years ago by sociologist Gaye Tuchman (1978) to describe the media's portrayal of women – "symbolically annihilated" through their absence.[2] At the heart of *African American Women in the News* is the call for a rethinking – and gendering – of our understanding of the representation of race and class within the news, a call to pull African American women from the margins to the center of study. This book is simply a step in – and an invitation to – that process.

NOTES

1 The Missing Black Woman in the News: An Introduction

1 See, for example, Campbell, 1995; Campbell, LeDuff, Jenkins & Brown, 2012; Dates & Pease, 1994; Dixon, 2006a, 2006b; Dixon & Linz, 2000; Entman, 1990, 1992, 1994, Entman & Rojecki, 2000; Ferguson, 1998; Gilens, 1996; Gray, 1989; Oliver, 2003; Shah & Thornton, 1994; Stabile, 2006; and Sommers, Apfelbaum, Dukes, Toosi & Wang, 2006.

2 See, for example, Campbell, 1995; Entman, 1990, 1992; Entman & Rojecki, 2000; and Dixon & Linz, 2000.

3 The terms "Black" and "African American" are used interchangeably throughout this book.

4 References to "mainstream" news, newspapers or media in this book indicate organizations and media that historically were developed to serve a primarily White audience. The terms "mainstream" and "White" will be used interchangeably throughout this book.

5 The critical cultural studies approach used here is within the theoretical framework of British cultural studies.

6 Audiences also may "read" or interpret texts in ways that challenge the dominant or "preferred reading" of a text based on individual decoding capabilities and strategies (Hall, 1980; Morley, 1980).

7 See, for example, bell hooks (1992), Melissa Harris-Perry (2011), Angela Davis (1983, 1989), Joy James (1998), and Patricia Hill Collins (1991, 2005).

8 Lubiano's (1992) definition of the overachieving Black lady differs from Collins's in that Lubiano's version also can be viewed as a Sapphire who emasculates the men in her life.

9 See, for example, Campbell, 1995; Campbell, LeDuff & Brown, 2012; Dixon, 2008a, 2008b; Entman, 1990, 1992; Entman & Rojecki, 2000; Dixon & Linz, 2000.

10 The terms can often be used interchangeably, although modern racism is most frequently used in the context of news coverage.

11 While some scholars have celebrated the idea of post-race as an opportunity to re-imagine outside the category of race, others warn of the dangers in dismantling the materiality and symbolism of race (Joseph, 2011, p. 57).

2   African American Women in Local TV News

1 The "tight weave" hairstyle, along with footage of African Americans in the vicinity where the shooting took place, was used to identify the victim as African American.
2 Hall later retired after becoming embroiled in a scandal involving the erasure of answers on standardized tests by staff at a number of schools in the district.

3   CNN and FOX News: African American Women in Cable Network News

1 See, for example, Campbell, 1995; Dixon, 2008b; Entman, 1990, 1992; Entman & Rojecki, 2000; and Dixon & Linz, 2000.
2 Looking at cumulative viewership, as opposed to ratings, during 2011 CNN placed first among viewers who tuned in for at least one minute over the course of an average month, with 99.4 million viewers, while FOX came in second with 82.8 million (Pew Research Center's Project for Excellence in Journalism, 2012).
3 Promos were included in this study and counted as separate stories, even though they referred to upcoming stories, both because they appeared as a separate unit, with the main story coming at a later time in the news show, and because the way they framed the story and its subjects could differ from the framing of the main story.
4 Given her strong performance against FOX's medical correspondent, Fegan is unlikely to be asked back as an expert on health care reform. Robert Greenwald (2004) suggests that FOX only hires little-known Democrats as correspondents, as opposed to better-known and more powerful Democrats who would be more likely to win a debate on-air.

4   'Tubing with Michelle Obama

1 Baby mama refers to young, unwed African American women who have babies.
2 The White House and Obama campaign maintain separate staff, including separate media production personnel.
3 No statistics are available for the number of times first ladies have appeared on magazine covers.
4 *AARP Magazine* is an official publication of the American Association for Retired Persons.
5 These publications featured Michelle Obama without her husband and children. Many more magazines ran covers that included Barack Obama and/or the Obama children with the first lady.
6 Whether Michelle Obama is post-feminist is open to debate; many would argue, as would this author, that she more accurately reflects a feminist sensibility.
7 Among those rules, according to Kantor, are that Sasha and Malia must write reports on what they have seen when they go on trips, even when not required by school, eat their vegetables or not get dessert or snacks, participate in two sports, and they are not allowed to watch television or use the computer for anything but homework except on weekends (p. A18).
8 Saartjie Baartman, a Khoi woman from what is now South Africa, was put on display in London and Paris in the early 1800s, her prominent buttocks seen as evidence of the wild and untamed sexuality of African women (Collins, 2005, p. 26).

9   Obama's Republican opponent in the 2012 presidential election, Mitt Romney, used similar technology, allowing visitors to his YouTube channel to donate, volunteer and share content.

10   This song is reminiscent of rapper Ludacris's 2009 single *Nasty Girl*, which is about sex with various girlfriends – a college student, a lawyer and a doctor – who are all a "lady in the street but a freak in the bed" – a woman who "walks so proper, talks with such class, but behind closed doors she a nasty girl."

11   A portion of this clip with a different title was reposted by the conservative Breitbart News, a blog founded by the late Andrew Breitbart.

12   Within this context, "hey" is a colloquial term for "hello."

13   The Act is frequently derided by opponents as Obamacare, although it is sometimes referred to as Obamacare by its supporters, as well.

14   Coast Guard Capt. Dorothy C. Stratton served as director of the Coast Guard Women's Reserve during World War II.

15   John Boehner, a Republican, is Speaker of the U.S. House of Representatives and a frequent critic of the president and his policies.

16   Trayvon Martin was a 17-year-old, unarmed African American who was shot by George Zimmerman, a Hispanic neighborhood watch coordinator in Sanford, Florida. The case made national and international news, and resulted in protests and demonstrations, when Sanford police initially refused to arrest Zimmerman, citing Florida's "Stand Your Ground" law and the possibility that Zimmerman acted in self-defense.

5   Juanita Bynum in Black and White (News)

1   Hard news is about a specific, recently occurring event; soft news includes features and other stories that are generally more in-depth and are not as time-sensitive.

2   Intimate partner violence is domestic violence that involves two individuals who are in or have been in a romantic relationship, whether they are married, divorced or dating.

3   The above statistics from the annual National Crime Victimization Survey (The Bureau of Justice Statistics, 2005) include both reported and unreported crimes.

4   Collins (2005) notes that "out LGBT African Americans are seen as being disloyal to the race," as well (p. 108).

5   The decisions by the *Amsterdam News* and the *Atlanta Daily World* to not cover the assault are likely tied to a general reluctance within the Black press to portray African American men in a negative light.

6   *Billboard*'s ranking of top gospel CDs, which included Bynum's CD, *A Piece of My Passion*, was excluded in this study.

7   The article erroneously states that the group has asked Bynum to step down, but then refers to this person as "he," and later "Weeks," indicating that the naming of Bynum here was simply a mistake.

8   Within this religious context, the adversary refers to the devil or Satan.

9   The portion or percentage to be contributed was not specified.

10   A version of this article also ran in the *New York Beacon*.

11   This same article appeared without crediting the AP in a slightly revised version in the Aug. 30–Sept. 5, 2007 *New York Beacon*, which ran a few sentences longer than in the Memphis newspaper.

12   The article is incorrect; the assault occurred in the parking lot of a hotel, not a church.

6   Violence Against African American Women in Local News: Freaknik as a Case Study

1   Cruising is a popular activity for high school and college-age young adults in the U.S. It involves driving slowly in designated areas, where the goal is to see and be seen. A related outcome is traffic jams and gridlock.

2   The number of rapes before, during and after Freaknik was provided by Nikki Berger, the former acting director of Grady Rape Crisis Centre, in personal communication, Sept. 18, 1996.

3   The late evening newscast of these three stations was chosen for uniformity. Earlier newscasts vary in length between the three stations. The FOX-affiliated station, WAGA, airs an hour-long, local news show beginning at 10 p.m., as opposed to the half-hour format at 11 p.m. of WSB, WXIA and WGNX. The UPN and WB affiliates do not provide local news.

4   The words "Freaknik," "Freaknic" and "Freak Nic" were used in a search of all *Atlanta Journal and Constitution* articles. Once the articles that were not specifically about Freaknik, but simply mentioned the event within the context of another topic, were eliminated, a systematic random sample of every 10th article was chosen. However, the goal was not to obtain a representative sample of all Freaknik articles, but rather to obtain a variety of Freaknik-related articles so as to enlarge the contextual framework for understanding the televised news coverage of violence against women. A total of 52 articles from 1994, 1995 and 1996 were examined.

5   WGNX and WXIA did not run a Freaknik story on April 25; WSB had no story on April 14.

6   The exception was a story about animal cruelty involving carriage horses during Freaknik that aired on WXIA on April 23.

7   Spelman and Morehouse colleges, Clark Atlanta University, Georgia State University, the Georgia Institute of Technology, Emory University, Agnes Scott College and a number of other four-year and two-year colleges serve the Atlanta area.

8   Auburn Avenue is also known as Sweet Auburn because of its historical role at the center of Black life in Atlanta during segregation. It was once home to some of the city's most successful Black-owned businesses and its most prominent Black families, including that of the Rev. Martin Luther King Jr.

9   Such comparisons are often fraught with difficulties because of the different contexts in which the events occur. For example, Atlanta is not a resort town with a beach, as are some coastal areas in Florida and elsewhere, which make them a destination for White students during spring break. In addition, those coastal areas actively work to attract students for spring break, while Atlanta officials attempted to discourage students from coming to Freaknik.

7   Crack Moms and the Narrative of Paternalistic Racism

1   The editorial is not included in the analysis because the conventions and purposes of editorials differ markedly from those of the news.

2   According to the *Atlanta Journal-Constitution*, "For ages 26–30, eight of 10 women arrested in Atlanta had cocaine in their system, the highest percentage among the 21 cities" in a study ("More Women Using Crack in Atlanta," September 27, 1998, p. A17).

3   Mary Shannon is likely the grandmother of Reginald, who was in the first installment.

4 An example is the reference in Tifiney's story to the "young men, old men, faceless men who promised to give her crack in exchange for sex."

8 Finding African American Women in the News: A Conclusion

1 The macro-level would be within the context of the larger society.
2 Tuchman argued that women were symbolically annihilated by the media through condemnation, trivialization or absence.

REFERENCES

Abbott, A.A. (1995). Substance abuse and the feminist perspective. In N. Van Den Bergh (Ed.), *Feminist practice in the 21st century* (pp. 258–277). Washington, DC: NASW Press.

Abramovitz, M. (1995). From tenement class to dangerous class to underclass: Blaming women for social problems. In N. Van Den Bergh (Ed.), *Feminist practice in the 21st century* (pp. 211–231). Washington, DC: National Association of Social Workers Press.

Afro-American Red Star. (2007). Minister writes about abuse. Oct. 27–Nov. 2, p. C5.

Alexander, A.L. (1995). She's no lady, she's a nigger: Abuses, stereotypes and realities from the Middle Passage to Capital (and Anita) Hill. In A.F. Hill, & E.C. Jordan (Eds.), *Race, gender and power in America: The legacy of the Hill-Thomas hearings* (pp. 3–25). New York: Oxford University Press.

Althusser, L. (1971). Ideology and ideological state apparatuses. In *Lenin and philosophy and other essays* (pp. 127–186). New York: Monthly Review Press.

Associated Press. (2007). Evangelist allegedly beaten by husband. *Memphis Commercial Appeal*, Aug. 24, p. A8.

Atlanta Journal and Constitution. (1996). Campbell shows little leadership, Feb. 14, p. 12A.

Atlanta Journal and Constitution. (1998). Resolution for Atlanta: No Freaknik in 1999, Dec. 30, p. 12A.

Barrett, M. (1988). *Women's oppression today: The Marxist/feminist encounter.* London: Verso.

Beasley, M. (2005). *First ladies and the press: The unfinished partnership of the media age.* Evanston, IL: Northwestern University Press.

Benedict, H. (1992). *Virgin or vamp: How the press covers sex crimes.* New York: Oxford University Press.

Bent-Goodley, T.B. (2006). Domestic violence and the black church: Challenging abuse one soul at a time. In R.L. Hampton and T.P. Gullotta (Eds.), *Interpersonal violence in the African-American community: Evidence-based prevention and treatment practices* (pp. 107–119). New York: Springer.

Berry, V.T., & Manning-Miller, C.L. (1996). *Mediated messages and African-American culture: Contemporary issues.* Thousand Oaks, CA: Sage.

Bhabha, H. (1983). The Other question: The stereotype and colonial discourse. *Screen*, 24(6), 18–36.

Black, M.C., Basile, K.C., Breiding, M.J., Smith, S.G., Walters, M.L., Merrick, M.T., Chen, J., & Stevens, M.R. (2011). *The National Intimate Partner and Sexual Violence Survey (NISVS): 2010 Summary Report*. Atlanta, GA: National Center for Injury Prevention and Control, Centers for Disease Control and Prevention.

Bourdieu, P., & Passeron, J. (1977). *Reproduction in education, society and culture*. Beverly Hills, CA: Sage.

Boxill, B.R. (1992). The underclass and the race/class issue. In B.E. Lawson (Ed.), *The underclass question* (pp. 19–32). Philadelphia: Temple University Press.

Bramlett-Solomon, S. (1991). Civil Rights vanguard in the Deep South: Newspaper portrayal of Fannie Lou Hamer, 1964–1977. *Journalism Quarterly*, 68(3), 515–521.

Brewer, R.M. (1993). Theorizing race, class and gender: The new scholarship of black feminist intellectuals and black women's labor. In S.M. James, & A.P.A. Busia (Eds.), *Theorizing black feminisms: The visionary pragmatism of black women* (pp. 13–30). New York: Routledge.

Brownmiller, S. (1975). *Against our will: Men, women and rape*. New York: Simon & Schuster.

Bumiller, K. (1990). Fallen angels: The representation of violence against women in legal culture. *International Journal of the Sociology of Law*, 18, 125–142.

Bureau of Justice Statistics. (2005). *National Crime Victimization Survey: Criminal Victimization, 2004* (BJS Publication No. NCJ 210674). Washington, DC: Shannan M. Catalano.

Burford, M. (2001, May). Carnal knowledge. *Essence*, 32(1), 185.

Byerly, C.M., & Wilson II, C.C. (2009). Journalism as Kerner turns 40: Its multicultural problems and possibilities. *Howard Journal of Communications*, 20(3), 209–221.

Campbell, C. (1995). *Race, myth and the news*. Thousand Oaks, CA: Sage.

Campbell, C.P., LeDuff, K.M., & Brown, R.A. (2012). Yes we did? Race, myth and the news revisited. In C.P. Campbell, K.M. LeDuff, C.D. Jenkins, & R.A. Brown (Eds.), *Race and News: Critical Perspectives* (pp. 3–21). New York: Routledge.

Campbell, C.P., LeDuff, K.M., Jenkins, C.D., & Brown, R.A. (2012). *Race and news: Critical perspectives*. New York: Routledge.

Chancer, L.S. (1987). New Bedford, Massachusetts, March 6, 1983–March 22, 1984: The "before" and "after" of a group rape. *Gender and Society*, 1, 239–260.

Chicago Tribune. (2007). Televangelist's husband breaks silence. *Chicago Tribune*, Sept. 16, p. 17.

Cloud, D. (1992). The limits of interpretation: Ambivalence and the stereotype in "Spenser: For hire." *Critical Studies in Mass Communication*, 9, 311–324.

Cohen, S. (1972). *Folk devils and moral panics: The creation of the mods and rockers*. London: MacGibbon and Kee.

Cole, H.J., & Jenkins, C.D. (2012). "Nappy-headed hos": Media framing, blame shifting and the controversy over Don Imus' pejorative language. In C.P. Campbell, K.M. LeDuff, C.D. Jenkins, & R.A. Brown (Eds.), *Race and news: Critical perspectives* (pp. 177–198). New York: Routledge.

Collins, P.H. (1989). The social construction of Black feminist thought. *Signs*, 14(4), 745–773.

Collins, P.H. (1991). *Black feminist thought: Knowledge, consciousness, and the politics of empowerment*. London: Routledge.

Collins, P.H. (2005). *Black sexual politics: African Americans, gender and the new racism*. New York: Routledge.

Conrad, L.T. (2008). Tattle: License shows Beyonce, Jay-Z hitched. *Philadelphia Daily News*, Apr. 23. Retrieved January 27, 2012 from Philadelphia Daily News Online: http://articles.philly.com/2008-04-23/entertainment/25252209_1_jay-z-shawn-carter- miley-cyrus.

Cuklanz, L. (1997). *Rape on trial: How the mass media construct reform and social change.* Philadelphia: University of Pennsylvania.

Dates, J., & Pease, E. (1994). Warping the world: Media's mangled image of race. *Media Studies Journal*, 8(3), 89–95.

Davis, A.Y. (1983). *Women, race and class.* New York: Random House.

Davis, A.Y. (1985). *Violence against women and the ongoing challenge to racism.* Latham, NY: Kitchen Table Press.

Davis, A.Y. (1989). *Women, culture and politics.* New York: Random House.

Davis, A.Y. (1998). Women and capitalism: Dialectics of oppression and liberation. In J. James (Ed.), *The Angela Y. Davis reader* (pp. 161–192). Malden, MA: Blackwell.

Davis, D.E. (1997). The harm that has no name: Street harassment, embodiment, and African American women. In A.K. Wind (Ed.), *Critical race feminism: A reader* (pp. 192–202). New York: New York University Press.

DeShay, A. (2010). Black Atlanta. Retrieved on April 10, 2012 from http://www.blackdemographics.com/atlantablackdemographics.html.

Dewan, S. (2007). A minister's public lesson on domestic violence. *New York Times*, Sept. 20, p. A1.

Dixon, T. (2004). Racialized portrayals of reporters and criminals on local television news. In R.A. Lind (Ed.), *Race/gender/media: Considering diversity across audiences, content and producers* (pp. 132–145). Boston: Pearson.

Dixon, T.L. (2006a). Psychological reactions to crime news portrayals of Black criminals: Understanding the moderating roles of prior news viewing and stereotype endorsement. *Communication Monographs*, 73, 162–187.

Dixon, T.L. (2006b). Schemas as average conceptions: Skin tone, television news exposure, and culpability judgments. *Journalism and Mass Communication Quarterly*, 83, 131–149.

Dixon, T.L. (2008a). Crime news and racialized beliefs: Understanding the relationship between local news viewing and perceptions of African Americans and crime. *Journal of Communication*, 58, 106–125.

Dixon, T.L. (2008b). Network news and racial beliefs: Exploring the connection between national television news exposure and stereotypical perceptions of African Americans. *Journal of Communication*, 58(2), 321–337.

Dixon, T.L. (2011). Teaching you to love fear: Television news and racial stereotypes in a punishing democracy. In S.J. Hartnett (Ed.), *Challenging the prison industrial complex: Activism, arts and educational alternatives* (pp. 106–123). Chicago: University of Illinois Press.

Dixon, T.L., & Linz, D. (2000). Overrepresentation and underrepresentation of African Americans and Latinos as lawbreakers on television news. *Journal of Communication*, 50, 131–154.

Douglas, S. (1995). *Where the girls are: Growing up female with the mass media.* New York: Three Rivers Press.

Dyson, M.E. (2003). *Open mike: Reflections on philosophy, race, sex, culture and religion.* New York: Basic Books.

Dyson, M.E. (2009). *Can you hear me now?* New York: Basic Civitas Books.

Eco, U. (1990). *The limits of interpretation*. Bloomington: University of Indiana Press.

Edney, H.T. (2007). Bishop T.D. Jakes: Don't give up on love. *Memphis Tri-State Defender*. Sept. 6. Retrieved January 20, 2012 from Tri-State Defender Online: http://tri-statedefenderonline.com/articlelive/articles/1818/1/Bishop-T-D-Jakes-Dont-give-up-on-love/Page1.html.

Edwards, A. (1987). Male violence in feminist theory: An analysis of changing conceptions of sex/gender violence and male dominance. In J. Hanmer, & M. Maynard (Eds.), *Women, violence and social control* (pp. 13–29). Atlantic Highlands, NJ: Humanities Press International.

Entman, R.M. (1990). Modern racism and the images of blacks in local television news. *Critical Studies in Mass Communication*, 7, 332–345.

Entman, R.M. (1992). Blacks in the news: Television modern racism and cultural change. *Journalism Quarterly*, 69, 101–113.

Entman, R.M. (1994). Representation and reality in the portrayal of blacks on network television news. *Journalism Quarterly*, 71(3), 509–520.

Entman, R.M., & Rojecki, A. (2000). *The black image in the white mind*. Chicago: University of Chicago.

Erickson, K.V., & Thomson, S. (2012). First lady international diplomacy: Performing gendered roles on the world stage. *Southern Communication Journal*, 77(3), 239–262.

Fair, J.E. (1994). "Black-on-Black": Race, space and news of Africans and African Americans. *Issue: A Journal of Opinion*, 22(1), 35–40.

Fears, D. (1995a). Opinions of annual festival are split along racial lines. *Atlanta Journal and Constitution*, May 10, p. 6B.

Fears, D. (1995b). Racial split over Freaknik renewed in vote to organize, not kill, '96 party. *Atlanta Journal and Constitution*, May 16, p. 2B.

Ferguson, R. (1998). *Representing 'race': Ideology, identity and the media*. London: Arnold.

Finn, G. (1989–1990). Taking gender into account in the "theatre of terror": Violence, media and the maintenance of male dominance. *Canadian Journal of Women and the Law*, 3, 375–394.

Fiske, J. (1994). *Media matters: Everyday culture and political change*. University of Minnesota Press.

Fourth Estate. (2012). Silenced: Gender Gap in 2012 election coverage. Found 10/31/2012 at http://www.4thestate.net/female-voices-in-media-infographic/#.T85TIJIYskX.

Gandy, O.H. Jr. (1998). *Communication and race: A structural perspective*. London: Oxford University Press.

Gardetto, D. (1997). Hillary Rodham Clinton, symbolic gender politics, and the New York Times: January–November 1992. *Political Communication*, 14, 225–240.

German, L. (1983). *The socialist case against theories of patriarchy*. Toronto: International Socialists.

German, L. (1989). *Sex, class and socialism*. London: Bookmarks.

Gibbs, N., & Newton-Small, J. (2008). The war over Michelle. *Time*. June 2, 171(22), 28–29.

Gilens, M. (1996). Race and poverty in America: Public misperceptions and the American news media. *Public Opinion Quarterly*, 60, 515–541.

Gilens, M. (2004). Poor people in the news: Images from the journalistic subconscious. In Heider, D. (Ed.), *Class and news* (pp. 44–60). Lanham, MD: Rowman & Littlefield.

Gilliam, F.D.J., & Iyengar, S. (2000). Prime suspects: The influence of local television news on the viewing public. *American Journal of Political Science*, 44(3), 560–573.

Glaser, B., & Strauss, A. (1967). *The discovery of grounded theory: Strategies for qualitative research*. Chicago: Aldine.

Gramsci, A. (1971). *Selections from the prison notebooks*. London: Lawrence and Wishart.

Gramsci, A. (1983). *The modern prince and other writings*. New York: International Publishers.

Gray, H. (1989). Television, black Americans and the American dream. *Critical Studies in Mass Communication*, 6, 376–386.

Greenwald, R. (2004). *Outfoxed: Rupert Murdoch's war on journalism*. Culver City, CA: Brave New Films.

Griffin, C. (1996). Experiencing power: Dimensions of gender, "race," and class. In N. Charles, & F. Hughes-Freeland (Eds.), *Practicing feminism: Identity, difference and power* (pp. 180– 201). London: Routledge.

Grove, S. (2008). "YouTube: The Flattening of Politics," *Neiman Reports*, summer 2008, 62(2), pp. 28–30.

Grove, S. (2010). "YouTube's Ecosystem for News," *Neiman Reports*, summer 2010, 64(2), pp. 50–51.

Guerrero, E. (1993). *Framing Blackness: The African American image in film*. Philadelphia: Temple University Press.

Haines, E. (2008). Televangelist's husband pleads guilty. *Philadelphia Inquirer*, Mar. 11. Retrieved January 25, 2012 from USA Today Online: http://www.usatoday.com/news/nation/2008-03-11-3046205615_x.htm.

Hall, S. (1977). Culture, the media and the "ideological" effect. In J. Curran, M. Gurevitch, & J. Woollacott (Eds.), *Mass communication and society* (pp. 315–348). Beverly Hills, CA: Sage.

Hall, S. (1982). The rediscovery of "ideology": Return of the repressed in media studies. In M. Gurevitch, T. Bennett, J. Curran, & J. Woollacott (Eds.), *Culture, society and the media* (pp. 56–90). London: Methuen.

Hall, S. (1997). The work of representation. In S. Hall (Ed.), *Representation: Cultural representations and signifying practices* (pp. 13–64). London: Sage.

Hall, S., (1980). Encoding/decoding. In S. Hall, D. Hobson, A. Lowe, & P. Willis (Eds.), *Culture, Media, Language* (pp. 117–127). London: Routledge.

Hall, S., Connell, I., & Curti, L. (1977). The "unity" of current affairs television. *Working Papers in Cultural Studies*, 9, 51–93. Birmingham, UK: Centre for Contemporary Cultural Studies, University of Birmingham.

Hall, S., Critcher, C., Jefferson, T., Clarke, J., & Roberts, B. (1978). *Policing the crisis: Mugging, the state and law-and-order*. New York: Holmes and Meier.

Harris, H.R. (2007a). Condemning violence from the pulpit: Project aims to give voice to domestic issue rarely mentioned in the pulpit. *Washington Post*, Oct. 11, p. T3.

Harris, H.R. (2007b). Marital strife roils ministry: Bishop Weeks charged with assaulting wife. *Washington Post*, Sept. 1, p. B7.

Journal and Constitution, Apr. 25, p. 8C.

Harris-Perry, M.V. (2011). *Sister citizen: Shame, stereotypes, and Black women in America*. New Haven, CN: Yale University Press.

Harrison B. (1995). Freaknik '95 behavior: Sexual hijinks not a sign of disaster, experts say. *Atlanta Journal and Constitution*, p. 8C.

Hartley, J. (1982). *Understanding news*. London: Methuen.

Heider, D. (Ed.). (2004). *Class and news*. Lanham, MD: Rowman & Littlefield.

Heider, D., & Fuse, K. (2004). Class and local TV news. In D. Heider (Ed.), *Class and news* (pp. 87–107). Lanham, MD: Rowman and Littlefield.

Helton, C. (1996). It all started in 1982 as friendly little picnic. *Atlanta Journal and Constitution*, Apr. 19, p. H4.

Higginbotham, E.B. (1992). African American women's history and the metalanguage of race. *Signs*, 17, 253–254.

Hill, A.F., & Jordan, E.C. (1995). *Race, gender, and power in America: The legacy of the Hill-Thomas hearings*. New York: Oxford University Press.

Holmes, K. (2007a). Celebrity watching. *Philadelphia Inquirer*, Oct. 17.

Holmes, K. (2007b). Celebrity watching. *Philadelphia Inquirer*, Sept. 7.

Holsey, S. (2007). A songwriter/singer's recollections. *Michigan Chronicle*. Sept. 19–25, p. D1.

hooks, b. (1981). *Ain't I a woman: Black women and feminism*. Boston: South End Press.

hooks, b. (1992). *Black looks: Race and representation*. Boston: South End Press.

Jackson, P. (2007a). What's the 411? *Philadelphia Tribune*. Dec. 28, p. 31E.

Jackson, P. (2007b). What's the 411? *Philadelphia Tribune*. Dec. 21, p. 31E.

Jackson, P. (2007c). What's the 411? *Philadelphia Tribune*. Dec. 14, p. 31E.

Jackson, P. (2007d). What's the 411? *Philadelphia Tribune*. Nov. 30, p. 31E.

Jackson, P. (2007e). What's the 411? *Philadelphia Tribune*. Nov. 9, p. 31E.

Jackson, P. (2007f). What's the 411? *Philadelphia Tribune*. Oct. 26, p. 31E.

Jackson, P. (2007g). What's the 411? *Philadelphia Tribune*. Oct. 19, p. 31E.

Jackson, P. (2007h). What's the 411? *Philadelphia Tribune*. Oct. 12, p. 31E.

Jackson, P. (2007i). What's the 411? *Philadelphia Tribune*. Sept. 21, p. 31E.

Jackson, P. (2007j). What's the 411? *Philadelphia Tribune*. Sept. 14, p. 31E.

Jackson, P. (2007k). What's the 411? *Philadelphia Tribune*. Sept. 7, p. 31E.

Jackson, P. (2007l). What's the 411? *Philadelphia Tribune*. Aug. 31, p. 31E.

Jackson, P. (2008a). What's the 411? *Philadelphia Tribune*. Jan. 18, p. 31E.

Jackson, P. (2008b). What's the 411? *Philadelphia Tribune*. Jan. 4, p. 31E.

Jackson, P. (2008c). What's Up? *Philadelphia Tribune*. Jan. 13, pp. 12–14.

Jacobs, R.N. (2000). *Race, media, and the crisis of civil society: From Watts to Rodney King*. Cambridge, England: Cambridge University Press.

James, J. (1996). *Resisting state violence: Radicalism, gender, and race in U.S. culture*. Minneapolis: University of Minnesota Press.

James, J. (1998). *The Angela Y. Davis reader*. Malden, MA: Blackwell.

Jeffries, J.L. (2002). Press coverage of Black statewide candidates: The case of L. Douglas Wilder of Virginia. *Journal of Black Studies*, 32(6), 673–697.

Jhally, S., & Lewis, J. (1992). *Enlightened racism: The Cosby show, audiences, and the myth of the American dream*. Boulder, CO: Westview Press.

Jones, Jeffrey M. (2012, May 30). Michelle Obama Remains Popular in U.S. Retrieved from http://www.gallup.com/poll/154952/Michelle-Obama-Remains-Popular.aspx.

Joseph, R.L. (2011). "Hope is finally making a comeback": First lady reframed. *Communication, Culture & Critique*, 4(1), 56–77.

June, L.N., & Parker, M. (1999). *Evangelism and discipleship in African-American churches*. Grand Rapids, MI: Zondervan.

Kahl, M.L. (2009). First Lady Michelle Obama: Advocate for strong families. *Communication & Critical/Cultural Studies*, 6(3), 316–320.

Kantor, J. (2012). Unheard, but speaking volumes in the race: Obama girls are important to father's image. *The New York Times*, Sept. 7, A18.

Katel, P. (2008, July 18). Race and politics. *CQ Researcher*, 18, 577–600. Retrieved from http://library.cqpress.com/cqresearcher/.

Kaufman Jr., G. (1993). The mysterious disappearance of battered women in family therapists' offices: Male privilege colluding with male violence. In E. Imber-Black (Ed.), *Secrets in families and family therapy* (pp. 196–212). New York: W.W. Norton.

Kellner, R., Ruether, R., & Cantlon, M. (Eds.). (2006). *Encyclopedia of women and religion in North America.* Bloomington: Indiana University Press.

Kitzinger, J. (2004). *Framing abuse: Media influence and public understanding of sexual violence against children.* Ann Arbor, MI: Pluto Press.

Klein, R.D., & Naccarato, S. (2003). Broadcast news portrayal of minorities. *American Behavioral Scientist, 46,* 1611–1616.

Koester, S., & Schwartz, J. (1993). Crack, gangs, sex, and powerlessness: A view from Denver. In M.S. Ratner (Ed.), *Crack pipe as pimp: An ethnographic investigation of sex-for-crack exchanges* (pp. 187–203). New York: Lexington Books.

Kraft, M., & Furlong, S. (2010). *Public policy: Politics, analysis, and alternatives.* Washington, DC: CQ Press.

Landry, B. (1987). *The new black middle class.* Los Angeles: University of California Press.

Lawson, B.E. (1992). Meditations on integration. In B.E. Lawson (Ed.), *The underclass question* (pp. 1–15). Philadelphia: Temple University Press.

LeDuff, K. (2009). *Tales of two cities: How race and crime intersect on local TV news in New Orleans and Indianapolis.* Saarbrücken, Germany: LAP Lambert Academic Publishing.

Leiblich, A., Tuval-Mashiach, R., & Zilber, T. (1998). *Narrative research: Reading, analysis and interpretation.* Thousand Oaks, CA: Sage.

Lester, N.A. (2010). Disney's *The princess and the frog: The pride, the pressure and the politics of being a first. Journal of American Culture, 33*(4), December, 294–308.

Liebler, C.M. (2004). Tales told in two cities: When missing girls are(n't) news. In D. Heider (Ed.), *Class and news* (pp. 199–212). Lanham, MD: Rowman & Littlefield.

Lincoln, C.E., & Mamiya, L.H. (1990). *The Black church in the African American experience.* Durham, NC: Duke University Press.

Lorde, A. (1992). Age, race, class, and sex: Women redefining difference. In M.L. Anderson, & P.H. Collins (Eds.), *Race, class and gender: An anthology* (pp. 495–502). Belmont, CA: Wadsworth.

Love, A. (2008). *The other inconvenient truth: The appropriate response to domestic violence within independent congregations.* Atlanta, GA: Black Church and Domestic Violence Institute.

Lubiano, W. (1992). Black ladies, welfare queens, and state minstrels: Ideological war by narrative means. In T. Morrison (Ed.), *Race-ing justice, en-gendering power: Essays on Anita Hill, Clarence Thomas, and the construction of social reality* (pp. 323–363). New York: Pantheon.

Lugo-Lugo, C.R., & Bloodsworth-Lugo, M.K. (2011). Bare biceps and American (in)security: Post-9/11 constructions of safe(ty), threat, and the first Black first lady. *Women's Studies Quarterly, 39*(1/2), 200–217.

Lule, J. (1995). The rape of Mike Tyson: Race, the press and symbolic types. *Critical Studies in Mass Communication, 12,* 176–195.

McAlister, J.F. (2009). Trash in the White House: Michelle Obama, post-racism, and the pre-class politics of domestic style. *Communication and Critical/Cultural Studies, 6*(3), 311–315.

McConahay, J.B. (1986). Modern racism, ambivalence and the modern racism scale. In J. Dovidio and S. Gaertner (Eds.), *Prejudice, discrimination and racism* (pp. 91–125). New York: Academic Press.

McCormick, C. (2010). *Constructing danger: Emotions and mis/representation of crime in the news*. Winnipeg, MB, Canada: Fernwood.

McDonald, R.R., & Cowles, A. (1995). Freaknik '95; Police say gangs played big role in weekend violence. *Atlanta Journal and Constitution*, Apr. 26, p. 6B.

Mama, A. (2000). Violence against Black women in the home. In J. Hanmer and C. Itzin (Eds.), *Home truths about domestic violence: Feminist influences on policy and practice – A reader* (pp. 44–56). London: Routledge.

Meyers, M. (1994). News of battering. *Journal of Communication*, 44, 47–63.

Meyers, M. (1996). Integrating the military: News coverage in the *Washington Post*, 1948. *Howard Journal of Communications*, 7(2), 169–183.

Meyers, M. (1997). *News coverage of violence against women: Engendering blame*. Newbury Park, CA: Sage.

Meyers, M. (2004a). African-American women and violence: Gender, race and class in the news, *Critical Studies in Media Communication*, 21, 95–118.

Meyers, M. (2004b). Crack mothers in the news: A narrative of paternalistic racism, *Journal of Communication Inquiry*, 28, 194–216.

Millner, D. (2007, December). I've come this far by faith. *Essence*, 38(8), 224–276.

Morley, D. (1980). *The "nationwide" audience: Structure and decoding*. London: BFI.

Morrison, T. (1992). *Race-ing justice, en-gendering power: Essays on Anita Hill, Clarence Thomas, and the construction of social reality*. New York: Pantheon.

Myrdal, G. (1964). *An American dilemma: The Negro in a white nation*. Vol. 1. New York: McGraw-Hill.

National Institute of Justice and the Centers for Disease Control and Prevention. (2000). *Full report on the prevalence, incidence and consequences of violence against women: Findings from the National Violence Against Women Survey* (DOJ Publication No. NCJ 183781). Washington, DC: Patricia Tjaden and Nancy Thoennes.

New York Beacon. (2007). Juanita Bynum assaulted by minister husband in hotel parking lot. Aug. 30–Sept. 4, 14(35), p. 4.

Nielsen Media. (2012). 2011–2012 media markets. Retrieved on April 10, 2012 from http://www.tvjobs.com/markets/market2.cgi.

Oliver, M.B. (2003). African American men as "criminal and dangerous": Implications of media portrayals of crime on the "criminalization" of African American men. *Journal of African American Studies*, 7(2), 3–18.

Oliver, S.S. (2011, December 8). A guidebook based on Michelle Obama's style. *The New York Times*. Retrieved from http://www.nytimes.com/2011/12/08/fashion/new-book-about-michelle-obama.html.

Painter, N.I. (1992). Hill, Thomas, and the use of racial stereotype. In T. Morrison (Ed.), *Race-ing justice, en-gendering power: Essays on Anita Hill, Clarence Thomas, and the construction of social reality* (pp. 200–214). New York: Pantheon.

Palser, B. (2006). Artful disguises. *American Journalism Review*, 28(5), 90.

Parisi, P. (1998a). A sort of comparison: The *Washington Post* explains the "Crisis in urban America." *Howard Journal of Communications*, 9, 187–203.

Parisi, P. (1998b). The *New York Times* looks at one block in Harlem: Narratives of race in journalism. *Critical Studies in Mass Communication*, 15(3), 236–254.

Parsons, C. (2008). Secrets and tall tales target Obama's wife. *The (Adelaide) Advertiser*, June 14, p. 67.

Patterson, O. (2007). Jena, O.J., and the jailing of Black America. *New York Times*. Sept. 30, p. 13.

Peters, J.W. (2012, Mar. 14). With video, Obama looks to expand campaign's reach through social media. *The New York Times*. Retrieved from http://www.nytimes.com/2012/03/15/us/politics/with-youtube-video-obama-looks-to-expand-social-media-reach.html.

Pew Research Center's Project for Excellence in Journalism. (2012). The state of the news media, 2012: Cable by the numbers. Found October 13, 2012 at http://stateofthemedia.org/2012/cable-cnn-ends-its-ratings-slide-fox-falls-again/cable-by-the-numbers/.

Philadelphia Inquirer. (2007). In the nation. Sept. 4. Retrieved January 27, 2012 from *Philadelphia Inquirer* Online: http://www.philly.com/philly/news/nation_world/20080312_In_the_nation.html?adString =inq.news/world/us;/category=world_us;&randomOrd=03130801251.

Philadelphia Inquirer. (2008). In the nation. Mar. 12. Retrieved January 27, 2012 from *Philadelphia Inquirer* Online: http://www.philly.com/philly/news/nation_world/20080312_In_the_nation.html?adString=inq.news/world/us;/category=world_us;&randomOrd=03130801251.

Phillips, J. (2007). Ministries bring domestic violence to fore. *Philadelphia Tribune.* Aug. 31, p. 6D.

Pickler, N. (2008). Fighting slurs, lies and videotape. *Toronto Star.* June 13, p. A2.

Poindexter, P.M., Smith, L., & Heider, D. (2003). Race and ethnicity in local television news: Framing, story assignments, and source selections. *Journal of Broadcasting & Electronic Media*, 47(4), 524–536.

Potter, G.W., & Kappeler, V.E. (1998). *Constructing crime: Perspectives on making news and social problems.* Prospect Heights, IL: Waveland Press.

Prince, Z. (2007). Domestic violence: A "love" tap?, *Afro-American Red Star.* Sept. 1–7, p. A6.

Rakow, L.F., & Kranich, K. (1991). Woman as sign in television news. *Journal of Communication*, 41(1), 8.

Ratner, M.S. (1993). *Crack pipe as pimp: An ethnographic investigation of sex-for-crack exchanges.* New York: Lexington Books.

Reeves, J.L., & Campbell, R. (1994). *Cracked coverage: Television news, the anti-cocaine crusade, and the Reagan legacy.* Durham, NC: Duke University Press.

Reinarman, C., & Duskin, C. (1996). Dominant ideology and drugs in the media. In G.W. Potter and V.E. Kappeler *Constructing crime: Perspectives on making news and social problems.* Prospect Heights, IL: Waveland.

Reinarman, C., & Levine, H.G. (1997). *Crack in America: Demon drugs and social justice.* Berkeley: University of California Press.

Reynolds, B. (2007). Pastors giving new meaning to "laying on hands." *New York Beacon.* Sept. 13–19, p. 9.

Richie, B. (1985). Battered black women and a challenge for the black community. *The Black Scholar*, 40–44.

Riessman, C.K. (1993). *Narrative analysis.* Newbury Park, CA: Sage.

Rivers, C. (2007). *Selling anxiety: How the news media scare women.* Lebanon, NH: University Press of New England.

Rolfe, E. (2007). Sounds of inspiration. *Chicago Defender*, Aug. 24–26, 21.

Rolfe, E. (2008). A warm "welcome" for Noel Jones' debut CD. *Chicago Defender*, May 21–27, 39–40.

Samuels, A. (2009, May 11). Michelle hits her stride. *Newsweek*, 153(19/20), pp. 40–41.

Scruggs, K., & Blackmon, D. (1994). City won't ban future Freaknik events. *Atlanta Journal and Constitution*, Apr. 26, p. 1A.

Scruggs, K., & McDonald, R.R. (1995). Freaknik '95; Sexual issues. *Atlanta Journal and Constitution*, Apr. 24, p. 5B.

Shah, H., & Thornton, M.C. (1994). Racial ideology in mainstream news coverage of black–latino interaction. 1980–1992. *Critical Studies in Mass Communication*, 11, 141–161.

Shah, D.V., Watts, M.D., Domke, D., & Fan, D. (2002). News framing and the cueing of issue regimes: Explaining Clinton's public approval in spite of scandal. *Public Opinion Quarterly*, 66, 339–370.

Sherr, L., & Murphy, M. (2012). A conversation with the Obamas. *Parade*, Sept. 2, pp. 6–9, 11.

Shipp, E.R. (1994). OJ and the Black media. *Columbia Journalism Review*, 33(4), 39–41.

Shoop, T. (2010). From professionals to potential first ladies: How newspapers told the stories of Cindy McCain and Michelle Obama. *Sex Roles*, 63(11/12), 807–819.

Smith, B. (1992). Ain't gonna let nobody turn me around. In R. Chrisman and R.L. Allan (Eds.), *Court of Appeal: The Black community speaks out on the racial and sexual politics of Clarence Thomas vs. Anita Hill* (pp. 185–193). New York: Ballantine Books.

Soderlund, G. (2002). Covering urban vice: The *New York Times*, "white slavery," and the construction of journalistic knowledge. *Critical Studies in Media Communication*, 19, 438–460.

Sommers, S.R., Apfelbaum, E.P., Dukes, K.N., Toosi, N., & Wang, E.J. (2006). Race and media coverage of Hurricane Katrina: Analysis, implications, and future research questions. *Analyses of Social Issues and Public Policy*, 6(1), 39–55.

Spillers, H. (2009). Views of the East Wing: On Michelle Obama. *Communication and critical/cultural studies*, September, 6(3), 307–310.

Stabile, C.A. (2006). *White victims, Black villains: Gender, race, and crime news in US culture.* New York: Routledge.

Steeves, H.L. (1997). *Gender violence and the press: The St. Kizito Story.* Athens, OH: Ohio University Center for International Studies.

Steiner, L. (1999). *New York Times* coverage of Anita Hill as a female cipher. In M. Meyers (Ed.), *Mediated Women: Representations in popular culture* (pp. 225–250). Cresskill, NJ: Hampton Press.

Sterk, C.E. (1999). *Fast lives: Women who use crack cocaine.* Philadelphia: Temple University Press.

Stoltenberg, J. (1989). *Refusing to be a man: Essays on sex and justice.* Portland, OR: Breitenbush.

Strangelove, M. (2010). *Watching YouTube: Extraordinary videos by ordinary people.* Toronto: University of Toronto Press.

Strother, T.E. (1978). The race-advocacy function of the Black press. *Black American Literature Forum*, 12(3), 92–99.

Suggs, E. (2000). Freak out: Rowdy party weekend morphs into job fair. *Atlanta Journal and Constitution*, Apr. 16, p. 1A.

Swan, J. (2010). Newspaper coverage of Cindy McCain and Michelle Obama in the 2008 presidential election. *Media Report to Women*, 38(2), 6–21.

Taylor, K.H. (2007a). Domestic violence knows no limits. *Detroit News*, Aug. 27. Retrieved January 27, 2012 from Religion News Blog: http://www.religionnewsblog.com/19137/domestic-violence-2.

Taylor, K.H. (2007b). Married co-pastors face stress: For unions similar to evangelists Juanita Bynum and Paula White's, ministerial couples say it takes a lot of work to avoid divorce. *Detroit News*, Aug. 31. Retrieved January 27, 2012 from http://www.christianitytoday.com/ct/2007/septemberweb-only/137-11.0.html.

Thomas-Lester, A. (2007). Abusers and victims told to get help: Dozens of Prince George's ministers focus their sermons on domestic violence. *Washington Post*, Oct. 15, p. B5.

Tuchman, G. (1978). Introduction: The symbolic annihilation of women by the mass media. In G. Tuchman, A.K. Daniels, & J. Benét (Eds.), *Hearth and home: Images of women in the mass media* (pp. 3–38). New York: Oxford University Press.

USA Today. (2012). 'Back to school' is first lady's theme, Aug. 13.p. B1.

van Dijk, T.A. (1991). *Racism and the press: Critical studies in racism and migration.* London: Routledge.

Van Zoonen, L. (1994). *Feminist media studies.* Thousand Oaks, CA: Sage.

Vavrus, M.D. (2002). *Postfeminist news: Political women in media culture.* Albany, NY: SUNY Press.

Vickers, R., & Helton, C. (1994). Council gives lukewarm invitation to Freaknik. *Atlanta Journal and Constitution*, Apr. 19, p. 1A.

Vine, S. (2008). Style, intellect: A new kind of First Lady. *The Times* (U.K.), Nov. 8, p. 8.

Washington Post. (2007). Religion briefing. Dec. 27, p. B9.

Weaver, C.K., & Carter, C. (2006). *Critical readings: Violence and the media.* London: Open University Press.

West, C.M. (2000). Developing an oppositional gaze toward the images of Black Women. In J.C. Chrisler, C. Golden, & P.D. Rozee (Eds.), *Lectures of the psychology of women* (pp. 220–233). Boston: McGraw-Hill.

Winfield, B.H. (1997). The making of an image: Hillary Rodham Clinton and American journalists. *Political Communication*, 14, 241–253.

Women, Men and Media Project. (1994a). *Arriving on the scene: Women's growing presence in the news.* Alexandria, VA: Unabridged Communications.

Women, Men and Media Project. (1994b). *Slipping from the scene: News coverage of females drops.* Alexandria, VA: Unabridged Communications.

Wright, E.A. (1998). Not a black and white issue: For battered and abused Latinas and black women, dialing 911 may be risky business. *On the Issues*, winter, pp. 42–47.

INDEX